T0305195

Entrepreneurial Imagination

Entrepreneurial Imagination

Time, Timing, Space and Place in Business Action

Björn Bjerke

Linnaeus University, Sweden

Hans Rämö

Stockholm University, Sweden

Edward Elgar

Cheltenham, UK • Northampton, MA, USA

Published by
Edward Elgar Publishing Limited
The Lypiatts
15 Lansdown Road
Cheltenham
Glos GL50 2JA
UK

Edward Elgar Publishing, Inc.
William Pratt House
9 Dewey Court
Northampton
Massachusetts 01060
USA

A catalogue record for this book
is available from the British Library

Library of Congress Control Number: 2010939261

ISBN 978 1 84980 178 2

Typeset by Servis Filmsetting Ltd, Stockport, Cheshire
Printed and bound by MPG Books Group, UK

Contents

Introduction

This book will discuss entrepreneurship along four themes:

1. Time, timing, space and place
2. Behaviour and action
3. Explaining and understanding
4. Phenomenology.

Using the terms 'time', 'timing', 'space' and 'place' as special analytical categories may sound futile to some. After all, everything takes time, is a matter of timing, is located in space and takes place? However, we do not intend to play with words. We are rather interested, as researchers, to discuss what it means, beyond what is taken for granted, to look at the world through some specific concepts. There are several such examples in science. For instance, all human beings have a language. But what does it mean to have a language? This has been discussed in many intellectual camps, for instance, in philosophy, history and philology. In a similar fashion, we all have a culture. But what does it mean to a culture? An entire scientific field, social anthropology, is devoted to answer this question.

As in the case of language and culture, just because we take time, timing, space and place for granted, we normally deem them not worthy of separate treatment. And because we say that we cannot choose in these matters, we believe that we do not have to think about such facticity to start with (Casey, 1993). However, when we think a bit longer about such concepts, they may assume unexpected meanings and raise questions we have not thought to ask. In fact, time and timing, as well as space and place, can be very complicated concepts, which is all the more confusing because, at first glance, they appear so obvious and common-sense. To look at the world as time, timing, space and/or place is to use dimensions to characterize the world into a special fashion and, like using any criterion, a special way to talk about and to understand the world. According to Cresswell (2004, p. 27), for instance, 'by taking space and place seriously, we can provide another tool to demystify and understand the forces that affect and manipulate our everyday life.'

Specifically looking at the world as a world of places we see different things:

> Looking at the world as a set of places in some way separate from each other is both an act of defining what exists (ontology) and a particular way of seeing and knowing the world (epistemology and metaphysics). Theory is a way of looking at the world and making sense of the confusion of the senses. Different theories of place lead different writers to look at different aspects of the world. In other words, place is not simply something to be observed, researched and written about but simply part of the way we see, research and write. (Cresswell, 2004, p. 15)

So, one fundamental ambition of this book is to look at entrepreneurship through the conceptual quartet of time, timing, space and place. More about this conceptual quartet in general and an introduction to its relevance to entrepreneurship will come later in the next chapter.

One conceptual pair that has been used for characterizing human beings and the way we look at human beings is behaviour and action. We will suggest that the concepts in this pair have a much stricter meaning in science than in everyday language. In science, in fact, these concepts stand for two different orientations in modelling and/or interpreting human activities. Entrepreneurship is normally associated with action more than with behaviour.

Another, somewhat related, but more fundamental duality as far as research orientation is concerned is that of explaining and understanding. Both orientations exist in entrepreneurship research and we will present examples of both. A general trend, however, is that attempts at understanding entrepreneurship seem to gain in pace in researching this phenomenon.

Several different philosophical and theories of science exist today. We stand for one of them, that is, phenomenology. Phenomenology aims at ascertaining the subjective nature of 'lived experience', by exploring the subjective meanings, explanations and understanding that individuals attribute to their experiences. We will see that this is highly relevant to entrepreneurial actions.

A more thorough discussion of the second, third and fourth themes will be presented in Chapter Two. A discussion of what could be seen as the most fundamental theme of the four (contained even in its title), that is, the theme of time, timing, space and place, will come already in the next chapter. We will see, however, that all four themes are reflected in entrepreneurship and related economic action, make a difference and, if taken seriously, force us to choose as researchers.

THE AMBITION WITH THIS BOOK AND ITS OUTLINE

This book offers a phenomenological investigation of the importance of time, timing, space and place in studies of contemporary entrepreneuring

and related business activities. To understand entrepreneurship phenomenologically is a somewhat ignored field of entrepreneurship studies
(Cope, 2005; Berglund, 2007). This book is (thus) an enterprise that,
although predominantly theoretical in character, is geared to the understanding of the concepts of time, timing, space and place that form the
subject matter of the empirical phenomenon of entrepreneurship. In other
words, the book is concerned with how the factors of time, timing, space
and place are integrated (or disintegrated) in entrepreneurial contexts. It
deals with epistemological matters of entrepreneurial studies. Since the
main focus of this book is on the understanding of time, timing, space and
place in entrepreneurial processes, some questions of human action and its
phenomenological characterization (as well as research aiming at providing
explanations versus research aiming at providing understanding) will be
provided in Chapter Two. The purpose of this book is not to engage solely
in theory and philosophy. However, if the complexity of time, timing,
space and place are to be understood, account must be taken of its more
intrinsic character before we can proceed with the elucidation of entrepreneurial action. This will be done in Chapter One.

Three possibilities can be drawn from incorporating the conceptual
quartet of time, timing, space and place into the entrepreneurial discourse
more extensively and more consistently than it has been up to now:

1. Having the possibility to use a lot of theories, models and interpretations from 'neighbouring' subjects when researching entrepreneurship, subjects which have been discussing their research areas
   through this quartet of concepts (or part of it) for quite some time, for
   instance, history, political studies, human geography, architecture,
   urban studies and regional economics
2. Truly being able to live up to the vision that entrepreneurship belongs
   to the whole society, not only to its economy
3. By using such a broad approach, the entrepreneurial paradigm can
   be unshackled from 'hangover biases' such as that entrepreneurship
   primarily has to do with economic growth, that the subject is a predominantly male gender issue, that it is associated with a hero focus,
   and that it does not have to consider culture and mundane activities in
   everyday life.

Entrepreneuring can be seen as intimately related to subjective time, or
as a matter of timing. However, different factors have a different bearing
on entrepreneurship if they are treated as either 'space factors' or as
'place factors'. Some space factors that can influence entrepreneurship
include:

- Degree of organization
- Separate departments for business development being started in existing companies
- Market growth
- Possibilities to act freely and/or transgress borders of various kinds.

Some place factors that can influence entrepreneurship include:

- Local role models
- Leadership
- Existing networks
- Possibilities to access locations where things can take place.

Based on the four themes presented at the beginning of this chapter, the rest of the book will discuss various entrepreneurship and related business matters:

- Chapter One will provide a discussion of our basic conceptual quartet, that is, time, timing, space and place
- Chapter Two will provide an overview of the development of the academic topic of entrepreneurship and discuss important topics such as behaviour and action, explaining and understanding, and phenomenology
- Chapter Three will look at entrepreneurship in all its varieties in our modern society
- Chapter Four will study, in more detail, one interesting type of entrepreneurship today, social entrepreneurship
- Chapter Five will explain the relationship of social entrepreneurship to local government
- Chapter Six will relate entrepreneurship to regional development
- Chapter Seven relates entrepreneurial action to various aspects of environmental concerns
- Chapter Eight discusses ICT-networking in the context of entrepreneurship.

    We look at Chapters One to Three as the foundation of the book and Chapters Four to Eight more as applications.

- Chapter Nine provides a short summary of the book and its conclusions.

1. Entrepreneuring – when and where?

TIME, TIMING, SPACE AND PLACE

'Time', 'timing', 'space' and 'place' are trivial in a sense, of course. Almost anything we do as human beings takes time, requires timing, occupies space and takes place. However, the idea here is to look at time, timing, space and place as active factors in the sense that a situation would not be the same without considering them. We want to bring time, timing, space and place into the open and turn them into analytical categories in order to better understand entrepreneurship and related economic action in all its different forms.

Nowadays, time is frequently reduced to clock-time (objective time), which is equated with speed, and is regarded as an important yardstick against which we measure the value of our activities at work. Action and communication based on right and timely moments to act judiciously in unique situations are also encouraged virtues in business. However, such timely judgement-based decisions cannot be depicted by using clocks only; impromptu situations do occur irrespective of the clock (subjective time). In a similar fashion, attention to the aspects of space and place to business has ranged from economic models of exchange, distribution and allocation in 'abstract' geometrical extensions, to more nuanced and contextual understandings of space and place in, for example, entrepreneurial processes and relationship building in organizational networks. The focus of time, timing, space and place in this book is based on a belief that analyses in social science settings remain crippled if there is a partisan focus on either time, timing, space or place only. As much new work in this area attests, including the present volume, the combined implication of time and timing as well as space and place must be the ontological basis of any investigation in the social sciences (see May and Thrift, 2001).

To comprehend the notion that time can be seen as something beyond the successive reading of a clock is intuitively easy because a human's ability to coordinate his or her activities has a history that is much older than the history of mechanical clocks. This non-chronological understanding of time is also discernible in humanity's ability to act judiciously and wisely at an opportune occasion.

Situations that develop under the influence of clock-time can be characterized as '*chronos*', a notion that has a long history. As early as Aristotle's *Physics* (IV, 11, 219b), *chronos* is defined as the 'number of motion with respect to the before and the after', which is a classical expression of the concept of (*chronos*) time as change, measure and serial order. Therefore, despite Aristotle's antiquated understanding of physics – and a possible circularity in the definition – in this book *chronos* is used as a definition of an exact quantification of time (for example, passing time expressed in successive readings of a clock). In studies of business performance in network organizations, this clock-time of *chronos* is the ruling factor, particularly in terms of efficiency, time management, administration, and in the improvement of what already exists and is already known in different industrial settings.

This omnipresent characterization of time as clock-time is, however, only one delimited way of understanding time. Although being an important and inescapable aspect of modern life, the clock-time of *chronos* eventually creates blinders. Analyses of the theory of time and its different representations include a vast field of ontological studies (see Macey, 1994). With reference to Snow (1959), there is subdivision after subdivision also within the field of time study, and it soon becomes meaningless to discuss not only two theories of time, but 102, or 2002 theories of time. Therefore, for the sake of practicality, the concept of *chronos* will hereafter be discussed together with a more timely and non-chronological aspect of time, namely *kairos*. These two ideas of time, *chronos* and *kairos*, should not be seen as two sharply distinguished categories, but rather as a complementary pair of human time concepts.

This second and more obscure Greek notion of time, *kairos*, and its '*kairic*' stem is little used in the social sciences. Terms such as 'due measure', 'proportion' and, above all, the 'right moment' are some of the English translations of *kairos* that connote ideas of wisdom and judgement in timely situations (see Kinneavy, 1986; Kinneavy and Eskin, 1994; Smith, 1969, 1986; White, 1987; on *chronos* and *kairos* in organizational settings, see Bartunek and Necochea, 2000; Berman Brown and Herring, 1998; Jaques, 1982; Kirkeby, 1998; Rämö, 1999, 2002, 2004a, 2004b).

In addition to working with (or to) the clock in terms of what already exists and is already known, all humans are expected to seize new opportunities, in 'windows of opportunity', that exist for a finite period of time. Furthermore, all humans face timely situations characterized as 'moments of truth', which might imply judicious actions beyond the mechanically learned and beyond timetables. Understanding timeliness is also crucial in dealings with effectiveness and trust in relationships. The chronological time of *chronos*, whether it is described as clock-time, linear, circular or spiral, remains inadequate in such timely situations and, as we will see, may even lead to a different understanding of what an 'opportunity' is. *Chronos* – and most notably clock-time manifestation – must be augmented by the non-chronological practice of time as *kairos*.

We move now from time and timing to space and place. What is it, then, that distinguishes space from place? Naturally, the difference is not very clearly delineated. Whereas space is commonly seen as a three-dimensional geometric extension, place is a specific contextual setting. Next to a virtual space that is mediated through different computerized boundaries, there are always concrete places that we as humans exist in all the time. The difference between space and place was emphasized in ancient Greece, where the two concepts *chora* and *topos* were (roughly) used to refer to space and place, respectively (though a strict framing into abstract/concrete is more restricted now than it was for the ancient Greeks). Certainly, the concept of space has shown its dominance over the concept of place in the natural sciences for over 300 years; however, the question is brought to a head when the virtual spaces of the Internet have come in on the side of the physical spaces.

The difference between the two ancient Greek spatial notions of space (*chora*) and place (*topos*) is that, whereas the former is an abstract geometric or cartographic extension, the latter (*topos*) is a concrete contextual localization, without sharp demarcations. Thus, they serve as a useful distinction between abstract and virtual space (*chora*) and concrete place (*topos*) (see Casey, 1993, 1998; Rämö, 1999, 2002, 2004a, 2004b).

So, the temporal and spatial notions proposed here make a distinction between two ideas of time/timing and space/place. *Chronos* time relates to the 'exact' quantification of passing time expressed in successive readings of a clock. This idea is complemented by *kairos* time, the non-chronological timely moments in which we manifest abilities to act judiciously and wisely at a concrete and possibly opportune occasion. In a similar way, a distinction is made between the abstract spaces (*chora*) of theory and virtuality, and concrete human-lived places (*topos*).

To summarize, the concepts of 'space' (*Raum* in German; *espace* in French) and 'place' (*Ort* or *Platz* in German; *lieu* in French) are basic components of the lived world and we take them for granted.

Space is normally seen as the more abstract one of the two concepts. When we speak of space, we tend to think of outer space or possibly spaces of geometry (Cresswell, 2004, p. 8). Space is something deterritorialized (de Certeau, 1984). It can be discussed without considering that it might contain any social life, inhabited by actual identifiable people. It is an opening and a result of possibilities, for instance, from a business point of view. Spaciousness is closely associated with the sense of being free. Freedom implies space, enough room in which to act (Tuan, 1977).

Space is generally seen as being transformed into place as it acquires definition and meaning. Brenner (1997, p. 137) expresses it as such: 'Space appears no longer as a neutral container within which temporal development unfolds, but, rather, as a constitutive, historically produced dimension of social practices.' Considering antonyms to place, we refer to words such as 'remove', 'take away', 'dislodge', 'detach' and 'take off' (Rämö, 2004b). When space feels familiar to us, it has become place (Tuan, 1977). In other words, place is then a meaningful location, to which people are attached (Altman and Low, 1992).

Places are significant to human life. We might even say, like Cresswell (2004, p. 33), that 'there was no "place" before there was humanity but once we came into existence then place did too'. Places are being made, maintained and contested. All over the world, people are engaged in place-making activities (Cresswell, 2004, p.33). Nothing we do is unplaced (Casey, 1998, p. ix).

However, places are not isolated. Cronon (1992) argues that we must pay attention to their connections. Places are something we occupy. The relationships between people and places are at least as complex as relationships between people, but of another kind. As mentioned, places give meaning to people. This is where people learn to know each other and themselves. Places become points which stand out in every individual's biography and a set of feelings for different places develop through social interaction (Ekman and Hultman, 2007). Altman and Low (1992, p. 7) phrase it as: 'The social relations that a place signifies may be equally or more important to the attachment process than the place qua place.'

Even though the term '*homo geographicus*' has been coined (Sack, 1997), place is more than geography. It is something, the meaning and usefulness of which is continuously created in social relations and networks, that is, in meetings and flows between people and objects. This is something which has gained increasing response within social as well as within human sciences (Ekman and Hultman, 2007). To put it differently, place is culturally defined (Casey, 1993, p. 33).

The political geographer J. Agnew (1987) has outlined three fundamental aspects of place as a 'meaningful location':

1. Location
2. Locale
3. Sense of place.

Location has to do with fixed objective coordinates on the Earth's surface (or in the Earth's case a specific location vis-à-vis other planets and the sun). By locale, Agnew means material setting for social relations – the actual shape of place within which people conduct their lives as individuals. By sense of place, Agnew refers to the subjective and emotional attachments people have to place. Place can vary in size from being very large (for example, the Earth, universe or nation), mid-sized (for example, cities, communities and neighbourhoods), small (for example, homes or rooms) or very small (for example, objects of various kinds) (Altman and Low, 1992). It may even be something completely imaginary such as in Sir Thomas More's *Utopia*. A place can be called a 'room for activities' (Massey, 1995b) or an 'arena' (Berglund and Johansson, 2008). 'Home' is an 'exemplary kind of place' (Cresswell, 2004, p. 115).

One concept that frequently appears alongside place in geography texts is 'landscape'. In most definitions of landscape, however, the viewer is outside of it. Places, on the other hand, are very much things to be inside of (Cresswell, 2004, p. 10). Another concept of interest here is 'region', which became very much a part of common sense during the twentieth century (Curry, 2002, p. 511). We will discuss entrepreneurship and regional development in Chapter Six.

Some views on space and place over the years include the following:

- For Aristotle place was 'prior to all things'. 'To be' for Aristotle was to be in place (Casey, 1993, p. 14). Aristotle's view on place was dominant for more than 1500 years
- Descartes identified space with matter. To him, place was also a subordinate feature of matter and space (Casey, 1998, pp. 152–6)
- Motte and Cajori (1934, pp. 6–7) explain that Newton claimed that 'absolute space, in its own nature, without relations to anything external, remains always similar and immovable' and that 'place is a part of space which a body takes up, and is according to space, either absolute or relative'. According to Newton, places do not exist on their own; they exist in name only. Newton's ideas of absolute space became very dominant for several hundred years. His contemporary 'competitor', Leibniz, who tried to promote the idea of a relative space, never had a chance (Casey, 1998)
- The increasing obsession with infinite space from the thirteenth century onward, due to the dominant position of the Catholic church in the Western world at that time and later supported by Newton's theories, had the predictable effect of putting place into the shadows (Casey, 1998). The subordination of place to space culminated in the seventeenth century (Casey, 1993). Renaissance thinkers remained capable of equating space with place and vice versa. However, space took eventually over. From the end of the eighteenth century, place was virtually excluded from the scientific

discourse (Rämö, 2004b, p. 854). It did not come back until the mid twentieth century when it returned in full force

- Kant tried to demonstrate that space, as well as time, are both conditions under which sense perceptions operate (Jammer, 1982). To him, space was no longer situated in the physical world but in the subjectivity of the human mind (Casey, 1998). Space was not something 'out there', but existed as a sort of mental structuring (Curry, 2002)

- According to Curry (2002), two opposing intellectual movements, one deconstructive and one constructive, gave rise to the recasting of thinking of space and, above all, place were coming up during the latter part of the twentieth century. The first of these, the deconstructive, is perhaps most clearly seen in the work of Heidegger. According to him, everything in the world could and should be an object of empirical inquiry. Place is the same as authentic experience, according to Heidegger (Cresswell, 2004, p. 22). Another body of work that took a deconstructive tack toward the concept of space was the later work of Wittgenstein. Words, including 'space' and 'place', only have meanings within the contexts of the individuals and groups that use them, in particular situations and particular places (Curry, 2000). Before 1960, place was seen ideographically and space was seen nomothetically. However, from the 1970s, constructive notions of place, which were as universal and theoretically ambitious as approaches to space had been, became more and more common. Some attempts in this direction existed already, for instance, Jacobs (1961), who discusses the notion that in social planning one needs to look both at the everyday activities of people who live and work in urban neighbourhoods and to attend to them as places constructed through these everyday activities; and Hall (1959), who pointed to the ways in which people interact with one another when in close proximity. More central to constructive attempts to move place to the centre of scientific inquiry, however, were geographers like Tuan (1974a, 1977), Relph (1976) and Buttimer and Seamon (1980). One element in this movement was a desire to rethink the role of people (and bodies) in the construction of places. Examples of such contributors are the poststructuralist Foucault, the phenomenologist Merleau-Ponty, the historian de Certeau and the Marxist-architect Lefebvre

- Foucault's historical inquiries reveal alertness to space, or, more precisely, to the way in which spatial relations – the distribution and arrangement of people, activities and buildings – are always deeply implicated in the historical processes under study (Philo, 2000). He claimed in one interview (Foucault, 1980, p. 149), that 'the history of powers' would at one and the same time amount to a history 'written of space'

- Merleau-Ponty claims that places we inhabit are known by the bodies we live. We cannot be implaced without being embodied. Conversely, to be embodied is to be capable of implacement (Casey, 1998). Merleau-Ponty teaches that the human body is never without a place or that place is never without body; he also shows that the lived body is itself a place. Its very movement constitutes place and brings it into being (Casey, 1998)

- De Certeau may seem to have a kind of opposite understanding of space and place to what is the most common one. To him, place is an empty grid over which practice occurs while space is what is created by practice (Cresswell, 2004). While we have to use the rules and structures of language to make sense, the same applies to place. As we live in places that become pre-structured, those places are not operational without practice in them. He stresses that tactics operate through a sense of timing (movements) whereas strategies operate through place (fixation) (Hjorth, 2004)

- Lefebvre presents a theory that 'urban revolution' was supplant-ing an 'industrial revolution' and that this urban revolution was somehow a 'spatial revolution' as well (Merrifield, 2000). According to Merrifield, Lefebvre talks about construction of space through a spatial triad: representations of space (also called 'firstspace' – empirically measurable and mappable phenomena), representa-tional space ('secondspace' – the domain of representations and image, a felt and cared for centre of meaning) and spatial practices ('thirdspace' – the lived world, which is practiced and lived rather than being material/conceived or mental/perceived) (Cresswell, 2004; Merrifield, 2000)

- There is a close interconnection between the technologies available for communication and representation and the ways in which space and place are conceptualized. The modern region was in important ways a product of new technologies like the printing press, modern transports and the breakthrough of statistics in social life (Curry, 2002, pp. 508–509)

- A genuine rediscovery of place, alongside space, in most of the social sciences today is obvious (Casey, 1998), like in the course of history (for instance, Braudel, 1993; Foucault, 1980), in the natural world (for instance, Berry, 1980; Snyder, 1968), in the political realm (for instance, Lefebvre, 1991; Nancy, 1991), in gender relations and sexual difference (for instance, Irigaray, 1993), in the production of poetic imagination (for instance, Bachelard, 1964; Otto, 1992), in geographic experience and reality (for instance, Relph, 1976; Tuan, 1977), in the sociology of the city (for instance, Arendt, 1958), in nomadism (for instance, Deleuze and Guattari, 1980), in architecture (for instance, Derrida, 1981; Tschumi, 1994) and in religion (for instance, Nancy, 1991). We can see it in economics (for instance, Fujita et al., 2001) and there are examples where space and place are used in business studies in general (for instance, Rämö, 2004a, 2004b) as in entrepreneurship in particular (for instance, Hjorth, 2004; Bjerke, 2010).

ENTREPRENEURSHIP AND RELATED ECONOMIC ACTION IN TIME, TIMING, SPACE AND PLACE

In the vast literature on the subject of entrepreneurship and business studies in general, a relatively neglected but fast-growing area is humanity's changing relationship with time, timing, space and place. Our everyday understanding of time is what is measured with clocks that count the duration and numerical order of motion. Space, on the other hand, is what is measured with a ruler, may it then be wooden or a light ray. Rightly so. These systems of measurement are handy coordinators of our everyday life and central in scientific explanations. Traditionally, our everyday relationships with time, timing, space and place are something we rarely give much thought to, but nonetheless exerts immense influence over our lives. However, an emergent body of thought devoted to these subjects sees the nature of time, timing, space and place within our contemporary society to be undergoing profound transformation; our relationships with, and in, time, timing, space and place are currently being recreated and reconstructed. Working times and working places, the schedules and places of production, the way in which we 'spend', 'save' and 'optimize' time, in situations of 'using', 'saving' and 'optimizing' space usage are no longer fixed due to the effects of contemporary economy. An ongoing miniaturizing and virtualization of space together with a quest for speed have affected traditional ideas of human time and space. So before elaborating on different forms of entrepreneurial action in Chapter Two, there is something further to be said already here about when and where, so to speak, these exercises are taking place. In other words a fuller understanding of what is meant by time and timing on one hand, and by space and place on the other, in human endeavours is necessary. The overarching objective in coming up with this book is to bring together new writing into a focused and themed publication that deals wholly with the subjects of time and timing, space and place in relation to entrepreneurship and related economic action.

Today entrepreneurship (and business studies in general) is much studied in social science literature, but it seems to be at an academic crossroads, somehow, having many different directions to choose from. A quartet spreading across the social sciences today is time, timing, space and place. It should be, in light of the title of this book, of interest to analyse and discuss to what extent these concepts could be an armament in mobilizing studies on entrepreneurship and related economic action, when fighting for various more or less prominent academic positions in the future. This book contains such discussions. The purpose is not, however, to replace ruling business and entrepreneurship discourses with a contextual relativism in time, timing, space and place, but to broaden the possibilities of the subject and supplement them with broader and more reflexive understandings of the importance of time, timing, space and place in contemporary research on entrepreneurship and related economic action.

Some aspects of time, timing, space and place have been part of economics, business studies and entrepreneurship for a long time, even if not explicitly so. Since the start of industrialism, for instance, it can be observed how similar types of operation tend to locate in specific places. Groups of firms are established near each other and specific industries are concentrated in certain cities and regions. In the early days of industrialization this was not particularly surprising given the great need for proximity to different raw materials and energy sources in the form of coal, timber and water, and shipping harbours. What is true today is that companies locate near to each other due to the value of being near to each other. This localization is a means of competition. Alfred Marshall was the first person in the early twentieth century to specifically recognize the mutual advantages that firms could obtain from locating geographically near to each other, especially if they are small- and medium-sized enterprises (SMEs) (Hansen, 2001). The idea was that a concentration of firms in close geographical proximity could allow all to enjoy the benefit from large-scale industrial production and of technical and organizational innovation beyond the scope of any individual firm. Theories and studies of localizations and concentrations of entrepreneurial activities are therefore central concerns in the study of entrepreneurship. However, by taking a step back and exploring time, timing, space and place as central elements gives us a chance to unfold the phenomenological aspects of entrepreneurship as a form of human action. More on entrepreneurship and localization will come in Chapter Six.

From the days of Cantillon's (1755 [1955]) coining of the term, the word 'entrepreneur' has had an ambiguous meaning. Ask average people on the street to describe an entrepreneur, and they will likely mention a work-devoted person with ideas for new enterprises. Entrepreneurs are those who bring together and involve people in a process of change. Nowadays, politicians as well as business leaders continuously stress the importance of entrepreneurs and SMEs to the economy, to competitiveness, to growth and to the potentiality to create employment. SMEs are of immense importance for many countries, both socially and economically. Hence the popularity in recent years of books and articles that attempt to distil and explain the field for students and practitioners. This book refrains from attempting to explain how to become an entrepreneur. Instead, the focus is on entrepreneurship as a collective phenomenon by relating it to concepts from recent research literature on time, timing, space and place as well as to practices as identified in localized field research.

Since the 1990s, entrepreneurial studies have become much more pluralistic in terms of their central themes and the theoretical framework through which they are analysed. This transformation in theories and methodologies also reflects deep-seated changes taking place in the wider institutional setting in which these forms are located. Most of the central theoretical questions and issues that define entrepreneurial studies seem to be matters of dispute and opinions regarding direction and development of the field. Some welcome this pluralism, seeing it as an overdue vindication of a development from stultifying coherence into a juncture characterized by theoretical and methodological diversity. Others, however, might see it as a sign of a once well-disciplined field in a state of disarray and dissolution. Whatever response one makes to this current state of affairs, there is an agreement that over the past 20 years or so, there has been a period of considerable intellectual upheaval within the field of entrepreneurial studies.

After all, the good thing is that we all have our personal understandings and experiences of entrepreneurship – from the smaller scale of bringing a project into realization at school, work or at home, to the more grandiose organized forms of business and social ventures – either as actors or spectators. Entrepreneurs can thus be found everywhere, doing just about everything – from starting a new restaurant to creating a new technology or invention. These people often put their money or their reputation on the line. Some wish to become rich and famous. Others wish to make themselves, their families or their communities better off. And some seek pure adventure – to challenge the limits of their capabilities. Regardless of motive, the entrepreneur's goal is to bring something new into existence. Some scholars, however, criticize this wide sense of understanding of what entrepreneurship is all about (Jones and Spicer, 2009).

Many commentators, however, assert that different forms of entrepreneurs are central actors in contemporary societies. This might sound like a cliché – a tale recounted over and over again, almost to the point of exhaustion – because it depicts such an attractive story, which is embraced by politicians and thinkers from many political abodes. Politicians are frequently asking for more entrepreneurial actions in societies. In most cases the more or less implicit focus is on entrepreneurship as business ventures. There are, however, many examples of entrepreneurship ventures that are not only for profit. In the rapidly expanding conversation about entrepreneurship, its different forms are becoming visible. One example is the social entrepreneurs who are individuals with innovative solutions to pressing social problems, which are also commonly based on voluntary and not-for-profit services.

Addressing the question of entrepreneurship in a wider sense instead of only as business-driven entrepreneurship, for instance as social entrepreneurship, is not simply another linguistic trick. Instead, it can shed new light on an ancient activity by elucidating the active form of entrepreneurship, and its objects and events as they are perceived and understood in time, timing, space and place. Different forms of entrepreneurship, in business ventures as well as in other forms of social systems, function as an increasingly central principle for organizing human action. Rather than following the old models in entrepreneurship, in this book a phenomenological focus on entrepreneurship unfolds new agendas. As such, this approach challenges how we think about the identity of entrepreneurship, its culture and its capacity to innovate and to set new ideas in motion. By embracing the active form of entrepreneurship, rather than the more passive entrepreneur, it becomes a framework that questions dominating views, by conceptualizing the entrepreneurial process as an active form of human action. That is the bottom line of this book: that the phenomenological understanding of entrepreneurship has become a new way of addressing and organizing a well-established research field.

The difference between space and place, and time and timing, coincides to a large extent with the difference between business studies and economics. In business studies the field of study mainly concerns different forms of how people deal with timely situations of scarce resources and incompatible preferences that occur in different places, such as in organizations. On the other hand, (neoclassical) economists have, during the past 100 years or so, endeavoured to create a more or less boundless 'science'. In economics there exists an attempt to replace the other social sciences in order to create a 'physics of social science' with boundless far-reaching ambitions (cf. Mirowski, 1989).

The difference between space and place, and time and timing, within entrepreneurial studies themselves coincides largely with the difference between theory and practice-based studies of entrepreneurs. In more practice-based studies, the field of study mainly concerns different forms of how people deal with all kinds of timely situations that occur in their daily life as entrepreneurs. The next chapter presents two views of entrepreneurial studies. These are referred to as the 'American view' and the 'Scandinavian view'. In the American view, 'opportunity' is a key concept. It has been widely discussed, however, whether opportunities exist to be discovered or whether they are to be created. In the former case, opportunity can be interpreted in objective time, while in the latter case, subjective time is more appropriate as a conceptual tool. In the American view 'market' is also a dominant concept. Market is, by and large, seen as a space concept. In the Scandinavian view, understanding entrepreneurship is dominated by subjective time and place. It is therefore seen as creating your own possibilities and doing things in a meaningful way for yourself and for others.

Overall, we have seen something of a 'spatial turn' spreading across all social sciences (Soja, 2008, p. 178). Foucault (2008, p. 145) claims that 'the present epoch will perhaps be above all the epoch of space'.

Lukermann (1964) analyses the concept of place and comes up with six major components:

1. The idea of location, especially location as it relates to other things and places, is absolutely fundamental. Location can be described in terms of internal characteristics (site) and external connectivity to other locations (situation); thus places have spatial extension and an inside and outside
2. Place involves an integration of elements of nature and culture: 'Each place has its own order, its special *ensemble*, which distinguishes it from the next place.' (p. 170) This clearly implies that every place is a unique entity
3. Although every place is unique, all places are interconnected by a system of spatial interactions and transfers: they are part of a framework of circulation
4. Places are localized – they are parts of larger areas and are foci in a system of localization
5. Places are emerging or becoming – with historical and cultural change new elements are added and old elements disappear. Thus places have a distinct historical component
6. Places have meaning: they are characterized by the beliefs of man.

> [We, the authors] wish to understand not only why place is a factual event in human consciousness, but what beliefs people hold about place. It is this alone that underlies man's acts which are in turn what give character to a place. (Lukermann, 1964, p. 169)

This fits well with the phenomenologist ambition to understand places as 'existential' and 'lived'.

Generally, there are few studies of entrepreneurship that include time explicitly. Few such studies recognize the historical dimension of it (Spinosa et al., 1997, p. 34). This is serious, as we see it. We would like to see more studies of entrepreneurship as a *process*. We agree with a statement by Paul Klee (Petranker, 2007, p. 174): 'To define the present in isolation is to kill it.' In the spirit of this, Chris Steyaert, for instance, who is a representative of the Scandinavian view, suggests that 'entrepreneuring' should be spoken about, instead of entrepreneurship. Steyaert (2007) writes somewhat regretfully that entrepreneuring has never achieved a breakthrough as the key concept that could elucidate the inherently process-oriented character of entrepreneurship. Dynamic and process-oriented approaches to human action are the exception rather than the rule in mainstream social science literature – not least in entrepreneurial studies.

It may sound like another play on words to talk about entrepreneuring instead of entrepreneurship. However, at the most basic level, the concept of entrepreneurship is about creative human action and endeavour. The use of the active form of entrepreneuring instead of the more static entrepreneurship, transforms how we understand and perceive this form of action, how we think of it and how we organize our attempts to study it. Simultaneously, using the word 'entrepreneuring' may shed new light on the methods, theories and understanding of different forms of entrepreneurial ventures.

To understand a phenomenon as a process, as an ongoing concern, can certainly provoke new thoughts:

> Goals and endpoints matter less. Learning is more urgent than storing information. Caring is better than keeping. Means *are* ends. The journey is the destination.
>
> When life becomes a process, the old distinctions between winning and losing, success and failure, fade away. Everything, even a negative outcome, has the potential to teach us and to further our quest. We are experimenting, exploring. In the wider paradigm there are no 'enemies', only those useful, if irritating, people whose opposition calls attention to trouble spots, like a magnifying mirror.
>
> The solid world is a process, a dance of subatomic particles. A personality is a collection of processes. Fear is a process. A habit is a process. A tumor is a process. All of these apparently fixed phenomena are recreated every moment, and they can be changed, reordered, transformed in myriad ways. (Ferguson, 1980, pp. 101–2)

We accept the interpretation that entrepreneurship is, above all, a process. Therefore, we will, as much as possible, use the term 'entrepreneuring' instead of 'entrepreneurship' in the present work.

Talking further about a central issue to us, no one should believe, however, that we have to choose between objective time and subjective time, between space and place. Adam (2004) claims, for instance, that an individual's pictures of society become more complete if they include objective as well as subjective time. She refers to such pictures as 'time-scapes'. One example from an entrepreneurial point of view is perhaps to say that people living in subjective time, including entrepreneurs, could be better understood if contrasted with people living in objective time and being directed by the clock.

On the matter of chosing between space and place, furthermore, Entrikin writes that:

> The tension between the relatively subjective and the relatively objective sense of place generally has been overlooked. The tendency to reduce one side to the other has made it easy to ignore. The theoretical reduction of place to location in space could not effectively capture, however, the sense of place as a component of human identity, and the opposing reduction tends to treat place solely as a subjective phenomenon. (1991, 24–5)

One example in entrepreneurship of the usefulness of looking at a situation as space as well as place is provided by Johnstone and Lionais (2004) in their study of depleted communities. Contrasting space with place, as does Hudson (2001), and by looking at the former as an economic evaluation of location based on its capacity for profit and the latter as a social location based on meaning, they claim that depleted communities can prosper only by combining the two. This is sometimes called 'community entrepreneurship' (more of this in Chapter Five).

2. A phenomenology of entrepreneurial action

INTRODUCTION

This chapter presents the foundation of our view on entrepreneuring. This is inevitably connected to how behaviour and action are normally seen and it is based on a social phenomenologist's approach to understanding reality.

The chapter begins with an overview of the development of the academic subject of entrepreneurship, what it has come to and its present standing in terms of different schools and views. This leads to a discussion about the differences between explaining and understanding, which relates to how action is commonly described as opposed to behaviour. This, in turn, leads to how the various logics of where and when can be used in the field of entrepreneuring, which is one theme in this book.

The chapter continues by presenting the authors' philosophical position as researchers – phenomenology – and ends by exploring the fourth theme of the book, that is, by discussing the consequences of the phenomenologist position on how to understand entrepreneurial action.

ENTREPRENEURSHIP AS AN ACADEMIC SUBJECT

Entrepreneurship as an academic subject has existed for about 300 years. During the first 250 years or so, this subject was only of interest to economists. However, the subject of entrepreneurship has never been part of mainstream economics.

For the purpose of this book, it is worth bringing up four classical scholars from the time, when only economists were interested in entrepreneurship, and present their ideas of what entrepreneurship is all about. They are Richard Cantillon (1680–1734), Jean Baptiste Say (1767–1832), Joseph Schumpeter (1883–1950) and Israel Kirzner (b. 1930).

Richard Cantillon, an Irish banker who mostly worked in Paris, was the first person to give the concept of entrepreneurship an analytical content. In his work *Essai sur la nature du commerce en general*, which was published posthumously in 1755, the entrepreneur was given a recognized role in economic development. Richard Cantillon, as most economists after him, was mainly interested in the entrepreneurial function, not so much in the entrepreneur as a person. He saw the entrepreneurial function as taking risks in the sense of buying at a given price and not knowing what demand will be or what the selling price will reach later.

The French economist Jean Baptiste Say distinguished three economic activities (1855):

1. Research generating new knowledge
2. Entrepreneurship applying this new knowledge to manufacture useful products by combining means of production in new ways
3. Workers doing the manufacturing.

Say claimed that entrepreneurs bring factors of production together and organize business firms. Say saw the entrepreneurial function as 'building units of production'.

The person often recognized as the most influential classical scholar of all in the theory of entrepreneurship is Joseph Schumpeter. Schumpeter was born in Austria but worked during the last 20 years of his life at Harvard University in the US. To Schumpeter, innovation was the critical function for the entrepreneur – the introduction of new products, processes or organizational units (see, for instance, Schumpeter, 1934). Schumpeter's considerable intellect was wide-ranging; beyond economics he was familiar with classical history, law, history of arts and sociology. He contributed many new ideas to the theory of entrepreneurship, including:

- That the main mechanism for economic development is 'creative destruction', that is, when entrepreneurs disturb existing market mechanisms and market shares
- That people cease to be entrepreneurs once they have introduced an innovation. The entrepreneurs may then become 'only' small business managers, that is, administrators of former innovations.

To Israel Kirzner, above all, entrepreneurs are alert to opportunities, that is, looking for imbalances in the economic system, which can be exploited to coordinate production resources more effectively than before (Kirzner, 1973).

Drawing on the work of these theorists, it is common to discuss entrepreneurship today as taking risks, building units of production, being innovative and/or being alert to opportunities.

Since the 1960s, entrepreneurship has mainly become a subject for business studies and related subjects. Some significant contributions are:

- Theories for technology development (Donald Schon, 1930–97)
- Behavioural research (David McClelland, 1917–98)
- Sociology (William Gartner, b. 1953)
- Small business research (David Birch, b. 1937; David Storey, b. 1947).

Donald Schon (for instance, 1983) pointed out the importance of what he referred to as 'champions' to all technological development. He came up with the following four conclusions:

1. At the outset, new ideas face strong resistance. Schon claimed that a social system's resistance to change can sometimes be extremely forceful. He called this the 'dynamic conservatism' of the social system
2. To overcome this resistance, selling becomes vital
3. The people who represent the new idea work mainly through the informal rather than the formal organization, at least to begin with.
4. Typically, one person acts as a champion for the idea.

David McClelland (1961) tried to come up with a picture of individual motivation in the context of management and entrepreneurship. According to McClelland, people in those areas are motivated by three principal needs: the need to achieve, the need for power and the need for belonging. The relative importance of these three needs varies between different people according to McClelland. He claimed that entrepreneurs are primarily driven by a need for achievement. He also stated that societies where the need for achievement is a norm are developing more dynamically than other societies. He wrote a classic book on this theme, *The Achieving Society*, which was published in 1961.

William Gartner, who is a sociologist, claimed in a seminal article (1988) that it is fruitless to ask who the entrepreneur is. According to him, the important question is: How are organizations created? He even defines entrepreneurship as the creation and establishment of new organizations.

David Birch presented pioneering work about the importance of small businesses in *The Job Creation Process* (1979). He claimed that in a country like the US, most new jobs are created by small firms. This conclusion was contrary to the established, taken-for-granted understanding, that big companies are the machine of the economy in all important aspects.

David Storey, a British scholar and contemporary of Birch refers to himself as a small business researcher, not as an entrepreneurship researcher. He points out, for instance that:

- Whether a small firm is growing or not is very much up to the entrepreneur/founder
- The government is important for the development of the small business sector in a society
- There are major differences between the frequencies in establishment of new firms in different regions of a country. (Storey, 1980).

Entrepreneurship is now a multidisciplinary subject. The phenomenon can be and is studied from many different points of view, from that of the economist, of the sociologist, of the financial theorist, of the historian, of the psychologist, of the anthropologist or of the geographer, just to name a few. Furthermore, much research on the topic probably still takes place in business-related areas and is market based, but, increasingly, the interest in the topic is broadened to other sectors of the society (there will be much more to say about this as the book moves on).

Interest in and research on entrepreneurship has simply increased exponentially during the past ten years or so. It is possible here, however, to see differences within various orientations. Two important orientations, containing definitely different views on the subject of entrepreneurship, are:

1. The American and the Scandinavian views on entrepreneurship
2. Explaining and understanding views on entrepreneurship.

We will see that this is related to how to look at behaviour versus how to look at action and how to look at entrepreneurship by different logics of where and when. The first will be discussed briefly in this chapter and the second will be a theme throughout the whole book.

TWO VIEWS ON ENTREPRENEURSHIP

As introduced in Chapter One, it is possible to speak of two different views concerning how entrepreneurship is seen today (see, for instance, Bill et al., 2010):

1. The American view: Entrepreneurship is basically an economic phenomenon and is a matter of tracing and exploiting opportunities and of creating something new, thereby satisfying demand in different markets, new or not. Entrepreneurs in all parts of society should, as much as possible, try to emulate those entrepreneurs who have been successful in business. Some representatives of this tradition are Amin et al. (2002), Dart (2004) and Dees et al. (2001)

2. The Scandinavian view (to some extent also the European view):
    Entrepreneurship belongs to the whole society, not only to its
    economy and is a question of creating something new and thereby
    satisfying demands and/or needs, new or not. To be a social entre-
    preneur is, at least partly, logically different from being a business
    entrepreneur. This tradition is represented by, for instance, Bjerke
    (2007), Hardt (2002), Hjorth and Steyaert (2003), Johannisson (2005)
    and Steyaert and Katz (2004). As aforementioned in Chapter One,
    this view sometimes wants to stress entrepreneur*ing* more than entre-
    preneur*ship*.

This geographic dichotomy is, of course, a simplification. There are many
examples of what we refer to as the American view also in Scandinavia
and, above all, in other parts of Europe. There are also a few examples of
the Scandinavian view in the US. Furthermore, both views can be found
in the rest of the world. What is clear, however, is that the American view
is dominant almost everywhere.

The difference between the American and the Scandinavian views on
entrepreneurship becomes very clear if you look at how the subject is
defined in American and Scandinavian textbooks. First some American
examples:

> Entrepreneurship is the process whereby an individual or a group of individ-
> uals use organized efforts and means to pursue opportunities to create value
> and grow by fulfilling wants and needs through innovation and uniqueness, no
> matter what resources are currently controlled. (Coulter, 2001, p. 6)
>
> An entrepreneur is one who creates a new business in the face of risk and
> uncertainty for the purpose of achieving profit and growth by identifying
> opportunities and assembling the necessary resources to capitalize on them.
> Although many people come up with great business ideas, most of them never
> act on their ideas. Entrepreneurs do. (Zimmerer and Scarborough, 2002, p. 4)
>
> Entrepreneurship is a dynamic process of vision, change, and creation.
> It requires an application of energy and passion towards the creation and
> implementation of new ideas and creative solutions. Essential ingredients
> include the willingness to take calculated risks – in terms of time, equity, or
> career; the ability to formulate an effective venture team; the creative skill to
> marshal needed resources; the fundamental skill of building a solid business
> plan; and finally, the vision to recognize opportunity where others see chaos,
> contradiction, and confusion. (Kuratko and Hodgetts, 2004, p. 30)

Compare these with some Scandinavian definitions:

> Entrepreneurial processes are about identifying, challenging and breaking insti-
> tutional patterns, to temporarily depart from norms and values in the society.
> (Lindgren and Packendorff, 2007, p. 29; authors' translation)

> Entrepreneurship is tangible action as creative organizing in order to realize something different. (Johannisson, 2005, p. 371; authors' translation)
> Entrepreneurship = to create new user value. (Bjerke, 2007, p. 17)

So, the Scandinavian view defines entrepreneurship less specifically than the American view does. Some consequences for approaching, tracing and describing entrepreneurship in the two views are:

1. The Scandinavian view, unlike the American one, does not specify what is required of a person to be an entrepreneur or which way is the best way to do something, if it is to be done entrepreneurially. The Scandinavian view is stressing the outcome of the entrepreneuring process more than anything else
2. The American view claims that entrepreneurs are something of an elite; the Scandinavian view does not
3. Similarly, the Scandinavian view does not say that entrepreneurship is to perform extraordinarily, which the American view does
4. The result of entrepreneurship, according to the Scandinavian view, is normally not very radical. Most entrepreneuring results, in that view, are better seen as more or less constructive imitations of what exists already. The American view asks for more.

To summarize, we can say that against the view of finding and exploiting opportunities, the result of which is to be sold to a market (the American view) we can conceptualize entrepreneuring as a way of improving your own situation and living, involving fellow members of the society (the Scandinavian view).

One Scandinavian researcher sees two developments in entrepreneurship research today (Lindgren, 2009):

- From a focus on individual to a focus on process (compare this with entrepreneuring)
- From individual activities to temporary collective organizational processes.

In terms of the logic of where and when, it is clear that the American view is a space-based view (even if not explicitly so), stressing opportunities and growth. It also points out the importance of subjective time for an entrepreneur. Finding and exploiting an opportunity is certainly a matter of timing. The Scandinavian view is much more open in these respects, even if it leans towards subjective time and place. The common belief for both views seems to be that entrepreneurs act, they do not just simply behave.

BEHAVIOUR AND ACTION

If a human being is abstracted according to the definition of behaviour it is seen as observable, that is, it can be perceived as empirical according to classic behaviourism. It is certainly true that 'behaviour' by many social scientists is used as an umbrella term for all kinds of human endeavours. Besides certain shortcomings in this, such an application of the term leads, as we see it, to a serious loss of information and a considerable confusion, if we are not to find what is meant by 'behaviour' or, if we do, to an extensive description. Here we suggest, like Werlen (2008) does, to use 'activity' as an umbrella term and 'action' and 'behaviour' as two specific possibilities to look at what humans do.

When looking at a human activity as a behaviour, we are neglecting all non-observable cognitive aspects of this activity, because it is necessary then to explain what is going on using (observable) 'stimuli' and (observable) 'responses'. Every object in the physical environment is representing a potential 'stimulus'. In empirical research an object is described as a 'stimulus' the moment it leads to a behavioural reaction. 'Response' is defined as 'anything the living being does' (Watson, 1970, p. 6). To reduce human activities to observable physical processes should, according to Watson and his followers, above all make a consistent application of (natural) science methods to society possible. The ambition with behavioural research is then to define behaviour causally within the framework of scientific theories so that, given certain 'stimuli', the corresponding response of a human being can be forecasted in a deterministic-nomological way.

Theories for cognitive behaviour constitute a development of classic behaviourism, as behaviour is then no longer described solely in terms of stimulus and response. 'Stimuli' is here conveyed *via* the elements of reflection, cognition and consciousness and not until then seen as relevant to behaviour. The cognitive (motives, needs, attitudes, level of aspiration, etc.) is seen as something of a perceptual filter for 'stimuli'. Stimuli, in turn, are now described in terms of information. Within these theoretical terms human behaviour is explained as responses to stimuli, which are chosen selectively and which go through cognitive processes and become information.

From an 'action' perspective things look different. 'Action' can generally be defined as a reflecting and intentional activity: a 'freely' performed activity which is goal directed. This may be brought about as an internal (mental) activity or as an external one (observable muscle activity) as opposed to just responding to stimuli. An action can be defined in its simplest form as 'intentionally effecting or preventing a change in the world' (von Wright, 1971, p. 83). But the discussion of action can lead further. Schutz makes a distinction between 'act' and 'action'. An act, in his opinion, 'shall designate the outcome of this ongoing process, that is, the accomplished action' (Schutz, 1962, p. 67). Furthermore:

> Schutz focused on different temporalities of the 'act' and 'action', respectively. An act, he suggested, can only be known retrospectively, once it has been performed. As a rationalized act it is explained with reference to the past. It can also be projected into the future as a potential act. Knowledge about any act as an act – past or future – therefore requires reflection. In contrast to the act, action is intimately tied to the present. It is a process with a forward direction, oriented towards projects. Action is always projected action and lived in an ongoing process. Action therefore, is always present, lived action in the direction of the future, while the act is always rationalized from a present (even the projected future present) in the direction of the past. This means meaning is inescapably attributed reflectively. (Adam, 2004, p. 67)

This means that we may even question whether it is possible to study entrepreneurship *ex ante*.

We do not mean that there are any human activities which lack a conscious intention at the time one acts. It is necessary here to decide whether a conscious and free act becomes so routinized that it is no longer necessarily planned consciously. If this is the case the activity can be described as 'quasi-behaviour', if not, simply as 'behaviour' (Werlen, 2008, p. 227). But simple behaviour (physiologically and biologically conditioned reflexes) is hardly relevant in a social context in general or an entrepreneurial context in particular.

'Quasi actions' are, on the other hand, described by Habermas (1984, p. 12) as the 'behavioural reaction of an externally or internally stimulated organism, and environmentally induced changes of state in a self-regulated system'. By this Habermas means processes which can be described 'as if they were expressions of a subject's capacity for action', which in reality can be described as activities of a mechanism which itself is not capable of providing any cause of its actions. This can be compared with the von Wright's distinction between 'quasi-causal' (causal descriptions of intentional action) and 'quasi-teleological' (intentional descriptions of causal processes in the sense of functional explanations) activities (von Wrights, 1971, pp. 84–5 and p. 58).

This work does not want to enter into any extensive analysis of the consequences of using the behavioural set of theories when analysing entrepreneurship. It is enough to say that its basic scientific orientation is to look at the environment as a cause. In this view, entrepreneurs live in a world full of circumstances, so to say. Bodies react in a deterministic fashion and they are fixed involuntarily. Those who represent this behavioural

*Table 2.1   The man of action and the non-entrepreneurial person,
according to young Schumpeter*

The Man of Action	The Non-Entrepreneurial Person
dynamic	static
breaks out of equilibrium	seeks equilibrium
does what is new	repeats what has already been done
active, energetic	passive, low energy
leader	follower
puts together new combinations	accepts existing ways of doing things
feels no inner resistance to change	feels strong inner resistance to change
battles resistance to his actions	feels hostility to new actions of others
makes an intuitive choice among a multitude of new alternatives	makes a rational choice among an existing multitude of existing alternatives
motivated by power and joy in creation	motivated exclusively by needs and stops when these are satisfied
commands no resources but borrows from a bank	commands no resources and has no use for new resources

Source: Swedberg (2006), p. 29.

orientation observe that subjective perceptions of the environment sometimes divert from 'objective' facts. But they go no further. Reasons behind
different subjective perceptions and their effect on different kinds of
behaviour are not studied closer. Nor are subjective perceptions seen as
related to subjective behaviour.

From an action point of view, entrepreneurs are living in a world full of
meaning. This means a distinctly different way to look at entrepreneurship
(as entrepreneuring) and at entrepreneurs. Swedberg (2006, p. 29) refers to
Schumpeter to draw up the distinctions between the man of action and the
non-entrepreneurial person (Table 2.1).

What makes people act? If we know the answer to that question we
would live in a different world to the one we live in now!

The authors of this present work would like to say that entrepreneurs
'just not are' – they act 'as if'. To be entrepreneurial means, as aforementioned, to do new things. It means, basically, to be more than, say, *just*
a manager, an employee or a citizen. Over and above this means to do
something for others (such as producing new products and/or services to
satisfy demand or starting new activities to satisfy needs). This also means
not feeling restricted by existing or expected resources – when doing something new it is done in such an interesting fashion or with such interesting
results for others, that new resources are generated in the process. Another

way to phrase this is to make a distinction between behaving managerially (administrative or bureaucratic behaviour) and acting entrepreneurially (see, for instance, Hjorth, 2001).

To act 'as if' (sometimes phrased as 'fake it till you make it') (Gartner et al., 1992) does not mean only to act as if you had the necessary resources already. It can also mean that:

- you can forecast the future; and
- before you have even embarked up on the road to success, you act 'as if' you have.

There is a metaphor that can be useful when discussing successful entrepreneurs (Bjerke, 2007). Such people must have four parts of their body actively involved:

1. The head: to have some ideas about what is required to be entrepreneurial in the specific case this can be referred to as 'to *know*'
2. The heart: to *want* to be entrepreneurial
3. The stomach: to have the guts to *dare* to take on something new.
4. The feet: to *start to move.*

All these parts must be present. If one of them is missing the entrepreneurial effort will not function very well. If you do not 'know', it will be a blind fumbling. If you do not 'want', it will be an act against yourself. If you do not 'dare', something constructive will not take place. The fourth part, 'feet', means that you actively do something. This is an example of the necessity to act as a venturesome person as somebody *acting*, not as somebody *behaving*.

This metaphor should not be taken as proof that the authors of this present work have, better than other researchers, found the formula for how entrepreneurs should best behave in order to succeed. Instead the metaphor should be seen as a special way of working with pictures, what Max Weber calls to work with 'ideal types'. He also calls them 'pure types'. One famous example of this is his three types of domination: legal domination with bureaucratic administrative staff, traditional domination and charismatic domination. Weber says you rarely find them in their pure types in reality but there are combinations, transitions and deformed varieties of these ideal types (Weber, 1975).

> [Weber] says they are not an average or a depicture of reality but bring the presentation of the idea clear-cut and unambiguous means of expression providing a uniform thought-picture free from contradictions. He further says that ideal

types should be logically consistent and free from value judgments and the ideal types are notions of limits – i.e., guidelines for the scientific work. (Ljungbo, 2010, p. 411)

Lately, a group of theories has come up which deals with how action in network is performed. Those theories are labelled as Actor Network Theories (ANT). They have had some influence in criticizing market as a fundamental arena for economic behaviour and might seem to be of some interest when discussing entrepreneurship as entrepreneuring. It started with Kuhn (1962) and his devastating critique of the naïve opinion of the relationship between natural scientific knowledge and nature (that is, the view that such knowledge reflects the true state of nature) and backed up with the assertion, for instance Winch (1958), that social science is fundamentally distinct from natural science. It led a group of sociologists to venture into the citadels of scientific activity – laboratories – to watch scientists at work (Murdoch, 2008). Their ambition 'was to create a legitimate space for sociology where none had previously been permitted, in the interpretation or explanation of scientific knowledge' (Shapin, 1995, p. 297). The resulting ethnographic studies dealt a further blow to the generally accepted simple correspondence between natural science knowledge and nature. They showed that scientists used a number of means to bring nature 'into order' in the laboratory (Hacking, 1983). Such means were technological instruments, such as 'inscription devices' (Latour and Woolgar, 1979), which transform material substances into figures and diagrams; literary techniques of persuasion, used within, for instance, scientific papers (ibid.); and political strategies, which might include coalition building in order to mobilize resources (Knorr-Cetina, 1981).

Actor Network Theories show that 'scientific results are not only "technically" manufactured in laboratories but also inextricably symbolically and politically constructed' (Knorr-Cetina, 1981, p. 152). Those results are interesting in themselves, but it will be seen later that such in-depth empirical and material-semiotic knowledge does not fit the phenomenological orientation that this book has.

We believe that acting is a better way to understand entrepreneuring than behaviour. We also believe that our modern society requires action. Change plays a dominant role in the working environment of today, but that is not all. Many changes are of a new kind in that they contain genuine uncertainty. Such uncertainty cannot be eliminated or erased by more extensive or more careful planning. Our 'changes have changed' (Ferguson, 1980). Furthermore, an increasing number of aspects of our modern society are affected by change. So, one consequence is that planning is less possible and action is more necessary today.

Behaviour and action have similarities with explaining and understanding, as investigated in the following section.

EXPLAINING AND UNDERSTANDING

To claim a clear difference between 'explaining' and 'understanding' may seem of little interest to some. However, it has become customary, though by no means universal, to distinguish between trying to get a picture of events or behaviour and trying to get a picture of acts. It is suggested that the term 'understanding', in contrast to 'explaining', ought to be reserved for the latter.

Since the inception of the disciplines of social science, lines of controversy have been drawn between those who do and those who do not make a principal distinction between two presumed alternative modes of thought, in the beginning represented by natural sciences and social sciences. Theorists rejecting any fundamental distinction between those modes have traditionally been called 'positivists'. They may be referred to as researchers interested in explaining. They assume that the methods which have proved their unparalleled value in the analysis of the physical world are applicable to the materials of social sciences, and that while these methods may have to be adapted to a special subject matter, the logic of explanation in physical and social sciences is the same. Theorists who draw a distinction between 'understanding' and 'explaining' can be labelled 'anti-positivists', and can be referred to as researchers interested in understanding. The critical element in anti-positivism is the insistence that the methods of physical sciences, however modified, are intrinsically inadequate to the subject matter of social sciences; in the physical world knowledge is external and empirical, while social sciences are concerned with interpretations and with various kinds of experience.

Many methodological and theoretical discourses within social sciences since the late nineteenth century have concerned modes of thought of 'understanding' and 'explaining' (Bottomore and Nisbet, 1979). These discourses reached a high point in the period immediately before World War I, and they have been part of social sciences ever since.

The controversy between explaining and understanding is deeply rooted in Western thought. In its most elementary sense it is based on a presumed intrinsic difference between mind and all that is non-mind. The controversy cannot be eliminated by choosing between explaining and understanding, because, basically, these two cannot be compared. Most explaining-oriented researchers, for instance, claim that everything, in the natural world as well as in the human world, can be explained, at least in principle; while understanding-oriented researchers claim that under-standing is only for humans. Furthermore, there is no neutral position where you can choose between explaining and understanding in a busi-nesslike and impartial way. One has to 'choose' at the same time as, by necessity, being positioned in either the explaining or the understanding camp. Which is really no choice at all! Furthermore:

- The purpose of explanations is to depict a factual (objective and/or subjective) reality in order to better predict its course from outside; the purpose of understanding is to develop means in order to better manage human existence from within
- One explanation can replace another explanation; one understand-ing can replace another understanding. However, an explanation cannot (according to understanding-oriented researchers) replace an understanding (which it can, according to an explaining-oriented researcher). Understanding-oriented researchers claim that these are two different scientific approaches.

According to von Wright (1971) and Apel (1984) the German philosopher of history J.G. Droysen (1808–84) was the first, within science, to intro-duce the difference between 'to explain' and 'to understand' (in German, *erklären* and *verstehen*, respectively), to ground historical sciences meth-odologically and to distinguish them from natural sciences. He did this in *Grundrisse der Historik*, which was published in 1858/1897:

> According to the object and nature of human thought there are three possible scientific methods: the speculative (formulated in philosophy and theology), the mathematical or physical, and the historical. Their respective essences are to know, to explain, and to understand. (Droysen, 1858 [1897], p. 13)

Droysen's term '*verstehen*' can be traced back to the modern founders of hermeneutics, F. Schleiermacher (1768–1834) and A. Boeckh (1785–1867); it was made more generally known through M. Weber (1852–1931). A his-torically significant form of the debate between understanding and expla-nation began with W. Dilthey (1833–1911). He utilized the dichotomy between understanding and explanation as the terminological foundation for distinguishing between natural sciences and *Geisteswissenschaften* (the humanities) as a whole. Initially, understanding gained a psychological character, which explanations lacked. This psychological element was emphasized by several of the nineteenth-century anti-positivist method-ologists, perhaps above all by G. Simmel (1858–1918), who thought that understanding as a method characteristic of the humanities is a form of empathy (von Wright, 1971). But empathy is not a modern way of separating understanding from explanation. Within hermeneutics, for instance, understanding is today associated with language (Gadamer, 1960/1997); within anthropology it is associated with *culture* (Geertz, 1973); and within phenomenology it is associated with intentionality in a way which explanation cannot be. (Phenomenology and intentionality will be discussed further later in this chapter).

Generally we can say that natural sciences require concepts which permit the formation of testable laws and theories. Other issues, for instance, those deriving from ordinary language, are of less interest. But in the social sciences another set of considerations exists as well: the concepts used to describe, explain and/or understand human activity must be drawn at least in part from the social life being studied, not only from the scientists' theories (Fay, 1996). Scientific concepts then bear a fundamentally different relationship to social phenomena from that which they bear to natural phenomena. In social sciences, concepts partially constitute the reality being studied; in relation to natural phenomena concepts merely serve to describe and explain (Fay, 1996).

> It is possible to explain human behaviour. We do not try to understand an area of low pressure because it has no meaning. On the other hand we try to understand human beings because they are of the same kind as we are. (Liedman, 2002, p. 280; authors' translation)

No one claims today that only natural sciences should aim for explanations and that only social sciences should aim for understanding. In practice, both attempts are made in the two scientific areas. Researchers are normally separating the two approaches, although in everyday usage it is harder to distinguish between what is meant by 'explain' and 'understand'. While it seems relatively clear that 'explain' means, by and large, to figure out the external circumstances around what has happened or what is happening, there is, however, a wide variety of opinions as to what could be meant by 'understand':

- to find out more details
- to get access to subjective opinions
- to get a picture of the larger context in which a phenomenon is placed
- to get a picture of relevant circumstances that have taken place earlier in a specific situation.

None of these equates to understanding; they are each just more detailed, more circumstantial or deeper aspects of explanation. From this book's point of view – phenomenologist – the crucial difference between explaining

Table 2.2   Explanation and understanding

Explanation	Understanding
Uses a depicting language	Uses a constituting language
Believes in a circumstantial world	Believes in a meaningful world
Sees behaving human beings	Sees acting human beings
Aims to depict a naturally complicated reality in models, that is, comes up with patterns in the law-bound reality by finding the most crucial circumstances in a situation and neglects those circumstances which are of less importance	Aims to problematize a socially constructed reality by using interpretations, that is, to construct pictures (maybe as metaphors) which can contain that meaning and those significances which are experienced in a situation and which, furthermore, provide openings for further construction of the social reality

and understanding is that explanation sees language as *depicting* reality and understanding sees language as *constituting* reality.

Thus, researchers interested in explaining, or explanation:

- look for factual (objective and/or subjective) data and use a depicting language
- want to find cause-effect relationships
- build models.

While researchers interested in understanding:

- deny that factual and depicting data exist (at least in the human world)
- want to look for actors' view on meaning, importance and significance and use a constituting and forming (even performing) language
- come up with interpretations.

In this, models are deliberately simplified pictures of factual reality; and interpretations are deliberately problematized pictures of socially constructed reality. It is natural for explaining-oriented researchers to build models and for understanding-oriented researchers to come up with interpretations. An interpretation is a theory-laden observation (Rose, 1980, p. 125). Table 2.2 offers a summary of the concepts of explanation and understanding.

EXPLAINING AND UNDERSTANDING ENTREPRENEURSHIP

According to Bjerke (2007, Chapter 3), there are four schools trying to *explain* entrepreneurship. They are:

1. Macro and micro schools
2. Entrepreneurial description schools
3. Supply and demand schools
4. Psychological and behavioural schools.

Bjerke (2007, Chapter 4) also presents four different attempts to *understand* entrepreneurship. They are looking at entrepreneurs as:

1. Sense-makers (Sanner, 1997; Weick, 1995)
2. Language-makers (Bjerke, 1989; Normann, 2001)
3. Culture-makers (Bjerke, 1999; Redding, 1993)
4. History-makers (Spinosa et al., 1997).

Below are, first, brief descriptions of the explanatory schools of entrepreneurship, and later are the four attempts to understand entrepreneurship being mentioned here.

Macro and Micro Schools

Kuratko and Hodgetts (2004) suggest a classification of entrepreneurial schools in two groups: macro schools (based on factors beyond the control of entrepreneurs) and micro schools (based on factors which the entrepreneur can control).

Macro schools can be broken down into the 'environmental school', which focuses on factors in the socio-political environment which positively or negatively affect the development of the entrepreneur, and the 'finance and capital school', which focuses on opportunities for the entrepreneur to look for and to find venture capital during different phases of the development of a business venture. Furthermore, the 'displacement' school is counted as a member of this group; this school considers the consequences for the entrepreneur of being outside certain political, cultural or economic situations.

Micro schools consist of the 'entrepreneurial trait school', which aims to identify the personality traits which characterize successful entrepreneurs; the 'venture opportunity school', which focuses on the process for searching for opportunities to develop a business; and the 'strategic formation school', which stresses the planning process for effective business development.

Entrepreneurial Description Schools

Cunningham and Lischeron (1991, p. 47) provide a list of models for describing entrepreneurs. It consists of the 'great person school', the 'psychological characteristics school', the 'classical school', the 'management school', the 'leadership school' and the 'intrapreneurship school'.

Supply and Demand Schools

A relatively common ground for classification is to divide studies of entrepreneurship into 'supply schools' focusing on the availability of suitable individuals to occupy entrepreneurial roles, and 'demand schools', where focus is on the number and nature of entrepreneurial roles which need to be filled (Thornton, 1999).

Factors influencing the supply of entrepreneurship can in turn be divided into population growth and density, age structure, immigration, participation, and income level and unemployment (Bridge et al., 2003). Similarly, factors that influence the demand for entrepreneurship can be divided into economic development, technological development, globalization, and industrial structure and clustering (ibid.).

Psychological and Behavioural Schools

These can be divided into the 'personality school', the 'social demographic school', the 'cognitive school' and the 'behavioural school'.

The personality school, as mentioned already, aims at finding the typical entrepreneurial personality. Personality can, in turn, be defined in terms of patterns and regularities in action, feelings and thoughts that are characteristics of the individual (Snyder and Cantor, 1998).

The personality school has endured much criticism. It has been unable to differentiate clearly between entrepreneurial small-business owners and equally successful professional executives in more established organizations (Carson et al., 1995). Most of the factors believed to be entrepreneurial have not been found to be unique to entrepreneurs but common to many successful individuals (Boyd and Vozikis, 1994). Most entrepreneurs do not possess all the enterprise traits identified, and many of the traits are also possessed by those who could hardly be described as entrepreneurs (Bridge et al., 2003).

Socio-demographic circumstances can explain entrepreneurs to some extent:

- Some regions or communities encourage entrepreneurship more than others because they have institutions ready to help small firms (Curran and Blackburn, 1991). Such localities could be said to be more favourably disposed to the notion of entrepreneurship (Bridge et al., 2003, p. 75)
- People who have self-employed parents are over-represented among those who are self-employed themselves (Delmar and Davidsson, 2000; Shapero and Sokol, 1982)
- Education and work experience influence entrepreneurship. Two groups are over-represented among those who start a business (Delmar and Davidsson, 2000, p. 4): individuals previously self-employed trying to start a new business, and unemployed individuals trying to start a business as a way of earning a living. As regards education most studies indicate a positive effect on self-employment, at least for low versus intermediate levels of education
- Ethnicity: self-employment is often suggested as a way for immigrants to establish themselves in a new society. However, the interest in self-employment differs widely between different categories of immigrants
- Those people who find themselves in an in-between situation in life seem to be more inclined to seek entrepreneurial outlets than those who are in 'the middle of things' (Dollinger, 2003, p. 43). Examples of such situations, apart from immigration, are between military and civilian life, between student life and career, and between prison and freedom.

However, no socio-demographic (or other individual level) variables have turned out to be particularly strong predictors of self-employment (Delmar and Davidsson, 2000, p. 2).

Theories which try to explain behaviour by how people perceive and comprehend information surrounding them are called 'cognitive theories' (Delmar, 2000, p. 138). Some general results within this area of interest to entrepreneurship (Baron, 1998) are that:

- many entrepreneurs seem to think counter-factually
- many entrepreneurs live more in the present and the future than in the past
- many entrepreneurs become very involved when making decisions and evaluating things
- many entrepreneurs underestimate costs as well as time required to succeed.

When modelling people, psychologists tend to make a distinction between 'distal' and 'proximal' factors affecting behaviour (Ackerman and Humpreys, 1990). A distal factor explains general behaviours (such as eating, sleeping or having sex). A proximal factor defines the more concrete situation in which the individual finds him- or herself. Actual behaviour is better explained by proximal factors (task characteristics) than by distal factors (traits and needs). Traits are, mostly, distal factors and they may therefore have little success in explaining actual behaviour, even less business performance (Delmar, 2000).

The behavioural school aims at looking at a larger complex of behaviour and how elements within it are related to supporting entrepreneurship. Examples of variables that may be contained in such a complex are the ability to make judgements and decisions, goal-oriented behaviour, planning behaviour, taking on responsibility, creativity, technical skills, networking ability and knowledge of project management.

With our research orientation as social scientists, and as we believe that action is a more interesting road to comprehend entrepreneuring than behaviour, we find theories trying to understanding entrepreneurship more significant than theories trying to explain it.

Entrepreneurs as Sense-makers

Sense-making is, philosophically, building on phenomenology. A few basic aspects of this are (more about phenomenology will come later in this chapter):

- The interesting world is the life-world: everyday life, that reality which is the constructed and experienced everyday reality, not the scientific world
- The life-world is socially constructed but individually based (Sanner, 1997, p. 39)
- Sense-making takes place in a continuous process that is characterized by dialogues and communicative exchanges between people
- This approach, which is based on phenomenology as presented originally by E. Husserl, has clear dialectic undertones.

This sense-making approach is described by Arbnor and Bjerke (2009) as the 'actors' approach'.

It is important here to separate three ways of looking at 'reality', that is, reality as objective, as perceived or as sense-made (Smircich and Stubbart, 1985). In the first case, reality is seen as something 'out there', a reality to discover and to depict. Reality is then seen as full of contexts and as objective *or* subjective (but still factual). In the second case, reality is seen as very complex. Human ability to generate more holistic and encompassing pictures of such a reality is limited. Only one part of such a reality can be looked at at a time. Reality can then be seen as perceived. The third case offers a different way of looking at reality. In this case, reality is not believed to be full of contexts, of which we, limited as we are as human beings, can see only a part. Instead it is assumed, consciously or unconsciously, to be controlled by our intentionality: we enact a reality which we have *made sense of*, a reality which means something to us. If this reality exists as such, or if it does not, is of less importance, as it is of no interest whether our perception is right or wrong. People act here as if reality were this way.

We claim that understanding entrepreneurs as sense-makers has much to offer in the understanding of their thinking and actions, for instance:

- Entrepreneurs live in a reality which they see as meaningful
- Entrepreneurs continuously construct a new social reality
- Entrepreneuring may probably never be understood without seeing entrepreneurs the way they see themselves
- Entrepreneurs must probably be understood by catching the content of their intentionality
- As aforementioned, entrepreneurs act 'as if', which means here to act as if reality is what they make sense of it.

Entrepreneurs as Language-makers

To catch entrepreneurs as language-makers means first of all to see language as reality. To work symbolically through language and by this transcend out of biological limits is a sign of mankind and may even be seen as the most significant characteristic of human beings. Our acts are not just controlled by our purposes; our acts, as well as our purposes, are controlled by the language we use. Genuinely new problems require genuinely new solutions. These new solutions will not be found if there is no language for them (Bjerke, 1989).

Language has certainly entered the theory and practice of business in the past 20–30 years:

- A company is defined by its language. The symbols, concepts, visions and focus of the senior managers offer a better understanding of the company in question than either its plans or decisions

- Every moment is a symbolic moment. Even to ignore this as a business leader is symbolic. Are you accessible? Is your door open? Who is invited to your meetings? Who is not? Are you present at the company's parties?
- The vocabulary of a company can be an important asset, but it can also be a major liability. Is the vocabulary of your company based on terms like 'efficiency', 'productivity', 'growth' and 'return' or is it based on terms like 'feeling', 'commitment', 'pleasure' and 'creativity'?
- To renew a company may require identifying those who hold on to relics of its old language (Arbnor et al., 1980). The point is to clarify the original ideas underlying the language being used in a company in order to reveal those who are still living in an outdated world
- To renew a company may also require changing the central building blocks of its language, that is, its memes. Think about mapping the genuine phenomenological language of starting a business used by an entrepreneur, that is, a personal language in an individual life-world.

Entrepreneurs as Culture-makers

Culture is a concept which is used in many parts of the society. However, no matter where we come across it, it seems, in general, to consist of the following (Bjerke, 1999):

1. Culture is something which unites a specific group of people
2. Culture is something you learn as a member of a group of people
3. Culture is intimately related to values.

All people have a culture and everybody is a unique combination of subcultures picked up from different contexts, like family, school, ethnic belonging, friends and work.

We claim that culture is intrinsically connected with entrepreneuring, for instance:

- Entrepreneurs around the world are different and very much dependent on the social culture, the business culture and the democratic culture, in which they live
- The relative number of entrepreneurs in society differs widely between different societies
- Those values influencing entrepreneurs are probably very different from one society to another.

- Different cultures have built up different structures for supporting their entrepreneurs.

Entrepreneurs as History-makers

We have presented three views of mankind, which are intimately related to each other and applied them to entrepreneurs. We are all, entrepreneurs or not, sense-makers, language-makers and culture-makers.

However, there is a fourth view of interest to the attempt to understand entrepreneurs, the notion devised by Spinosa et al. (1997): that only some people are history-makers. Entrepreneurs belong to this category.

We occasionally experience anomalies or disharmonies in our lives. These happen in our socially constructed life when things do not seem to fit together. Most of us merely note such situations. But there are those, including entrepreneurs, who act when faced with such disharmonies, thus disclosing a new reality for the rest of us. By doing so, they change the way something in society is done – what Spinosa et al. (1997) call the 'style'. This can be done in three different ways:

1. 'Articulation' is the most familiar type of style change. It occurs when a style, which so far 'is in the air', that is, only potential, is brought into sharper focus. Entrepreneurs act instinctively. In articulating change, the style does not alter its core identity, but becomes more recognizable for what it is. There are two forms of articulation. All articulation makes what is implicit explicit. If what is implicit is vague or confused, then we can speak of 'gathering from dispersion'. If what is implicit was once important and has been lost, we can call it 'retrieval'. Articulation is the most common form of entrepreneurship
2. 'Reconfiguration' is a more substantial way in which a style can change. In this case some marginal aspect of the practices coordinated by a style becomes more dominant. This kind of change is less frequent in everyday life than articulation. In the case of reconfiguration, a greater sense of integrity is generally *not* experienced (as in the case of articulation). Rather, one has the sense of gaining wider horizons
3. 'Cross-appropriation' takes place when one disclosive space takes over a practice from another disclosive space, a practice that it could not have generated on its own but that it finds useful.

Articulation, reconfiguration and cross-appropriation are three different ways in which disclosive skills can work to bring about meaningful historical change of a disclosive space. All of these three changes are called 'historical' by Spinosa et al. (1997) because people sense them as a continuation of the past: the practices that become newly important are not unfamiliar. Spinosa et al. (1997) are, therefore, contrasting their notion of historical change with discontinuous change.

One may ask, of course, why it is that our potentialities as history-makers are discovered by so few? Spinosa et al. (1997) assert that there are three ways to understand this. All of them can be seen as aspects of phenomenology:

- Our common sense works to cover up our role as possible disclosers of new reality. Common sense practices cover the situation that everyday common sense is neither fixed nor rationally justified. The ultimate 'ground' of understanding is simply shared practice – there is no *right* way of doing things
- Once we have become habituated to a style, it becomes invisible for us. It becomes part of what we take for granted in our everyday reality. If someone behaves in a way that does not fit in with our dominant style, we can fashion his or her behaviour to fit with ours
- Because we do not cope with the style of, for instance, our culture or our company or our generation directly – we simply *express* this style when we cope with things and with each other – we have no direct way to handle it or come alive to it and transform it. Our practices are designed for dealing with things but not for dealing with practices for dealing with things and especially not for dealing with the coordination of practices for dealing with things. We do not normally sense our potential as disclosers, because we are more interested in the things we disclose than in the disclosing as such.

> Through these three ordinary tendencies to overlook our role as disclosers, we lose sensitivity to occluded, marginal, or neighboring ways of doing things. By definition an occluded, marginal, or neighboring practice is one that we generally pass over, either by not noticing its unusualness when we engage in it or by not engaging at all. Special sensitivity to marginal, neighboring, or occluded practice, however, is precisely at the core of entrepreneurship. This sensitivity generates the art, not science, of invention in business. (Spinosa et al., 1997, p. 30)

Spinosa et al. (1997) claim that three widespread ways of thinking about entrepreneuring right now (entrepreneurship as theory, entrepreneurship as pragmatism and entrepreneurship as driven by cultural values) are not enough for several reasons:

- They are not genuinely innovative; to reduce entrepreneurship to a number of fairly stable and regular procedures which place us virtually outside of change

- They only try to satisfy those needs that exist already or which can be discovered or created without talking about how a person as an entrepreneur is changing the *general* way in which we handle things and people in some domain
- They are deeply ahistorical.

The authors of the present work instead suggest a composite case of entrepreneurship which:

- has the ability to act on the links between innovation and implementation
- exists to develop a feeling for the roots of our way of being
- creates domains for history-makers by attaching itself to perceived anomalies. The essential issue is what they call historical, unlike the dominant ways of thinking by developing specific skills, by being pragmatic or by living according to one's culture
- plays a leading role in determining which needs are important and in making change occur as it does; and
- brings up and makes central what is only implicitly understood but still moves with its time (articulation), takes up an innovation and, above all through speech acts, turns it into a practice (reconfiguration) or finds other domains for entrepreneurship (cross-appropriation).

Spinosa et al. (1997, p. 66,) claim that entrepreneurship is human activity at its best. Entrepreneurship as history-making is a good example of what we have referred to as the Scandinavian view of entrepreneurship.

PHENOMENOLOGY AS WE SEE IT AND USE IT

In general, it is possible to see (at least) three levels at which time, timing, space and place is approached:

1. A descriptive approach: This approach most closely resembles the common-sense idea of the world being a set of combinations of when and where, each of which can be studied as a unique and particular entity. This is also referred to as an 'ideographic' approach. The concern here is with the distinctiveness and particularity of combinations of when and where
2. A social constructionist approach: This approach is still interested in the particularity of combinations of when and where but only

as instances of more general underlying social processes. Marxists, feminists and post-structuralists might take this approach. Looking at the social construction of a combination of when and where involves explaining the unique attributes of a combination of when and where by showing how these combinations are instances of wider processes of the construction in general under conditions of capitalism, patriarchy, heterosexism, post-colonialism and a host of other conditions (Anderson, 1991; Clayton, 2000; Forest, 1995; Till, 1993)

3. A phenomenological approach: This approach is not particularly interested in the unique attributes of particular combinations of when and where, nor is it primarily concerned with the kinds of social forces that are involved in the construction of such particular combinations. Rather, it seeks to define the essence of human existence as one that is necessarily and importantly 'in time' and 'in place' and is more of an understanding approach than an explaining one. This approach is less concerned with, for instance, 'time' and 'places' and more interested in 'Time' and 'Place'. Humanistic geographers, neo-humanists and phenomenological philosophers all take this approach (Casey, 1998; Malpas, 1999; Sack, 1997; Tuan, 1974b)

Phenomenology is primarily concerned with how we perceive, experience and act in the world around us. What differentiates it from other approaches is its central emphasis on the actual phenomena of experience, where other approaches might be concerned with abstract world models. Traditional approaches would suggest that each individual has an understanding of the elements of which our world is constructed and an abstract mental model of how these concepts are related. This information, abstractly encoded in our heads, guides our actions in the world. Armed with a model of appropriate concepts and relations – an ontology – we can look around us and recognize what we see.

In contrast, the phenomenologists argue that the separation between mind and matters, or between what Descartes called the *res cogitans* and the *res extensa*, has no basis in reality (Dourish, 2004, p. 21). Thinking does not occur separately from being and acting. Phenomenology has attempted to reconstruct the relationship between experience and action without this separation.

Phenomenologists are trying to get at what Husserl calls 'the primary world' (what he later renamed as '*Lebenswelt*'). However, there are several differences between Husserl's transcendental phenomenology and Heidegger's hermeneutic phenomenology (Table 2.3). The authors of us lean towards the latter.

Table 2.3   Summary of differences between Husserlian and Heideggerian phenomenology

	Husserl	Heidegger
Metaphysical focus	Epistemological	Ontological
Description of the individual	Person living in a world of objects	Person exists as being in and of the world
Knowledge	Ahistorical	Historical
Enabling the social	Essences are shared	Culture, practices and history are shared
Method for gaining knowledge	Bracketing affords access to true knowledge	Cultural interpretation 'grounds' any knowing

Source: Berglund (2007), p. 80.

The phenomenological approach, as used in this book, is based on a belief that we, as human beings, always already exist in an interpreted wider context of the world. Our understanding of things surrounding us is therefore not as objects of perception and knowledge only, but as instruments, equipment and other artefacts that fit into our ordinary everyday practical activities. Our existence is understood as being concerned with how we fit in relation to others. This approach thus goes beyond an everyday understanding of phenomenology referring to that which is the immediate object of experience of things themselves. We do not have such 'immediate' data of pure consciousness, bringing forth a pure descriptive science of essential being (as proclaimed by, for example, Husserl, 1931, 1964). Instead, our phenomenological understanding requires interpretation of the *intentionality*, of, for instance, actions. It also means that our ordinary use of the word intention, meaning 'to have a plan or expectation', remains insufficient, and must be complemented with an understanding of 'our directedness' and 'attention directed to'. Intentionality in this sense is always practical rather than cognitive and the primary form of intending is doing something for a purpose rather than being only conscious of something.

The ideas that knowing and practice are intertwined as 'something we do' is a common trait in anti-foundationalist knowledge theories (cf. Rorty, 1981). By appreciating individuals as socially and culturally located beings also means that social and private aspects of action and practice are interwoven as a natural component of everyday practice. Practice, therefore, constitutes the ontological level against which any human epistemic relations become possible. Such anti-foundationalist approaches are therefore practice-oriented and often practice-based in their approaches (Dreyfus and Dreyfus, 2005).

Recent development in organization and business studies have proposed grounds for an exploration of knowledge and action as forms of social and material practice, that is, knowledge ability in action situated in the historical, social and cultural contexts in which it arises and embodied in a variety of mediators and materials (see Nicolini et al., 2003). Economists and sociologists tend to agree that economic action refers to the acquisition and use of scarce means. Motives on the array of economic action and the socially patterned influence hereon, is less agreed upon. The neoclassical perspective in economics adopts a set of simplifying assumptions about human action, in which humans (as rational agents) are reduced to pursuers of personal utility. This view is perhaps an extreme in a pendulum between constructions of mathematical models in social science and phenomenological – and more recently – practice-based approaches and understanding of human action.

Authors such as Bhaskar (1998), Bourdieu (1977, 1990, 1998, 2000), Garfinkel (1967), Giddens (1984, 1991), Goffman (1959), Heidegger (1927/1962), Merleau-Ponty (1962) and more recently Latour (1987) and Schatzki (1997, 2003, 2005, 2006) have attempted to frame a systematic presentation of material objects in social worlds, a 'theory of social practices', which can also help us explore the contextuality of entrepreneuring as lived experience. According to Schatzki (1997, 2003, 2005, 2006), the proper site of the social is not the individual or the collective mind but social practices. As such, social practice is a regular bodily activity held together by a socially and contextually situated way of understanding and knowing.

The interest in practice-oriented inquiry in social science has been widely acknowledged recently (e.g. Orlikowski, 2000; Schatzki, 1997, 2003, 2005; Schatzki et al., 2001). The term practice can also be seen in the wake of a renewed interest in (critical) materialist approaches in qualitatively oriented social science, which has been much under the influence of constructionist approaches over the last ten decades. The practice turn is an attempt to describe and understand human action in view of external environmental conditions as well as internal subjective dispositions. The practice focus is concerned with the ways in which human action is linked to the cultural, historical and institutional conditions and in accordance with the various practices within specific communities.

In the growing interest in practice-based approaches to knowledge and other forms of human action, at least four conceptualizations of the relationship between practice and knowledge have become discernible in the literature. One group focuses on approaches in which knowledge is not a property of the individual but is located instead within social gatherings in different communities and/or networks of practice (for example, Brown and Duguid, 2002; Wenger, 1998). A second group pays attention to the interaction and co-emergence of practice and knowledge and on the ways in which ongoing knowledge is constituted and reconstituted as actors engage with the organizational world in practice (Orlikowski, 2002). A third and more recent group focuses on the mutual inclusion of social and material arrangements (Schatzki, 1997). Finally, there is a more 'radical' group that eschews the idea of a pre-existing entity or substance of knowledge, which is the 'used' in action between human and non-human artifacts (for example, relationalist ethnomethodology and Actor Network Theory; cf. Latour, 2005).

Schatzki (2001, 2002, 2005), deriving inspiration from Heidegger and Wittgenstein, has recently defined the concept of site ontologies. By following Heidegger (1927/1962), to discern an object or a subject we always already have a context in which entities can show up and make sense, that is to say, Heidegger roots philosophy in everydayness, in practical agency and in the flow of life itself. This ontological context is provided by different forms of social practice. By discerning and identifying objects and subjects, we first need to have experienced in some way what constitutes these objects and subjects. The practices into which we are socialized provide a necessary understanding of what counts as objects and subjects and what counts as real. It is only because of this understanding of 'what it means to be' (which is embodied in the ways of doing, the tools and the institutions of a society) that we can direct our minds towards things and people (Dreyfus, 1991). It follows that 'the clearing is neither on the side of the subject nor the object – it is not a belief system or a set of facts – rather it contains both and makes their relation possible' (Dreyfus, 1989, p. 42).

Schatzki et al. (2001, p. 1) proposes to see the site of any social life as a 'mesh of practices and orders'. Sites are thus arrangements and 'arenas or broader sets of phenomena as part of which something – a building, an institution, an event – exists or occurs' (Schatzki, 2005, pp. 467–8). Doings, actions and practices are the locus of signification and meaning, and the 'primary generic social thing'. Consequently, the practice of entrepreneuring provides concrete and concise examples of how timely social sites, social orders, practices and agency provide a coherent and adequate account of social life. The understanding of 'site' is thus a broad reference to the many kinds of spaces humans inhabit: spatial, temporal and teleological. A site is a location in the widest sense where something is or takes place in a localized context, as the set of activities that make up a practice, and as a plurality of the configurations of practices. 'Each action, moreover, is considered to be an event, in the sense of something that occurs, or takes place (as opposed to the sense of event as mere happening in which events contrast with intentional doings)' (Schatzki, 2006, p. 157). Such an understanding of phenomenology – which is proposed by, for instance, Schatzki – is thus more indebted to Heidegger's ontological inquiries into our 'being in the world' as acting in practical contexts and, in contrast to Husserl's, conceptualized human life primarily as a flow of experiences and transcendental intentionality. Site ontology therefore makes a case for a social ontology centered on practices, and in the course of it rethinks contributions to 'practice theory'. Following this perceptual and practice-oriented view on phenomenology also means that learning and acting are not purely cognitive or social processes but corporeal processes of practical wisdom (cf. Merleau-Ponty, 1962. See also Küpers, 2005; Noë, 2004).

The understanding of site ontologies, in this sense, contends that human social coexistence is inherently tied to the contextual sites in which it occurs. This understanding of site ontology maintains that social phenomena can only be analysed by examining the sites where human coexistence takes place. By highlighting this type of site ontology, this 'approach differentiates itself from societies' ontologies that emphasize wholes, *sui generis* facts, or abstract structures' (Schatzki, 2003, p. 176).

'Social fields' such as entrepreneuring or 'institutions' such as entrepreneurial ventures are nexuses and sequences of social practices, and forms of practical understanding that organize practices. In this phenomenologically oriented practice theory, the smallest unit of social analysis of time and place is not found in qualities of the individual 'entrepreneur'. The things handled in entrepreneuring must instead be treated as necessary components for a practice to be 'practised'. Both the entrepreneur's body/mind and the artefacts provide requirements or components necessary but not sufficient to a practice. Certain things act as 'resources' that enable and constrain the specificity of a practice. The practice turn facilitates phenomenological investigations of everyday actions, such as entrepreneurship – processually understood as entrepreneuring (on entrepreneurship and phenomenological inquiry, see Cope, 2005; on entrepreneuring and site ontology, see Johannisson, 2009).

The site ontological and phenomenological approach suggested here resembles the science of geography, which has been asserted as a discipline that 'derives its substance from human's sense of place,' (Tuan, 1979, p. 387). 'Place' and site interconnectedness, in this sense, are more substantial than the word location suggests; they are unique entities with history and meaning. Place incarnates the experiences and aspirations of a people. Place is not only a fact to be explained in the broader frame of space, it is also a reality to be clarified and understood from

the perspectives of the people who have given it meaning. Looking at
the ordinary usage of 'place' and 'site' indicates that it has reference to
either somebody's position in society (that is, their sociology) or spatial
location (geography). There are reasons to believe that the former is
the primary. Finding somebody's bodily place and position in society
dominates over the more abstract quest of understanding a location in
space (compare with Plato's elaboration on abstract *chora* and concrete
topos in *Timaios*, section 52a-d; see also, for instance, Rämö, 2004b).
Following this trait opens a way towards the ontological concept
of implacement and practice-bound site ontology. These concepts of
placement and implacement are central in understanding the difference
between space and place as we do not live in space – we live in places.
Any kind of human endeavour is place-bound and our bodily implacement is the origin of any action. We are thus bodily implaced without
necessarily being securely in place. This contextual bodily implacement
also involves attempts at orientation and other forms of actions, with
or without surrounding artefacts (tools and other resources). Curiosity
in action and language are the only guides we have in our devotion to
express a statement upon the situated condition of our existence and
agency in the doing.

   The full implications of the practice-based approaches discussed here
cannot be addressed in detail in this book. Such practice-based approaches
would require substantial in-depth case studies to explore the human
implacement and orientation in everyday work encounters. Nevertheless,
a phenomenological understanding of entrepreneuring and its relation to
timely places remains a central theme for this book. A phenomenological
inquiry into the embodied aspects of entrepreneuring is also an attempt
to recognize how human action in timely places constitutes different
expressions of the concept (for example, in social entrepreneuring, environmental management, regional development, etc.). Recognizing bodily
practice as a primordial form of any human action is also an attempt to
consider that entrepreneuring which occurs in contexts 'not traditionally
considered within the domain of entrepreneurship, including the activities
of explorers, scientists, artists, freelancers, and social cooperatives, as well
as the many small-scale initiatives through which individuals and groups
seek to change their worlds' (Rindova et al., 2009, p. 489). Already the
literal translation of entrepreneurship – 'going between' – proposes such
a processual boundary-spanning activity of entrepreneurship as practice,
which is based on a phenomenological understanding of human action in
timely places. Again, that is why it is preferable to speak of entrepreneuring instead of entrepreneurship.

3. Our entrepreneuring society

RESEARCHING ENTREPRENEURING

There are many ways of doing research. One classification which fits our purposes can be seen in Table 3.1.

Entrepreneurship research is both the second and the third (the second in the case of the American view and the third in the case of the Scandinavian view). The American view, which is dominating entrepreneurship in research as well as in public discussions, is market based and does not explicitly position entrepreneurship in time, timing, space or place (when compared with the Scandinavian view; however, it is possible to say that the American view positions entrepreneurship in space more than in place). Three things come naturally with such theories:

1. Discussing growth as something primary (which again points at the fact that the American view could be analysed in terms of space, not place) (Coulter, 2001; Wickham, 2006; Allen, 2010)
2. Looking at 'opportunity recognition' as a distinctive and fundamental entrepreneurial behaviour (Gaglio, 1997; Kirzner, 1979; Stevenson and Jarillo, 1990; Venkataraman, 1997)
3. Viewing entrepreneurship as a (special) kind of management (Drucker, 1985; Hjorth, 2004; Wickham, 2006).

This kind of entrepreneurship research can be divided into four interest areas (compare with Bjerke and Hultman, 2002): the role played by entrepreneurship in the society; the characteristics of entrepreneurs and their thinking; entrepreneurial environments, including intrapreneurship; and entrepreneurial courses of events.

One alternative view of entrepreneurship, what we refer to as the Scandinavian view, has another orientation. It may, for instance, mean to look at entrepreneurship as an effort to bring about a new economic, social, institutional and cultural environment through the actions of an individual or a group of individuals. This differs from the perspective of change initiatives to create something new, say in terms of a new

Table 3.1   Different types of scientific knowledge

	Exact knowledge	Experience and experimental knowledge	Knowledge in humanities
Foundation	Mathematics	Natural (science)	History
Status	Independent from experience	Observable or provoked	(not) Observable
Purpose	Tautological statements	Universal statements	Meaningful statements
Logical starting point	Axioms or postulates	Hypotheses	Known events or occurrences
Conclusion	Apodictic beyond time and space	Assertoric prediction	Interpretation, when/where
Inference	Deduction, from general and explicit to particular and implicit	Induction, from particular and known to general and unknown	Intentional, from particular known to particular unknown
Veracity	Analytical	Synthetic	Questions-answers
Proof	Compulsive	Permissive (compulsive if the conclusion is negative)	

Source: Adapted from Ramírez (1995), as in Rämö (2010).

product; it rather draws attention to the emancipatory aspects of entre-preneurship (Hindova et al., 2009). This is about the 'everydayness of entrepreneurship as creating your own situation and being' (Steyaert, 2000).

> In the world-risk society, where the borders between public and private, politi-cal and nonpolitical have become blurred and political institution seems to be in a profound crisis, interest in direct participation, in civic initiatives and forms of nontraditional collective action, is growing. With 'politics' and 'political institutions' no longer coinciding, the sphere of everyday life tends to politicize more and more. This renaissance of political subjectivity, closely linked to the expressions of twentieth- and twenty-first-century cosmopolitanism, material-izes in and through everyday life. Everyday life is not only the arena where these unconventional forms of engagement are expressed, but it is also the privileged dimension through which the world becomes meaningful. (Jedlowski and Leccardi, 2003, as in Alberti, 2003)

This brings us naturally to the subject of what is in our modern society.

OUR MODERN SOCIETY

There are several aspects of our modern society that are of relevance when discussing entrepreneurial action, that is, entrepreneuring, in space, place, time and timing. One was mentioned in the previous chapter, that is, we have a new kind of change today. But one change is not like another. As Kelly (1998) puts it, changes come on different wavelengths. There are changes in the way the game is played, changes in the rules of the game and changes in how those games are changed. The most complicated one is the third, of course. Then, changes become so complicated that it is impossible to identify separate and individual causes. Old change paths are turned upside down.

Changes can also be classified by distinguishing between variations, structural changes (also called displacements) and paradigmatic changes (also called paradigmatic shifts) (Bjerke, 2007). Variations could also be called 'changes with retrogression'. This means a variation around a normal position, for instance, when a hard winter forces traffic to use land transport around a frozen lake, where shipping on the lake is the normal case.

Structural and paradigmatic changes constitute changes without retrogression. A structural change (structural displacement) means that a situation takes a permanent new position. One example could be a new law governing when shops are allowed to open and to close.

Neither of these two first models of change is adequate to conceptualize a paradigmatic change (paradigmatic shift). In this case, changes in the environment have become so large (or so numerous) that previous explanatory patterns no longer suffice and new ways of explaining events must be found. A paradigmatic shift in a situation can only be understood in the context of a complete change in our frame of reference. Anomalies will be placed in a new frame and in consequence they will no longer be perceived as anomalies, but will be understandable and natural. One example is a story that was told when Margaret Thatcher came to power in England in 1979. One of her promises when coming to power was to reduce income tax so 'it should pay to work'. To her surprise (and to the surprise of many), this led taxi drivers in England to work *less* than before. The reason turned out to be that they now could afford to take more time off. So, the model where there is a relationship between pay and work had to be replaced by a model where there was a relationship between pay and appreciation of spare time.

There are similarities between Kelly's third level of change (changes in how the games are changed) which, in his opinion, characterizes the new economy and what are here referred to as paradigmatic shifts. Conceptions of the so-called 'new economy' are, according to Martin (2008, p. xxv):

- A new information-based, knowledge-driven networked economy: Revolutionizing effects of new information-communications technologies and industries of the social and spatial organization of economic life. 'Space of flows rather than space of places'; territorial innovation systems
- A new form of 'dematerialized capitalism': New model of economic organization, accumulation, work, consumption and regulation based around (increasingly global) digital information, products and processes. The 'death of distance' and the rise of the 'global bazaar' (Coyle, 1997; Friedman, 2005; Leadbeater, 1999; Reich, 2001)
- A new 'cultural capitalism': Driven by prominence of cultural production and consumption, a 'new economy' of symbols, signs and sensations. Cities as the new sites of cultural production (Power and Scott, 2004; Scott, 2000, 2006; Thrift, 2005)
- A new era of 'creative capitalism': The rise of new creative and entrepreneurial classes as the key drivers of innovation and growth. Cities and regions as creative spaces (Cooke and Schwartz, 2007; Florida, 2003).

Do we have a new economy? Discussing the matter a bit further could provide a body of evidence to claim that our modern society is 'new' somehow and that it even deserves the name an 'entrepreneuring' society.

IT and other technologies play a decisive role in our modern society. Castells has even provided a date for and localized the start of what he calls 'the new economy':

> The new economy emerged in a certain point in time, the 1990s, at a given space, the United States, and around/from specific industries, mainly information technology and finance with biotechnology looming on in the horizon. It was in the late 1990s that the seeds of the information technology revolution, planted in the 1970s, seemed to come to fruition in a wave of new processes and products spurring productivity and stimulating economic competition. Every technical revolution has its own tempo for diffusion in social and economic structures. For reasons, that historians will determine, this particular technical revolution appeared to require about a quarter of a century to retool the world – a much shorter span than the predecessors. (Castells, 1998, pp. 147–8)

Technology is more than information technology (IT), but it is this technology that is most widely associated with our modern society. IT can be defined as the infrastructure and knowledge necessary to make information quickly and easily accessible (increasingly it applies to the software and the communication services that link the hardware).

However, IT is not essentially about new firms in a new sector but about new conditions for the whole economy:

> The popular distinction between the old and the new economy completely misses the point. The most important aspect of the new economy is not the shift to high-tech industries, but the way that IT will improve the efficiency of all parts of the economy, especially old-economy firms. (*The Economist*, 2000, p. 13)

IT is central to our modern society. It moves faster and faster. It invades all sectors; all that can be digitalized will be. It has created completely new industries (for instance, e-commerce, information services online and mobile communication) and it eases boundaries between nations, industries, companies, goods and services, working time and leisure time. In addition to lowering prices, IT has four other noteworthy features (*The Economist*, 2000, p. 10):

1. It is pervasive and can boost efficiency in almost everything a firm does, from design to marketing and accounting, and in every sector of the economy
2. By increasing access to information, IT helps to make markets work more efficiently
3. IT is truly global
4. IT speeds up innovation itself, by making it easier and cheaper to process large amounts of data and reducing the time it takes to design new products.

IT can give the same advantages to small firms as to big ones but, as has been noted already, not only IT but technology in general is characterizing our modern society. Technology occupies a strategic role like never before. 'Technology has become our culture, our culture technology.' (Kelly, 1998, p. 49) Technology increases the rate at which our economy is changing and it is spread at an accelerating rate (Coulter, 2001, pp. 34–8).

Society has also become a society of knowledge. Knowledge and competency are its key resources, 'the' only meaningful resource. Peter Drucker said a long time ago (Drucker, 1969, p. ix) that *the* only meaningful resource at that time was knowledge. We have seen that knowledge workers are the dominant group in the workforce today. The economy is about services as never before:

> Economies are increasingly based on knowledge. Finding better ways of doing things has always been the main source of long-term growth. What is new is that a growing chunk of production in the modern economy is in the form of

> intangibles, based on the exploitation of ideas rather than material things: the so-called 'weightless economy'. In 1900 only one-third of American workers were employed in the service sector, now more than three-quarters are. (*The Economist*, 2000, p. 29)

But, according to Castells (1998), the relevant border line is not between the industrial and post-industrial economies but between two types of production. The analytical emphasis should, according to him, be moved from post-industrialism to informationalism. Our modern society concerns difficult immaterial entities like information, relationships, copyrights, entertainment and security, and what is derived from them (Kelly, 1998, p. 11).

One interesting aspect of knowledge is that it does not obey the traditional economic laws of scarcity. It does not matter how much knowledge is used, it is still not used up! The most revolutionary aspect of our modern society is possibly that it defies the traditional economic laws of diminishing returns. This has also led to industrial borders becoming less distinct and often impossible to maintain. Traditional industries either invade each other's territory or merge. One example is telecommunications, computers and entertainment. We refer to the three as infotainment today. It could be said that in our modern society opportunities are greater than ever, but so are the chances of failure (*The Economist*, 2001, p. 4).

New kinds of organization appear as hierarchical and centralized structures decline. But society does not collapse. Far from it. Some ambitious people transform society from below in order to make it stronger, more well balanced and more multi-faceted. Contemporary society is underpinned by all-encompassing electronic networks, but it is more than that: the network is the primary symbol of our modern society (Holmberg et al., 2002, p. 13). The logic of networks permeates almost all systems and arrangements of relationships today. It is even possible to say that network thinking is changing our identities. What matters today is whether a person belongs to 'the network' or not. However, at the same time, the more high-tech we become the more 'high-touch' we need (Naisbitt et al., 2001).

But we do not only need each other more as individuals. We also need each other more as nations. Our modern society is global because its central activities and its components are organized globally (Castells, 1998). Jonung (2000) associates this new globalized economy with a free and extremely fast flow of ideas, information and capital, a flow that to a large extent is a result of the IT revolution. Others, such as Eriksson and Ådahl (2000), discuss 'the new economy' in somewhat more political terms, with the market economy (heavily promoted by the United States) as a model. The supporters of globalization claim that it facilitates high economic growth for all participants. Its opponents claim, on the other hand, that it is increasing the rifts between rich and poor countries.

At any rate, global markets add to our inability to make meaningful forecasts. They have, furthermore, gone hand in hand with the fact that limitations of physical distance and actions in our companies and organizations as well as limitations of time have, by and large, disappeared. 'The linear time-regime of industrial society has been substituted by a time which has no beginning or end, which operates worldwide in real time and without respect to geographical demarcations' (Benner, 2002, p. 136). The winners in the competition between participants in our modern society often seem to concentrate on being the fastest rather than being the fittest (Bjerke and Hultman, 2002).

Finally, the view on capital has changed in our modern world. We speak less and less of financial capital and more and more of, for instance, human capital, social capital, cultural capital, structural capital and visual capital.

Giddens (1990) has some thought-provoking points to make about our modern society. He notes, like many others, some specific features involved in modern societies: the higher pace of change, the wider scope of change and the fact that modern societies are ordered according to different principles than those of pre-modern societies. Giddens discusses the development of societies in two themes: security versus danger and trust versus risk.

> Modernity is a double-edged phenomenon. The development of modern social institutions and their worldwide spread have created vastly greater opportunities for human beings to enjoy a secure and rewarding existence than any type of pre-modern system. But modernity also has a somber side, which has become very apparent. (Giddens, 1990, p. 7)

Giddens (1990) comes to several conclusions:

- The dynamism of modern societies derives from the separation of time and space and space from place and their recombination. In pre-modern societies, space and place largely coincided because, for most of the population, the spatial dimensions of social life were localized activities. The modern societies tear space away from place by fostering relations between 'absent' others, locationally distant from face-to-face interaction. We are increasingly influenced by social powers distant from ourselves
- The separation of time and space is crucial to the extreme dynamism of modern society for three reasons: 1. We experience an increasing number of standardized 'empty' dimensions in social activities and their 'disembeddedness' in the particularities of contexts of presence. Disembedded institutions greatly extend the scope

of time-space distanciation, depending upon coordination across time and space. We get an increasing number of 'expert systems'; 2. An increasing number of rationalized organizations also appear, organizations that connect the local and global in ways that would have been unthinkable in more traditional societies; and 3. Modern societies depend on modes of 'insertion' into time and space unavailable to previous civilizations. A standardized dating system, now universally acknowledged, provides for an appropriation to focus a unitary past – time and space are recombined to focus a genuinely world-historical framework of action and experience

- We live today by reflexively appropriating knowledge. The production of systematic knowledge about social life becomes integral to system reproduction, rolling social life away from fixities of tradition
- Risk has become globalized in modern societies. We have to live in the presence of the danger of expanding numbers of contingent events that affect everyone or at least large numbers of people on the planet. Risk stems from the created environment or socialized nature – the infusion of human knowledge into the material environment. Furthermore, many of the dangers we face collectively are known to wider publics.

Mariavelias (2009) takes a somewhat related tack on the subject of modern societies, concentrating on freedom. In traditional societies, freedom as autonomy was celebrated by all who could. In modern societies, we have another understanding of freedom – freedom as potential – which implies that we become entangled with the environment and that such intimate interaction is celebrated, because without it, the potential of doing and accomplishing things does not exist (de Carolis, 1996). This has, as we see it, several consequences. It will be harder to see how power is exerted. Furthermore, as the possibilities to exploit possibilities are so different in societies today, we may now have increased inequality.

The point is whether it is best to look at our modem society from an entrepreneurial point of view as a space for 'managing opportunities', or as a place for 'improving your own situation and living'. Maybe it is both, depending on which of the two you start from when looking!

MANAGING OPPORTUNITIES

Wickham (2006, p. 16) claims that he can say with confidence that an entrepreneur is a manager, that is, somebody who manages in an entrepreneurial way. Entrepreneurial management, as he sees it, is characterized by three features: a focus on change, a focus on opportunity and organization-wide management. Drucker (1985, p. 131) suggests that no matter where entrepreneurship is happening in a society, the rules governing it are pretty much the same, the things that work and those that do not are pretty much the same, and so are the kinds of innovation and where to look for them. He claims that in every case there is a discipline that can be called 'entrepreneurial management'. Furthermore:

> Unless a new venture develops into a business and makes sure of being 'managed', it will not survive no matter how brilliant the entrepreneurial idea, how much money it attracts, how good its products, nor even how great the demand for them. (Drucker, 1985, p. 172)

One outcome of looking at entrepreneurship as a kind of management is the common statement in the American view of the subject that successful entrepreneurship starts by coming up with a good business plan. Entrepreneurship is commonly defined in the American view as the process by which individuals pursue opportunities without regard to resources they currently control (Stevenson and Jarillo, 1990). The essence of entrepreneurship behaviour is there seen as identifying opportunities and putting useful ideas into action (Ireland et al., 2003). This may sound the same as the statement in Chapter 2 that entrepreneurs just not simply are, that is, that they do not behave administratively or bureaucratically. But we never said that this must be triggered by a special kind of management or by the recognition of an opportunity!

According to Gaglio and Katz (2001, p. 95), 'understanding the opportunity identification process represents one of the core intellectual questions for the domain of entrepreneurship'. Mariotti and Glackin (2010, p. 13) assert that there is a simple definition of 'entrepreneur' that captures the essentials: 'An entrepreneur recognizes opportunities where other people see only problems.' According to Baron and Shane (2008, p. 5), entrepreneurship involves the key actions of identifying an opportunity that is potentially valuable in the sense that it can be exploited in practical business terms and yield sustainable profits. 'The entrepreneur always searches for change, responds to it, and exploits it as an opportunity' (Drucker, 1985, p. 25). Kirzner (1979) asserts that the mentality of entrepreneurs differ because they are driven by 'entrepreneurial alertness', which he suggests is a distinctive set of perceptual and cognitive processing skills that direct the opportunity recognition process.

An opportunity is seen by Barringer and Ireland (2006, p. 28) as 'a favorable set of circumstances that creates a need for a new product, service, or business'. Coulter (2001, p. 53) sees opportunities as 'positive external environment trends or changes that provide unique and distinct possibilities for innovating and creating value'.

> The opportunities themselves often emerge from changes in economic, techno-logical, governmental, and social factors. When entrepreneurs notice links or connections between these changes, ideas for new ventures may quickly follow. (Baron and Shane, 2008, p. 13)

Timmons (1999) defines a business opportunity as an idea with four characteristics:

1. It is attractive to customers
2. It will work in your business environment
3. It can be executed in the window of opportunity (which is the amount of time you have to get your business idea to the market) that exists
4. You have the resources and skills to create the business or you know someone who does and who might want to form a business with you.

Opportunities may be internal, that is, come from inside you or your organization – from a hobby, an interest or even a passion; or opportunities, may be external, that is, generated by a noticeable outside circumstance. Such outside circumstances may be (Mariotti and Glackin, 2010, p. 16):

1. Problems that your business can solve
2. Changes in laws, situations or trends
3. Inventions of totally new products or services
4. Competition. If you can find a way to beat the competition on price, location, quality, reputation and reliability of speed, you may create a very successful business with an existing product or service
5. Technological advances. Scientists may invent new technology, but entrepreneurs figure out how to use and sell them.

Opportunities generally arise from two major sources – the information people have that helps them to notice new business opportunities, and changes in the external world that generate opportunities (Baron and Shane, 2008, p. 39). According to the economist Acs (2002, p. 12), opportunities for discovering or creating goods and services in the future exist precisely because of the dispersion of information. This dispersion creates the opportunity in the first place. Second, the very same dispersion presents hurdles for exploiting the opportunity profitably, because of the absence or failure of current markets for future goods and services. It is therefore, according to Acs (ibid.) necessary to understand how opportunities for the creation of new goods and services arise in a market economy, and how and in what ways individual differences determine whether hurdles in the discovering, creating and exploiting of opportunities are overcome.

What differentiates entrepreneurial opportunities from other profit-making opportunities is that to exploit entrepreneurial opportunities you have to discover a new means to an end, with unknown outcomes and resources not yet under the control of the entrepreneur (Amit et al., 1993). The way Wickham (2006, p. 236) phrases it is that an opportunity is the possibility to do things *differently* from and *better* than how they are being done at the moment. In economic terms, 'differently' means an innovation has been made. This might take the form of offering a new product or of organizing the company in a different way. 'Better' means the product offers a utility in terms of an ability to satisfy human demands, that exist-ing products do not. The new organizational form must be more *produc-tive*, that is, more efficient at using resources than existing organizational forms. According to the same author, we may think of business opportuni-ties as looking at a landscape representing the possibilities open to us. As we look across the landscape we will see open ground, untouched and full of new potential. We may see areas that are built up but where the build-ings are old and decrepit, waiting to be pulled down or for something new to be built in their places. Effective entrepreneurs know the landscape in which they are operating. They know where the spaces are and how they fit between the built-up areas. They know which buildings can be pulled down and which are best left standing.

The highly recognized Global Entrepreneurship Monitor studies on the variation of entrepreneurship inclination across countries are very much the product of the American view on entrepreneurship. Those studies have come to the conclusion (Bosma and Harding, 2007), that early-stage entrepreneurship is more likely to be opportunity-driven in high-income countries than in middle or low-income countries, where entrepreneur-ship in many cases may be the only option for making a living, that is, it is necessity-based. Two major drivers of opportunity entrepreneurship are identified in these same studies: those who are attracted to entrepreneur-ship primarily because they desire independence, and those who are pri-marily attracted because they want to increase their income compared to, for instance, being an employee (Bosma and Harding, 2007, p. 19).

There has been a debate in the field of entrepreneurship on whether opportunities exist in the external world or are created by human minds (see, for instance, Forbes, 2005). Baron and Shane (2008, p. 84) believe that there is no basis for controversy over this issue. Opportunities as potentials, according to them, come into existence in the external world as a result of changes in social conditions. However, they remain mere potentials until they are recognized by somebody's perceptual and cognitive skills. In a sense, therefore, according to Baron and Shane, opportunities both exist 'out there' and are a creation of human thought (compare this with the discussion in Chapter 2 around the differences between behaviour and action).

Hjorth (2004, p. 429) asserts that an opportunity is not waiting to be discovered: 'An opportunity has to be actualized in its own way, through creating its own difference. This, however, can only happen with a certain timing.' This brings us to the Scandinavian view on entrepreneurship.

IMPROVING YOUR OWN EVERYDAY SITUATION AND LIVING

> We believe that a managerial perspective already marginalizes entrepreneurship as forms of creativity due to the principle mandate of management to secure control and efficiency. (Hjorth, 2004, p. 413)

As the authors of this book, we agree with Steyaert and Katz (2004, p. 186) that there is a danger that 'an already dominant economic discourse becomes more widespread, or that other discourses are solely brought in to support the economic discourse'. There is a need, as they claim, to develop a 'more varied discursive repertoire and develop the very dimension of civic and cultural' (ibid.).

> The possibilities of entrepreneurship as a concept are at stake and the stakes for entrepreneurial scholars are high, to indulge a multi-sided view on entrepreneurship, so that creative possibilities are just not economized, again in the public sector, again in civic society. (Steyaert and Katz, 2004, pp. 188–9)

To adopt what we call the Scandinavian view on entrepreneurship as entrepreneuring is a kind of protest against constructing the subject using the enterprise discourse (Weiskopf and Steyaert, 2009, p. 200). It 'increases the possibilities of life that are not yet known' (ibid.). Its content can never be programmed, nor even defined, in advance. It has no foundation other than practice itself. It is not an 'acceptance of being', but rather the 'creation of being' (Hardt, 2002, p. 117). It favours 'the nonaction of suspending established stimulus-response circuits to create a zone where chance and change may intervene' (Massumi, 1992, p. 99). Steyaert refers to this as 'a prosaic study of entrepreneurship' which, to him, means to 'take a route towards a study of the conversational processes that account for the everydayness of entrepreneurial processes' (Steyaert, 2004, p. 9). It is based on 'the belief that the everyday is the scene where social change and individual creativity take place as a slow result of constant activity' (Steyaert, 2004, p. 10). Thousands of small steps can make a difference. Things are then not just happening but are related to a meaningful whole. We enter, so to say, a dialogue with ourselves while becoming, and every process of becoming is seen as social and meaningful (Boutaiba, 2004, pp. 23–4).

With the same orientation and using de Certeau's (1984) definition of space as something created as practice, Hjorth (2004) looks at entrepreneurship in existing organizations as the process of creating space for play and invention. He notices (Hjorth, 2007) that for some time, focus in entrepreneurship studies has shifted from individuals to processes or, more generally, from what something is to how it becomes. Along this line, he claims that the popular focus on opportunity recognition should attend to the creative opportunity of entrepreneurial processes; that is, entrepreneurs should associate themselves with the desiring, playful, creative person rather than the economic and modular composition of humans that has so far dominated modernist management theory.

> I believe that dominant thinking on entrepreneurship prevents us from studying entrepreneurship in relation to organisation in a way that affirms the playful, moving, creative and dramatic characteristics of entrepreneurial processes so often lost in representations dominated by economism and managerialism. In addition, I find a challenge in approaching processes of opportunity creation as part of the everydayness life, and, as such, escaping the 'strategic' purpose of opportunity exploitation (being the *telos* of opportunity discovery and recognition).
> A start is always created as a response to the openness of life's ongoingness. I therefore suggest, as a response to this openness, that stories of entrepreneurship start not from a focus on opportunity recognition/discovery that is already locked into the anticipated and strategised process of opportunity utilisation. Instead, we can start with tactical opportunity creation in everyday practices, expressing a desire to become another, and to increase the productive/creative powers of organising. That is, the opportunity of creating life would be life as potential (life as constituent power) rather than life as potestas (as a constituted power, an idea of presenting itself as a sovereign power). (Hjorth, 2007, pp. 715–6)

For the opening up of the subject of entrepreneurship and to move it in a more favourable direction as entrepreneuring, Steyaert and Katz (2004) formulate three propositions. The first proposition says that entrepreneurship takes place in multiple sites and spaces in society. The second proposition claims that these spaces are political spaces that can be constituted by a variety of discourses overcoming the sole economic definition that impacts and is impacted by entrepreneurship. The third proposition states that entrepreneurship is a matter of everyday activities rather than actions of elitist groups of entrepreneurs.

ENTREPRENEURING IN DIFFERENT SECTORS, SITUATIONS AND CONTEXTS IN SOCIETY

Most entrepreneurship researchers today, like the two authors of this book, do not want to limit entrepreneurship to specific personality criteria or to some specific (say economic) behaviour. The Scandinavian view on the subject (which we belong to) claims furthermore that entrepreneurs exist in all parts of the society, not only in its economy. Johannisson (2005, p. 27; our translation) expresses it as: 'entrepreneurship is something that is part of all human life' or 'the market is too small an arena for entrepreneurship, only the whole human existence is big enough.' (ibid., p. 39; authors' translation)

Three sectors, where entrepreneuring takes place, can be seen in society (Figure 3.1):

- The common sector
- The business sector
- The citizen sector (or the 'third sector').

Furthermore, only a part of each of these three sectors is made up by entrepreneuring, that is, by individuals who 'do, not simply are' and act 'as if' (individuals who are satisfying demands and needs through new business ventures or new activities over and above just being employed in the common sector, running a business or being citizens). They are seen in the subsets surrounded by dashed lines in Figure 3.1:

- E(com): Entrepreneurs in the common sector
- E(bus): Entrepreneurs in the business sector
- E(cit): Entrepreneurs in the citizen sector.

It is possible to associate the above three types of entrepreneurs with three different situations in which they act (compare with Bjerke, 2010):

1. In institutions in the common sector
2. In markets in the business sector
3. In private or public places in the citizen sector.

With this view, we find three kinds of entrepreneurs in a society:

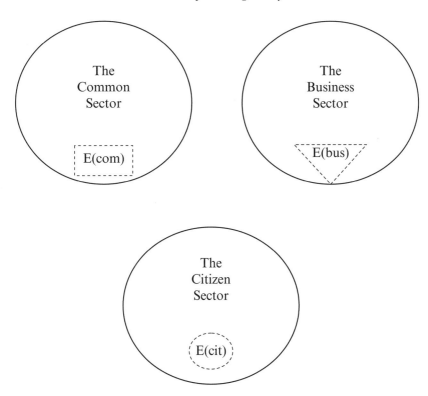

Figure 3.1   The three sectors of a society

1. The entrepreneurs in the common sector: People employed in differ-
    ent institutions in the common sector, who act 'as if' for the common
    good over and above 'just being' employed there
2. Business entrepreneurs: Entrepreneurial people who are economically
    motivated and who satisfy demand in different markets by providing
    new products and/or services
3. Citizen entrepreneurs: Entrepreneurial people who are motivated by
    social ideas and who satisfy needs through new activities. These can
    take place in private places (for instance, in sheltered workshops or
    in the homes of old people) or in public places (for instance, in city
    libraries or on the Internet).

This broad classification is in line with the Scandinavian view on entrepreneurship as entrepreneuring. Berglund and Johansson, as representatives
of this view, state that:

To see that entrepreneurship in fact manifests itself in a number of places and not localized to only, say, incubators or science parks. To see that people, through their entrepreneurship, create a number of values for the society and not only the economic ones which so easily come into focus. (2008, p. 2; authors' translation)

It is important to realize that Figure 3.1 intends to show that not all that is going on in society is entrepreneuring. There are many activities in the traditional sectors of the society which are not entrepreneurial. To phrase it differently, it is of course possible to be a citizen, employed in the common sector and/or be a business person without being entrepreneurial. Furthermore, entrepreneurial activities can take place in situations where many non-entrepreneurial activities also take place. Institutions are associated with what is traditionally called the public sector (we prefer to call it the common sector), markets are associated with the business sector, and private or public places are associated with what sometimes is referred to as the third sector (we prefer to call it the citizen sector).

If the entrepreneurial subsets in Figure 3.1 are enlarged, Figure 3.2 results. We see all entrepreneurs in the common sector and all entrepreneurs in the citizen sector, but only some business entrepreneurs, as social entrepreneurs (represented by the shaded fields in Figure 3.2). We see all entrepreneurs as social entrepreneurs who are not run by a profit motive but by a social idea or entrepreneurs who, next to their profit motives, have a clear objective to satisfy non-commercial citizen needs in a society. The rest we see as business entrepreneurs, that is, the majority of entrepreneurs in the business sector.

There are all kinds of connections between the different entrepreneurial parts of Figure 3.2 and between these parts and the rest of the society, for instance:

- From or to entrepreneurs in the common sector and other parts *of* the same sector. This can be people who go from just being employed in this sector to coming up with new ways to perform their tasks, or people who after having done so go back to 'just' administering them as part of their employment (These connections are marked with *1* in Figure 3.2)
- From or to entrepreneurs in the business sector to social entrepreneurs in the same sector. This can be business entrepreneurs who change their entrepreneurial ventures in a more socially oriented direction or social entrepreneurs within the business sector who, after having developed new socially oriented activities within the business sector, move into running them in a more commercial, but

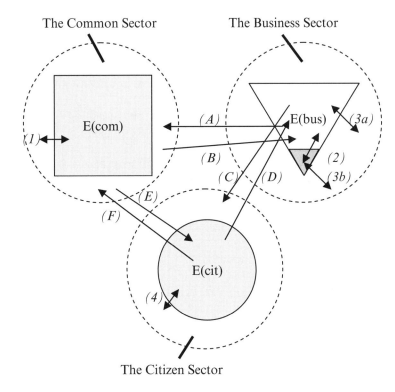

Figure 3.2   Entrepreneurs in different sectors of a society

still entrepreneurial, way (These connections are marked with *2* in
Figure 3.2)

• From or to entrepreneurs in the business sector and other, non-
entrepreneurial parts of, the same sector. This can be traditional
business people who move between being entrepreneurial business people and being non-entrepreneurial business people (*3a*)
and socially oriented business entrepreneurs who move between
being socially business entrepreneurs and being non-social non-
entrepreneurial oriented business people (*3b*)

• From or to citizen entrepreneurs (that is social entrepreneurs in
the citizen sector) to another part of the citizen sector. This can
be people who have run citizen sector entrepreneurial ventures as
a project and who move to 'just be' citizens, or citizens who move
from what it means to be a citizen and start citizen sector entrepreneurial ventures (as citizens) (These connections are marked with *4*
in Figure 3.2).

- There are several possible connections *between* the different sectors. Some examples (which are also marked in Figure 3.2) are:
  - *(A)* From market to institution: A consulting company which helps a local community with its place marketing
  - *(B)* From institution to market: A local community which privatizes its waste disposal management
  - *(C)* From market to private or public place: A company which applies Corporate Social Responsibility in a more tangible way
  - *(D)* From private or public place to market: An organization which is mainly operated by volunteers and assists women in starting their own businesses
  - *(E)* From institution to private or public place: Three employees in a local community who start a soccer club among teenagers
  - *(F)* From private or public place to institution: Two citizen entrepreneurs who run a seminar in a local community where the participants are members of a locally dominant political group.
- Finally, there are several different possibilities to a *cooperation* between the three sectors (entrepreneurial or not). (There are no such connections marked in Figure 1.2).

A model similar to the one in Figure 3.1 has been suggested by Nicholls (2006). It is presented in Figure 3.3.

A clear difference between Figures 3.1 and 3.2 compared to Figure 3.3 is that in Figures 3.1 and 3.2, different entrepreneurs are seen as clearly separated from each other, while social entrepreneurs in Figure 3.3 bridge over the traditional sectors of the society. We prefer Figures 3.1 and 3.2 for at least two reasons:

1. Even if social entrepreneurs in general may appear in any sector of the society, we assert that those social entrepreneurs of interest to us, that is, citizen entrepreneurs, act in a sector of their own, which we refer to as the citizen sector
2. We also claim that business entrepreneurs and social entrepreneurs build on clearly different logic, which cannot be combined in any straightforward or simple way.

However, as has been mentioned a number of times already, in all situations where you act entrepreneurially, it is necessary:

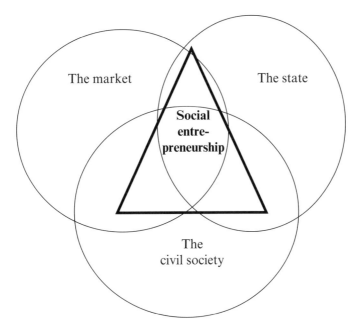

Source: Nicholls, 2006, p. 229.

Figure 3.3   The three estates of society

1. 'To just not be', that is, to, for instance, not just be employed in the common sector as a business person or citizen, but to come up with new solutions to satisfy a demand or need (it does not matter if you do this in the same sector or move to another one). Another aspect of this is that entrepreneurs can never be appointed; they have to act from their own free will

2. 'To act as if', that is, not to be restricted by existing or clearly predictable resources (which probably would lead you to behave as you have done before) but to think and act in a new way (entrepreneurially) instead of as you were before (administratively); to show yourself to be so interesting that you generate new resources (resources then seen in a wider sense, not only financial ones).

It is important in this context to realize that by 'increasing the connections between entrepreneurship and society, we get the chance to see the new multiverse of entrepreneurship with its variety of social, cultural, ecological, civic and artistic' possibilities (Steyaert and Katz, 2004, p. 193). There are however, as aforementioned, limits on applying the results of research onto business entrepreneurs and social entrepreneurs:

- Even if social entrepreneurs as well as business entrepreneurs are good at networking, social entrepreneurs exploit network relations in a much broader field (BarNir and Smith, 2002; Blundel and Smith, 2001; Dennis, 2000)
- Social entrepreneurs use their networks not only to leverage resources and strengthen their own ventures, which is primary to business entrepreneurs, but also to deliver impact and to create new social value (Nicholls, 2006, p. 225)
- Social entrepreneurs operate in a more diversified and dynamically strategic landscape than traditional business entrepreneurs do (O'Gorman, 2006). Even if they never compromise their social mission, social entrepreneurs are looking for alliances and cooperative possibilities where they can most easily find them. Many social entrepreneurs work at the same time with local governments, welfare institutions, volunteering groups and banks (Nicholls, 2006, p. 225)
- Social entrepreneurs often show a much larger variation in the form of organization under which they operate than business entrepreneurs do (Nicholls, 2006, p. 225–6)
- Economies of scale are not as obvious for social entrepreneurs as they are for business entrepreneurs. The former may often get maximum impact by remaining small and local and through deepening their activities rather than broadening them (Nicholls, 2006, p. 226)
- Social entrepreneurs are often looking for a social space where traditional business activities and the common sector have not shown any major interest and they improve on and create new social capital through institutional or gradual improvement and innovation (Nicholls, 2006, p. 226)
- Social entrepreneurs are often very politically involved (which is not the same as working for a specific political party) and they are often effective activists and/or campaigners and catalysts of a wider social change than is the case for business entrepreneurs (Nicholls, 2006, p.226)
- The urge to change the terms of engagement within their own sector, not for their own benefit but for the benefits of their stakeholders, often marks social entrepreneurs out as quite distinct from business entrepreneurs (Nicholls, 2006, p. 226)
- The ultimate aim (even if it may not be attainable) for social entrepreneurs is to do so well that they are no longer needed. This is not the case for business entrepreneurs (Nicholls, 2006, p. 226).

The important interest among social entrepreneurs is to satisfy different needs, while for the business entrepreneurs it is to satisfy different demands.

As we know, the academic subject of entrepreneurship is about 300 years old and has, until recently, mainly been of interest to economists. Most entrepreneurship theories are therefore based on the economic discourse (Steyaert and Katz, 2004), market-based and presented as explanations (instead of as a result of research in order to understand the phenomenon). 'Market' is a rather space-based concept and most entrepreneurship theories are not positioning themselves in place or in time, that is, they are very ahistorical and not specified in terms of in what culture they are valid. A majority of research in entrepreneurship is therefore following the American view rather than the Scandinavian one (as aforementioned). When business entrepreneurs are discussed in terms of place, this is commonly done by using narratives (see, for instance, Johansson, 2004 or Hjorth and Steyaert, 2004), by bringing networking and social capital into the picture (see Chapter 4) or by discussing cases like indigenous entrepreneurship (Anderson et al., 2006).

What we call the 'common sector' has traditionally been called the 'public' sector and the term 'public entrepreneur' is still used in the English-speaking world in this context (Cohen et al., 1999; Osborne and Gaebler, 1992; Osborne and Plastrik, 1997). However, the traditional distinction between public and private in terms of ownership seems less adequate when discussing entrepreneurship today (Hjorth and Bjerke, 2006, p. 99). Traditionally, public duties like schooling, sanitation and official transportation are in many countries often taken care of by private enterprises, and private businesses are often run by governments, nationally or locally. The common sector can be looked at in terms of space as well as in terms of place. The public sector has occupied a space to act economically by requiring people in a society to pay taxes, tariffs and charges to an amount that in a country like Sweden is more than half its gross national product. However, at the same time, activities in the common sector take place in institutions like schools, hospitals, courts and common political and quasi-political offices at national, regional and local levels. Movements like labour unions and producers' and consumers' cooperatives have today become rather institutionalized and may very well be seen as belonging to the common sector (or to the business sector in the latter case), even though they once started in the citizen sector.

Common activities at the central political level of a nation can be understood in terms of space and seen as a more collective form of entrepreneurship that focuses on broader actions and outcomes as a response to changes characterizing the global age (de Bruin, 2003). It is clear that there is a need for a new terminology to be developed to better convey the nature of the state and to conceptualize the reconfiguration of the role of the state in our modern society. The 'welfare state' concept is now outmoded. Jessop (1994, p. 251) argues that 'a Schumpeterian workfare state is more suited in form and function to an emerging post-Fordism state'. Similarly, Audretsch and Thurik (1999) observe that industrialized countries have changed from the 'managerial economy' of the previous industrial era to a knowledge-based 'entrepreneurial economy'. de Bruin (2003, p.156) suggests the term 'the strategic state': 'The strategic state could be the principal actor in laying the foundations for building a strong, socially inclusive economy within the globally connected world.' Some small city-states are doing just that. According to Pereira (2004), the Singaporean government has chosen to evolve from a development to an entrepreneurial state.

When going to the local level of government, the discussion becomes different than the above. Place then takes a front position:

> Economic processes are often regarded as provoking a more basic level of exploitation, while cultural and political change is interpreted as a dependent variable which is caused or heavily conditioned by the economy. While there is no doubt that what is conventionally understood as 'the economic' has important effects on all aspects of urban life, the view of the economy as foundational is flawed for a number of reasons. First, it is based on a false division between economic, cultural and political realms. None of these areas is independent of the others. Second, the very idea of a foundational explanation is suspect. Even if it is possible to explain some aspects of (say) political change with reference to economic processes, this does not exhaust the explanatory task, since the economic processes themselves require explaining. Third, economic changes always have a wide range of preconditions, some of which may well be cultured and political.
>
> Thus an entrepreneurial urban economy will only emerge if certain preconditions are in place. The precise specification of these preconditions is likely to vary from case to case, since it is possible that slightly different combinations of conditions could be compatible with the emergence of entrepreneurial cities. (Painter, 1998, p. 266)

Local communities and entrepreneurs will be discussed further in Chapter 5.

Figure 3.4 shows a distinction between social entrepreneuring, citizen entrepreneuring and public entrepreneuring. By social entrepreneuring we mean all entrepreneurial activity in society which does not have as the main purpose profit or an activity which aims at profit, but has a clear social objective as a purpose, no matter where in society it takes place.

We found a reason, as presented earlier, to separate three sectors in the society and situations associated with them, where entrepreneuring may take place. These are institutions in the common sector, business situations in markets and private or public places, which do not exist in

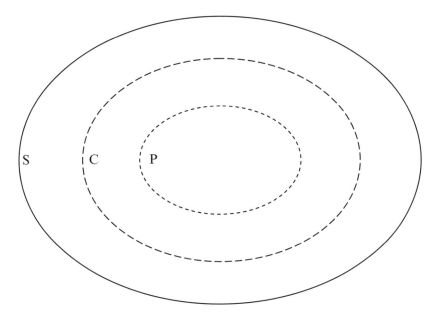

Figure 3.4 *Social entrepreneuring (S), citizen entrepreneuring (C) and public entrepreneuring (P)*

institutions or in markets but in what we call the citizen sector. We refer to this as citizen entrepreneuring. There are social entrepreneuring activities taking place in the common sector. Examples can be to talk about schools or hospitals as entrepreneurial (Mair et al., 2006, p. 256ff), entrepreneurial cities (Hall and Hubbard, 1998) or state entrepreneurship (de Bruin, 2003). There are also social entrepreneuring activities taking place in the business sector. One example of this is seen from the results of a study pointing out the 'natural' tendencies among small firms to feel responsible for the local environment where they operate (Sundin, 2009). This book is mainly interested in social entrepreneurs acting in the citizen sector, or in other words, citizen entrepreneuring.

Nicholls (2006, p. 229) provides a list of contexts for social entrepreneurship (Table 3.2). Referring to this table we want to speak of citizen entrepreneuring (as different from social entrepreneurship as social entrepreneuring) only in the first case (grassroots) and to some extent the next three (institutional, political and spiritual), however, only before they have become too institutionalized. The fifth (philanthropic), we do not count as entrepreneurial at all, because it does not contain any new approach (even if such attempts may be financed through this channel).

Table 3.2   Contexts for social entrepreneurship

Origins	Social market failure	Means	Ends	Example
Grassroots	Lack of institutional support	Critical social innovation	Coordinated creation of social capital through local/community action	Housing associations
Institutional	Changing social landscape	Normative social innovation	Social entrepreneurship champions new social institutions	Open University
Political	Retreat of centralized government control from society	Market socialism	Introduction of enterprise/private sector market philosophy into public sphere	Public-private finance initiatives (e.g. London Underground)
Spiritual	Decline of church influence in society	Commercial-ization of congregation- and church-based activities	Revitalize role of faith in public affairs	CAFOOD/ Fair Trade Foundation
Philanthropic	Lack of finance for development of social capital	Foundations coordinating charity giving as social entrepreneurial start-up funding	Link business and social innovation	Skoll Foundation and community education

Source: Nicholls (2006).

According to Dees and Anderson (2006) it is possible to separate two branches of the meaning of social entrepreneurship (or of citizen entrepre-neuring in our terminology): 'the social enterprising school' (for instance, Borzaga and Defourney, 2001a; Martin and Thompson, 2010) and 'the social innovative school' (for instance, Bornstein, 2004; Steyaert, 1997, 2004). Social enterprisers are spreading welfare to more citizens, for instance, by organizing care for older people in their homes, often assisted by volunteers, or having parents help each other with childcare. Another example of social enterprisers is sheltered workshops of various kinds, that is, providing meaningful work for handicapped people. Social enterprisers work in private places, for instance, homes, or in semi-private places like sheltered workshops. Social innovators are trying, in all possible ways, to build more citizenry and to reduce the amount of alienation in the modern society – they do so by operating in public places. A public place is any physical, virtual, discursive or emotional arena, which in principle all citizens have the right to participate in, which all citizens have responsibility for and no citizen can disclaim responsibility from. More often than not, social entrepreneurship (or citizen entrepreneuring) is used without clarifying which of the two is referred to or as an umbrella term, which is used deliberately to cover both possibilities (Grenier, 2009, p. 175). Social enterprising is, by and large, in a country like Sweden, taken care of by its large common sector. There are even those who claim there is no third sector in Sweden (Boli, 1991; James, 1989). Researchers of entrepreneuring (like the authors of the present work, who are Swedes) are therefore more interested in the second type of citizen entrepreneurs that is, citizen innovators. The name 'public entrepreneurs' was a concept that was coined some years ago to refer to these citizen innovators (Hjorth and Bjerke, 2006). To public entrepreneurs do not belong protest movements like Attac and Reclaim the City as we see them. They are also operating in public places, but it is possible to separate between citizen entrepreneurs *creating values* and *critical* social entrepreneurs (Nicholls, 2006, p. 235). We are more interested in the first of these two (the distinction between the two is, of course, not very clear).

If we look at 'space' like Hudson (2001) does, as mainly an economic evaluation of location based on its capacity for generating profit, and 'place' as a mainly social evaluation of location based on its capacity to provide meaning, then it is clear that citizen entrepreneurs operate in 'place' more than in 'space'. This is supported even further by the importance of networking and social capital to these entrepreneurs.

The next chapter will discuss social entrepreneurs, citizen entrepreneurs, public entrepreneurs, networking and social capital in more detail.

4. Various kinds of social entrepreneuring, networking and social capital

A STARTING POINT

Chapter Three presented three fundamental variations on the theme of social entrepreneuring:

1. Social entrepreneurs represent any entrepreneurial effort in a society, no matter where it takes place, that has a social mission as its only or as a major objective
2. As Citizen entrepreneurs represent any social entrepreneurial effort that takes place in the citizen sector of the society, that is, not in the common sector or the business sector
3. Citizen entrepreneurs are of two kinds: social enterprisers and social innovators. The first kind aims at spreading welfare to as many citizens as possible. The second kind aims at building more citizenry in the society, that is, at reducing alienation so that as many individuals in a society feel that they are citizens and not excluded for whatever reason. The first kind operates mainly in private or semi-sheltered places and the second mainly in public places. Some social innovators are operating very critically against the established society and could be called social critics. Some social innovators, on the other hand, are more or less cooperating with the established society to build more citizenry in general and more inclusiveness in particular. The name given to the second type is public entrepreneurs.

So, some social entrepreneurs are citizen entrepreneurs and some citizen entrepreneurs are public entrepreneurs.

This chapter will continue the discussion of various kinds of social entrepreneurs and introduce the concepts of networking and social capital.

RESEARCHING SOCIAL ENTREPRENEURING

The discussion of and research on entrepreneurs that are not mainly devoting themselves to business is very young, say 12–15 years old. The relationship between social entrepreneuring and business entrepreneuring is seen differently in the American view and in the Scandinavian view. In the American view the relationship between the two is often seen as rather close. A common definition of social entrepreneurship in that view can be taken from Austin et al. (2006, p. 3): 'Social entrepreneurship is innovative, social value creating activity that can occur within or across the nonprofit, business, and public sectors.'

Sometimes, social entrepreneurs are in this tradition seen as just another, even if special, kind of manager. And all entrepreneurs are normally seen here in economic terms and as operating on different markets. A somewhat more sophisticated version in the same view claims that all entrepreneurs create value but business entrepreneurs create economic value and the measure of success of the latter 'is not how much profit they make but the extent to which they create social value' (Dees et al., 2001, p. xxxi). However, both kinds of entrepreneurs are commonly described in very rational terms and the social entrepreneurs act as change agents in the social sector by (ibid.):

- adopting a mission to create and sustain social value
- recognizing and relentlessly pursuing new opportunities to serve that mission
- engaging in a process of continuous innovation, adaptation, and learning
- acting boldly without being limited to resources currently in hand; and
- exhibiting a heightened sense of accountability to the constituents served and for the outcomes created.

Change the word 'social' to 'economic' above and the description could be of a business entrepreneur. Bornstein, (2004, p. 92), for instance claims that ideas in society, no matter where they come from, 'need champions – obsessive people who have the skill, motivation, energy, and bullheadedness to do whatever is necessary to move them forward: to persuade, inspire, seduce, cajole, enlighten, touch hearts, alleviate fears, shift perceptions, articulate meanings and artfully maneuver them through systems'.

The influence of what we have referred to as the American school is very obvious as seen from the statement by one American scholar, when he claims that 'practically all of the definitions [of social entrepreneurship] contain one or more of the following concepts, articulated by major writers on the subject' (Brooks, 2009, p. 4):

1. Social entrepreneurship addresses social problems or needs that are unmet by private markets or governments
2. Social entrepreneurship is motivated primarily by social benefits
3. Social entrepreneurship generally works with – not against – market forces.

Another example based on the same view can be taken from Perrini and Vurro (2006, p. 65):

> Current literature is in agreement in recognizing three main steps which, although typical of business entrepreneurship, take on a new value and therefore become useful in the overall comprehension of the social entrepreneurship phenomenon. They are:
> (i)   Opportunity definition
> (ii)   Organizational launch and functioning
> (iii) Financial resource collection and leveraging
> These phases are not temporarily consequent but can both follow one another in a totally different order as well as be concomitant.

One proponent of the American view, Austin, outlines three avenues for social entrepreneurship research (2006, pp. 24–31):

1. The comparative avenue
   - Time
     - Dynamic vs static?
     - Retrospective vs prospective?
     - Are there stages in the entrepreneurial process?
     - Scaling up: How does the entrepreneurial task change?
   - Place
     - Context matters: regions, countries, localities?
     - Which contextual elements (political, legal, economic, sociocultural, demographic, and so on) impose barriers or enable opportunities?
     - Which elements foster innovation and how?
     - How can contextual forces be effectively exploited or managed?
   - Form
     - What are the determinants of optimal organizational form?
     - Does optimal organizational form vary by institutional sector (business, civic or government)?

- Does this vary with the problem focus of a social enterprise (environment, advocacy, health, and so on)?
- Does it vary by place? By time?
- Actor
  - What are the key attributes of social entrepreneurs compared to commercial entrepreneurs?
  - How do these change over time?
- Practice
  Financial
  - What are the comparative advantages and disadvantages of different revenue sources?
  - How do you determine the optimal financing mix?
  - How does the financing choice interact with organizational culture, values, and missions as well as capabilities?
  - What are the motivations, expectations and behaviour of funders and social investors in different places?
  Measurement
  - How can the entrepreneur demonstrate his or her value proposition to stakeholders?
  - How to quantity social outcomes and returns?
  - How do performance measurements get integrated into the management and incentive system?
- Governance
  - What are the key capabilities and functions of governing entities and individuals for entrepreneurial social undertakings compared to commercial businesses?

2. The corporate avenue
    - Why should companies engage in Corporate Social Responsibility (CSR)?
    - How can social value creation generate business value and vice versa?
    - How can CSR best be carried out in terms of strategy, organizational structure and management processes?
    - Do companies have a comparative institutional advantage for generating social value?

3. The collaborative avenue
    - What are the barriers, enablers, benefits, and key success factors for:
      - Intra-sector alliances?
      - Cross-sector alliances (business-nonprofit, business-government, government-nonprofit)?
      - Tri-sector partnerships?

- How can one most effectively create, manage, and govern social purpose networks?
- How can one create maximum value through collaborations?

The Scandinavian view criticizes the American view as being too much dominated by a managerialist approach, as presented by typical American scholars in the field like Anderson and Dees (2006) and Austin (2006). Based on the literature, Grenier (2009, pp. 177–8), for instance, identifies three main critiques of social entrepreneurship as it is presented most of the time:

1. It focuses too much on the characteristics and role of exceptional individuals, thereby crediting individuals with more power and effect than they can realistically have. It individualizes what are societal and structural problems, undermining the role and responsibility of the state and fragmenting social welfare (Amin et al., 2002; Edwards, 2002; McDonald and Marston, 2001)
2. It mimics the mainstream by privileging business and crediting being businesslike and market oriented with attributes and effects that extend inappropriately in the arenas of social and political action. This undermines the role of communities as sources of creative alternatives (Amin et al., 2002; Dart, 2004)
3. It sidelines political and social issues and processes, including the place of social justice, the effects of power inequalities, and the implications of economic inequality and the inherent nature of the social as contested (Cho, 2006; Dey, 2006; McDonald and Marston, 2001).

Grenier (2009, p. 178) summarizes the main implication of his critique by stating: 'Social entrepreneurship is ineffective in practice in bringing about the kind of radical change with which it has been associated or in introducing alternatives to outdated institutions. It "plasters over the cracks" rather than creates systemic change.'

The Scandinavian view sometimes presents business entrepreneurs and social entrepreneurs as people that are rather different from each other. Mair and Noboa (2006, p. 123), for instance, look at social entrepreneurs as a special kind of people, who, in their opinion, have a 'relentless motivation to change the whole society'. One difference between the American and the Scandinavian views has a linguistic background. In Latin languages like English (from where the expression 'social capital' originates) and French (in which the term *'economie sociale'* is coined), there is not much difference between social and societal, which there is in Germanic languages. This leads, for instance, Sundin (2009, p. 110; author's translation), a Swede, to claim that: 'Social and societal entrepreneurship cannot be seen as synonyms. Societal entrepreneurship is always social but social is not always completely societal.'

THE CITIZEN SECTOR

Westerdahl (2001) provides three proposals to why there is a 'citizen sector'. Other names proposed are the 'third sector' or the 'independent sector' (Bornstein, 2004):

1. The vacuum hypothesis: The shrinkage of the common sector in many countries together with decline in large areas of the business sector creates a space for other actors. This hypothesis is, according to Westerdahl, the most important one of the three
2. The influence hypothesis: We are experiencing an increased questioning of the common sector's handling of tax revenues connected with a wish of a greater influence over the way in which this is done
3. The local identity hypothesis: At the same time as we are experiencing more globalization we also note a greater wish for local and regional identity.

> Thus the three hypotheses – if they are correct – show that the transformation of society currently under way in the Western world exhibits certain development features suggesting a probability that, whether by necessity or by voluntary commitment, certain social elements of the economy will assume increased importance for certain actors. This makes it possible for activities conducted under social-economic forms to expand. The extent to which these activities can make use of this potential for expansion is determined primarily by their strength, their competitiveness and the attitude towards them of other actors in society. (Westlund, 2001, p. 435)

Things have changed for social entrepreneurs. Democracy has spread and a vigorous citizen sector has become very obvious over the past few decades. Today hundreds of universities offer courses on the citizen sector. Working in this sector has become socially acceptable, even status-worthy. In the opinion of Bornstein (2004, pp. 267–8), the citizen sector is going through changes that are comparable to those that occurred in the business sector over the past three centuries. Dees et al. (2001, pp. 12–13) characterize the new spirit in social organizations by several trends that have emerged and gained strength over the past couple of decades:

- Heightened concerns about the effectiveness of traditional government and charitable approaches to meeting social needs
- A search for more innovative solutions that lead to sustainable
  improvements
- An increased openness to experimentation with market-based
  approaches and businesslike methods in the social sector
- A growing shift toward the privatization of public services, leading
  to government contracting with both for-profit and nonprofit
  providers
- A parallel shift toward outcomes-based (rather than needs-based)
  approaches to funding on the part of both private philanthropies
  and government agencies
- A new, more engaged and strategic approach to corporate involvement in social and community issues.

Together, according to Dees et al. (ibid.), these trends are creating major
changes in how societies around the world are dealing with providing
public goods and services.

Estimated employment in the citizen sector is 8–10% in Western Europe
(somewhat less in Sweden due to its large common sector and considerably
more in, for instance, Greece). Studies show that the increase of employment in the third sector is increasing in the whole Western world. Between
1980–90, the increase was 40% in France, 36% in Germany and 41% in
the USA (Salomon and Anheier, 1994); in 20 Western European regions
the increase was 44% (Westlund and Westerdahl, 1997). All numbers are
very uncertain here (and in a sense misleading), due, among other things,
to the large proportion of part-time work in the citizen sector (Vasi, 2009,
p. 169) and its many volunteers. The so-called 'not-for-profit sector' in the
USA (which refers to all social entrepreneurs, not only those in the citizen
sector) is much higher than in Europe and is estimated to 7% of GNP,
which is probably twice as high as in Great Britain (Burns, 2007, p. 454).

> In almost all industrialized countries, we are witnessing today a remarkable
> growth in the 'third sector', i.e. in socio-economic initiatives which belong
> neither to the traditional private for-profit sector nor to the public sector. These
> initiatives generally derive their impetus from voluntary organizations, and
> operate under a wide variety of legal structures. In many ways they represent
> the new or renewed expression of civil society against a background of eco-
> nomic crisis, the weakening of social bonds and difficulties of the welfare state.
> (Defourney, 2001, p. 1)

Social entrepreneurs (or citizen entrepreneurs) are not new in society.
Just think about names like Florence Nightingale and Mahatma Gandhi.

What is new now, however, is that the amount of social entrepreneurial activities is much bigger than ever before in history (Bornstein, 2004, pp. 3–6). There are also, according to Nicholls (2006), studies in, for example, Great Britain that show that the number of newly started social entrepreneurial projects there is larger than the number of newly started pure business entrepreneurial projects. During 2003 it is estimated that 6.6% of the adult population of Great Britain was involved in some kind of activity which basically had a purpose of use to the society as a new or ongoing operation. This was higher than what GEM (Global Entrepreneurship Monitor) estimates the business entrepreneurial start-up activities to be in Great Britain, which was 6.4%. Among other things, a new social entrepreneurial minister was appointed in Great Britain in 2001.

This increased interest in social entrepreneurial activities probably has a rather broad explanation:

> The buzz surrounding has as much to do with the person and personality of the entrepreneur him or herself as it has to do with making change in society. The need to prove oneself, the drive, commitment – all these things may result in positive change, but they arise from, and in fact depend on, a personal calling, and perhaps a sense of personal anger or injustice for the problems of others. (Boddice, 2009, p. 147)

It has been claimed that the concept of 'social entrepreneur' appeared for the first time in the literature with Banks (1972). There are many who assert that the Englishman Michael Young (1915–2002) is the world's most successful social entrepreneur (for instance, Mawson, 2008). He started more than 60 social enterprises during his lifetime, including the School for Social Entrepreneurs (SSE) in Great Britain and the country's first university for distant learning (The Open University).

Historically, areas in which social entrepreneurs have been operating have been (Nicholls, 2006, p. 228):

- poverty alleviation through empowerment (for example, the micro-finance movement)
- healthcare, ranging from small-scale support for the mentally ill 'in the community' to larger-scale ventures tackling the HIV/AIDS pandemic
- education and training, such as widening participation and the democratization of knowledge transfer
- environmental preservation and sustainable development, such as 'green' energy projects
- community regeneration, such as housing associations

Table 4.1 Nicholls's positioning of social entrepreneurship by level of community involvement and level of strategic engagement with social need

Level of community involvement	High	Cooperatives	Social entrepreneurship
	Low	Conventional private sector enterprise	Conventional public sector welfare
		High	Low

Level of strategic engagement with social need

Source: Nicholl's (2006, p. 230).

- welfare projects, such as employment for the unemployed or homeless and drug and alcohol abuse projects; and
- advocacy and campaigning, such as Fair Trade and human rights promotion.

ARE CITIZEN ENTREPRENEURS SOCIAL ENTERPRISERS, SOCIAL INNOVATORS OR PROPONENTS OF SOCIAL MOVEMENT?

There are many presentations of the differences between business entrepreneurs and social entrepreneurs (who, in this book's terminology, should better be called 'citizen entrepreneurs'). Wickham's suggestion (2006, p. 184) is presented in Table 4.2.

There are many examples of what could be meant by social entrepreneurs as citizen entrepreneurs:

- social enterprisers
- entrepreneurs in the social economy
- participants in associations
- participants in protest movements
- business entrepreneurs devoted to CSR
- cultural activists.

Table 4.2   Distinguishing between the business entrepreneur and the social entrepreneur

	Pure 'classic' entrepreneur	Pure 'social' entrepreneur
Personal motivation	Maximize personal wealth	Maximization of 'social value'
Sector of activity	Commercial	Not-for-profit/public
Organizational form created	Traditional business hierarchy with entrepreneur taking leadership role	Non-traditional organizational form with an emphasis on egalitarianism rather than efficiency
Strategies adopted	Focused on competition and maximizing return to entrepreneur/investors	Avoid competition; focused on creating and delivering social value
Definition of, and relationship with, stakeholders	Relationship with investors considered critical; relationship with customers seen as means to an end	Stakeholders defined over wide and broadly defined groups
Interaction with wider social environment	Aspires to no wider social legitimacy	Seeks broad based social legitimacy with wide group of parties
Ethical reflections	Self-interested; not altruistic. Ethically neutral or unethical?	Altruistic at expense of self-interest. Ethical?

Source: Wickham (2006, p. 184).

- proponents of Fair Trade
- environmental activists
- arrangers of public events
- public entrepreneurs.

It has been suggested that social entrepreneurs as citizen entrepreneurs can express themselves in at least three different ways (Vasi, 2009, pp. 160–61):

1.   Some initiatives focus on disseminating a package of innovations needed to solve common problems. This form of entrepreneuring attempts to serve widespread needs because it assumes that 'information and technical resources can be reconfigured into user-friendly forms that will make them available to marginalized groups' (Alvord et al., 2002, p. 10). Once such packages are constructed by various experts – a difficult task, because it requires substantial creativity to adapt materials and resources for low-cost usage – they can

be disseminated by individuals and agencies with relatively few
resources

2. Some forms involve building capacities or working with marginalized
    populations to identify capacities needed for self-help. This approach
    is based on two main assumptions: local groups possess the best
    knowledge about which issues are most important, and local actors
    may solve their problems if they have access to more resources and a
    better capacity to act. Therefore, entrepreneuring directed at capacity
    building requires paying special attention to local constituents and
    resource providers

3. Some initiatives focus on mobilizing grassroots groups to form alli-
    ances against abusive elites or institutions. As noted by Alvord et al.
    (2002), the assumption underlying this approach is that marginalized
    groups can solve their own problems if they have increased access to
    political institutions. This form of entrepreneurship is highly politi-
    cized and may involve activities that challenge powerful antagonists.

Vasi (2009, pp. 161–2) points out that the above description of expressions
of social entrepreneuring has similarities as well as differences with social
movement activism. There are at least two similarities:

1. Because social entrepreneuring and social activism are inherently
    political phenomena, they both have to overcome resistance to social
    change by mobilizing resources, taking advantage of political oppor-
    tunities and engaging in framing activities

2. Both are complex phenomena that are irreducible to organizational
    creation and growth. Social entrepreneuring as citizen entrepreneur-
    ing can never be reduced to the creation of a viable business or social
    activism to its sheer size; a more adequate measure of their success,
    which is not easy to apply in practice, is to what extent they have
    secured medium- and long-term collective benefits for their constitu-
    ents as well as for the larger population (Amenta and Young, 1999;
    Amenta and Caren, 2004).

But the two concepts of social entrepreneurship as citizen entrepreneuring
and social movement are not interchangeable:

1. Unlike social movements, social entrepreneurship may consist of indi-
    vidual action; movement activism is limited to collective actions

2. Social entrepreneurship may attempt to create social change without
    challenging an existing authority, by working within the institutional-
    ized channels and reproducing 'the rules of the game'.

Table 4.3 Communities likely to work with and need social entrepreneurs

Types of communities	Defining features
Geographical	Historically isolated and underresourced or abused areas
Marginalized	Stigmatized groups often viewed as nonconformist particularly with regard to work, personal and residential maintenance and sexual practices
Age groupings dependent on working population	Populations segmented by virtue of their need for services, support and control they seem unable to provide for themselves
Special interest groups	Affiliations that advocate for recognition, preservation or expansion of issues or entities that cannot speak for themselves
Groups that self-identify through religious, ethnic, racial or national membership	Alliances built through a sense of common history, often shared hardships and hopes for a better future
Affiliate groups aligned through pursuit of similar activities	Devotion to what are often leisure activities or specialized ways of carrying out particular types of work

Source: Dees et al. (2002, p. 143).

There are many different communities in a society that may gain from cooperating with social entrepreneurs as citizen entrepreneurs (Dees et al., 2002, p. 143). A list is provided in Table 4.3.

There are many suggestions as to what names should be given to those whom we refer to as citizen entrepreneurs:

- social entrepreneurs (Boschee, 1998; Brinckerhoff, 2000)
- community entrepreneurs (De Leeuw, 1999; Dupuis and de Bruin, 2003; Johannisson and Nilsson, 1989; Johannisson, 1990)
- non-profit entrepreneurs (Skloot, 1995)
- civic entrepreneurs (Henton et al., 1997)
- idealistic entrepreneurs (Piore and Sabel, 1984)
- mundane entrepreneurs (Rehn and Taalas, 2004)
- public entrepreneurs (Hjorth and Bjerke, 2006).

There are also many suggestions as to adequate definitions of social entre-preneurship. There are possibly more definitions of the social (and citizen) entrepreneur than of the business (and commercial) entrepreneur. For instance, it can be loosely defined as: 'Social entrepreneurship combines the passion of a social mission with an image of businesslike discipline, innovation, and determination commonly associated with, for instance, the high-tech pioneers of Silicon Valley' (Dees, 1998, p. 1), or 'Social entrepreneurship is the use of entrepreneurial behavior for social rather than profit objectives' (Burns, 2007, p. 454). An example of a Scandinavian definition is: 'A social entrepreneur is a person who takes an innovative initiative in order to develop functions which are useful for society.' (Gawell et al., 2009, p. 8; author's translation)

So, the field of a social or citizen entrepreneurship is very unclear, but not fussy. The concepts of social or citizen entrepreneurship are far from unambiguous. One reason, of course, is that there is no (and will probably never be) neutral view on what a social entrepreneur *is* doing as a citizen entrepreneur and what he or she *should* be doing. Political aspects enter here (Boddice, 2009, p. 137; Steyaert and Katz, 2004, p. 180). Social entrepreneurship, especially as citizen entrepreneuring, is, by its very nature, a political phenomenon (Cho, 2006, p. 36). Some order can be brought by first separating social entrepreneurs operating in the common sector or in the business sector from those entrepreneurs operating in a sector of their own. Mainly, this book discusses only the second type citizen entrepreneurs. Citizen entrepreneurs can in turn be separated into social enterprisers, social innovators and proponents of social movements. This second separation is first of all related to *where* in the citizen sector the entrepreneurs act – on which arena, so to say. Some citizen entrepreneurs, for example, are trying to find an answer to the question of how more people in a society should gain in welfare. They do so by taking part in the management of children's care and the care of older people (often in nursing homes), or by assisting in providing opportunities for handicapped people (in the wider sense of the term) to become involved in society (open in sheltered workshops). These citizen entrepreneurs are commonly called 'social enterprisers'. Other citizen entrepreneurs are trying to find an answer to the question of how more people in a society can truly feel like citizens and experience inclusiveness instead of alienation. The entrepreneurs may do this by operating on public arenas and so are referred to as 'social innovators' (compare this with the Scandinavian definition of 'social entrepreneur' from Gavell et al., 2009, p. 8). Protest movements like Attac and Reclaim the City are examples of social innovators. However, a final distinction can be made (Nicholls, 2006, p. 235) between social innovators who operate as social critics (that is, as proponents of social movements), and social innovators who operate as social-value creators (often in cooperation with other organizations in the established society). The name used in this book for citizen entrepreneurs who act as social-value creators is 'public entrepreneur'. It should be noted that it is very difficult to draw a strict line between social enterprisers, social critics and public entrepreneurs.

SOCIAL ENTERPRISERS

So, there are two kinds of citizen entrepreneurs, social enterprisers and social innovators (public entrepreneurs). The first will be presented in this section and the second will be discussed in Chapter Five.

Defourney (2001, pp. 16–18) suggests four criteria as far as the economic and entrepreneurial dimensions of social enterprises are concerned:

1. A continuous activity producing goods and/or selling services
2. A high degree of autonomy
3. A significant level of economic risk
4. A minimum amount of paid work.

He adds five more criteria to encapsulate the social dimensions of social enterprises:

1. An explicit aim to benefit the community
2. An initiative launched by a group of citizens
3. A decision-making power not based on capital ownership
4. A participatory nature, which involves the persons affected by the activity
5. Limited profit distribution.

Social enterprises are commonly seen as initiated by groups of citizens who seek to provide an expanded range of services and more openness to the local community (Laville and Nyssens, 2001, p. 312). According to Borzaga and Defourney (2001b, p. 351), social enterprises appear to engage in one of two different activities:

1. Work integration: From the traditional sheltered workshops in the context of passive labour-market policies to new work-integration social enterprises as tools of active labour-market policies to the same group of workers
2. Social and community care services provision: Enterprises initiated by citizens to spread social welfare to more people, for instance, to homeless people, to the elderly and to parents.

THE STARTING AND DEVELOPMENT OF SOCIAL ENTREPRENEURIAL EFFORTS

A social entrepreneur can be seen as something of a social leader, who has several significant leadership qualities with a distinct personal trustworthiness which allows him or her to mobilize other citizens in terms of social value and which expresses itself as a strong common purpose. Leadbeater, an American, adds to this that this person has the ability to identify gaps in a market and related opportunities. He describes social entrepreneurs as (1997, p. 10):

> Socially driven, ambitious leaders, with great skills in communicating a mission and inspiring staff, users and partners. In all cases they have been capable of creating impressive schemes with virtually no resources. Creating flat and flexible organizations, with a core of full-time paid staff, who work with few resources but a culture of creativity.

In the UK, compared to elsewhere, claims Burns (2007, p. 458), social entrepreneurs are predominantly better qualified, older already occupied and with a higher income than average, even if the level of social entrepreneurship is higher among disadvantaged groups. He also claims that women and ethnic minorities often become social entrepreneurs rather than business entrepreneurs. These statements must, of course, be interpreted very carefully as the definition of social entrepreneurship is so broad that it may refer to practically anything that is run by an individual (or joint) power and is characterized as a social, community or voluntary activity.

In essence, social entrepreneurs are entrepreneurs in a social or not-for-profit context. As aforementioned, the difference between social entrepreneurs and business entrepreneurs is that the former satisfy needs in the society and the latter satisfy demand on various markets. Social entrepreneurs may act as adventurous people at the same time as they run a business and have a 'guiding' social idea; they may be extra-active employees within the common sector or they may develop social ventures or social innovations within the citizen sector itself.

Mort et al. (2003) assert that social entrepreneurship is so complex that it necessitates a multidimensional understanding of it. They conceptualize social entrepreneurship as in Figure 4.2. They claim, first of all, that a social entrepreneur is driven by a mission to create a better social value than common citizens that requires that they act entrepreneurially virtuous. Secondly, they claim that social entrepreneurs show a balanced judgement and an ability to see through the situation they face. Thirdly, they say, similarly to business entrepreneurs, social entrepreneurs have an ability to find situations where they can create better user value than other people can.

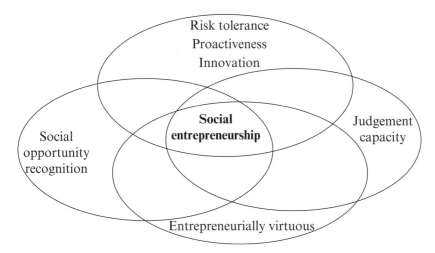

Source: Mort et al. (2003).

Figure 4.1 The multidimensional social entrepreneurship construct

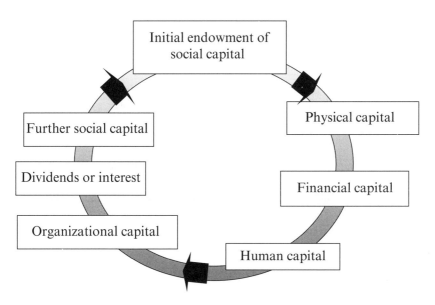

Source: Leadbeater (1997).

Figure 4.2 The virtuous circle of social capital

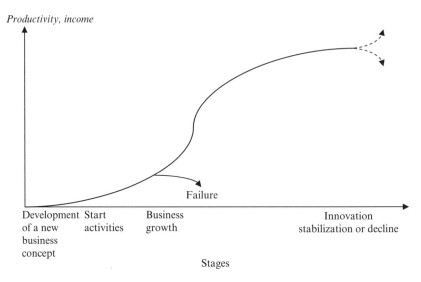

Productivity, income

Failure

Development   Start   Business   Innovation
of a new   activities   growth   stabilization or decline
business
concept
                                            Stages

Source: Adapted from Kuratko and Hodgetts (2004, p. 547).

Figure 4.3   A stage model for growth

Finally, according to Mort et al. (2003), social entrepreneurs show an innovative, proactive and risk-willing ability when making decisions. Only when
these four elements are combined, can social entrepreneurship be created.

Virtue is a key element here according to Mort et al. (2003). It under-
lines the balanced judgement of the social entrepreneur. It can be seen with
positive and good values such as love, integrity, honesty and empathy,
which are acted upon to become genuine. This is similar to what can be
talked about as important dimensions in citizenry.

Leadbeater (1997) places great emphasis on the development of social
capital in a social entrepreneurial process. He calls this a 'virtuous circle'.
It is based on access to social capital. The trick for the entrepreneur is to
lever this up to gain access to more resources: firstly, physical resources
such as buildings, and after this financial capital to get the wheels rolling,
and then human capital in order to deliver. Organization capital is generated when the project begins to reach its goals and more resources are
attracted. The resulting increase in cooperation and trust that is generated
in a successful project can lead to new injections of social capital when the
contact net and its contacts expand. This is shown in Figure 4.2.

It is relevant now to talk about the success and growth of social entrepreneurial efforts. Let us start by doing the same for business entrepreneurs in order to provide a basis for comparison.

Success and growth in a business startup can be seen as any increase in level, amount and type of the company's work and its result. This means to expand, enlarge or widen the business activities (Coulter, 2001, p. 283). Possible measures of success and growth for business entrepreneurs can be shareholder value, profit, employment, turnover, return on investment, profile/image, number of customers, market share, number of goods and/or services, and added value (Bjerke, 2007, p. 162–3).

Measuring the growth and success of social entrepreneurial projects is very different to that of business entrepreneurial projects. They often do not have any customers in the genuine sense, nor do they operate in markets or base their activities so explicitly on finances. There is also much voluntarism in social entrepreneuring.

Very little is known about the start and growth of social entrepreneurial activities but some relevant questions to ask could be:

- Is there a risk that you do not get any more support from outside if you become *too* successful as a social entrepreneur?
- Resources related to social entrepreneurial activities are not restricted to financial capital. However, how much financial resource is required to become a social entrepreneur?
- What is meant by an unsuccessful social entrepreneurial attempt?
- Do you find the majority of social entrepreneurs in cities, as is the case for business entrepreneurs?

Descriptive models for growth of business firms often separate between five stages, as seen in Figure 4.3 and described below:

1. Development of a new business concept: The first stage is to build the foundation of the entrepreneurial process, which requires creativity as well as analysis. To build networks is also vital here. The purpose is to formulate the general philosophy, vision, purpose, extent and direction of the business
2. Start activities: These activities encompass the basic work that is necessary to develop a formal business plan, to possibly search for necessary capital, to implement various marketing activities and to build up an entrepreneurial team if the venture is to contain more than one person
3. Business growth: Competition and other market forces may mean that a modification and sometimes even a major reformulation of the business strategy is required. These new challenges are to be part of the entrepreneur's effort to put a more complete set of business qualities in place

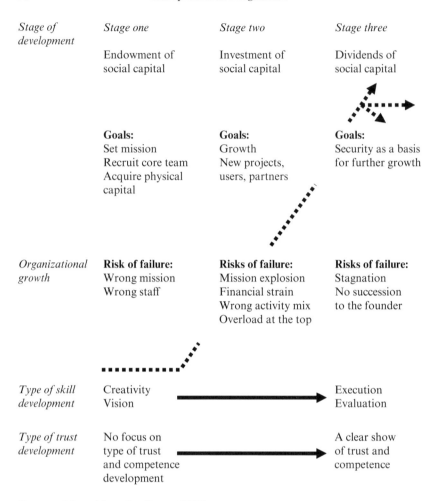

Stage of development	*Stage one*	*Stage two*	*Stage three*
	Endowment of social capital	Investment of social capital	Dividends of social capital
	Goals: Set mission Recruit core team Acquire physical capital	**Goals:** Growth New projects, users, partners	**Goals:** Security as a basis for further growth
Organizational growth	**Risk of failure:** Wrong mission Wrong staff	**Risks of failure:** Mission explosion Financial strain Wrong activity mix Overload at the top	**Risks of failure:** Stagnation No succession to the founder
Type of skill development	Creativity Vision		Execution Evaluation
Type of trust development	No focus on type of trust and competence development		A clear show of trust and competence

Source: Adapted from Leadbeater (1997).

Figure 4.4   Life cycle of a social entrepreneurial operation

4. Business stabilization: This is a result of the market as well as of the entrepreneur's efforts. Maturity will develop on the market as, it becomes saturated. The entrepreneur needs to think about how he or she is to proceed during the next three to five years
5. Innovation or decline: Those businesses that do not renew themselves, which is necessary sooner or later, will die. Financially successful companies often try to acquire other innovative companies in order to secure their own growth.

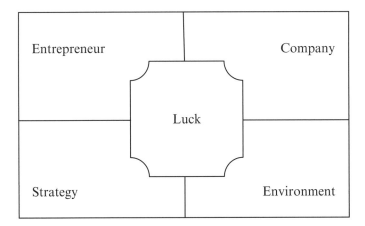

Figure 4.5   Factors favourable for growth of a business

It is more difficult to see the natural stages of a social entrepreneurial case compared to a business entrepreneurial case. However, there is one suggestion from Leadbeater (1997), which indicates the life cycle of a social entrepreneurial activity (Figure 4.4). Figure 4.4 suggests three stages in the growth of a social entrepreneurial activity. Every stage has its demand and requires its own skills.

1. Stage one is where the organization tries to establish itself. The key question is to formulate the foundation idea. But as the organization grows this idea must be reconsidered as the operation is expanded and possibly broadened. This formulation needs to be handled very sensitively having possible citizen users of the operation in mind. There is always a risk that somebody 'hijacks' the mission, makes it his or her own and thereby alienates it. This may be a greater risk for an operation with a shortage of resources and therefore run by some financier, who is interested in a special direction for this operation. The whole thing is a matter of governance, which becomes more and more complicated as the operation grows

2. As the social entrepreneurial activities widen they may need to change the need they satisfy due to changed citizen needs. Such changes can be very political if there is no awareness of how changes are made and in what direction they are going. This means that the organization must be very adept at how the operation is to be evaluated – how to ask for accountability so to say. At the same time it may become necessary to be more professional and to show a real entrepreneurial leadership. To be effective becomes more important as the operation

moves on. The organization needs to build a good reputation based on what it does – in the commercial world this would be called 'branding'

3. The final challenge is the same as for the commercial entrepreneur – how to handle the fact that the champion is dying out?

Very little is known of which factors are favourable to the growth of social entrepreneurial operations and how they work. For a business entrepreneurial project the factors may be classified as in Figure 4.5, that is as:

- luck
- entrepreneur
- company
- strategy
- environment.

Luck

Growth, particularly for new business ventures, can never be completely planned in advance. If that would be the case the venture would almost, definition-wise, be new. Growth is therefore partly a result of luck, for instance, in terms of timing, an unexpected financial windfall such as an inheritance or a chance meeting with a person who will later become the most important customer.

Entrepreneur

Growth is not only a result of chance in a business company. The characteristics of the entrepreneur are important:

- Growth interest: The entrepreneur behind the business must be proactive and have a willingness to expand and a positive belief in the future development of the company in order for growth to be possible
- Attitude to risk: This may influence the business entrepreneur's willingness to use available external financial resources for growth
- Competency: In order to grow a business entrepreneur should not just have an interest in growth and a good attitude to risk but also an ability to adapt to any new demands that arise as the venture moves on
- Innovation ability: If growth is not possible on the basis that the company stands, the business entrepreneur should have an ability to innovative and to lead the operation into other, more growth-friendly areas – if growth is of interest
- Willingness to delegate: Empirical studies show that one of the most

important factors for a venture to grow is the business entrepreneur's willingness to delegate (Storey, 1994). This may, for instance, provide more time for the business entrepreneur to think about issues of growth and problems related to this. Lack of time is generally regarded as a major obstacle to growth (this will be discussed further later in this chapter)

- Age: The results are not clear here for the researcher interested in explaining facts. The probability to belong to the growth group declines with a higher age among business leaders ('Tillväxt i småföretag', 2003). At the same time, a higher age may mean more experience to successfully launch and further develop the business, thus making it grow
- Willingness to spread ownership: A willingness to spread ownership with external individuals and organizations is often perceived as a central factor in growth.

Company
Characteristics of the company that are important for its growth include:

- A growth culture: One part of the business culture must contain the willingness to grow. This is probably more important than the structure of the business
- Age: The younger the company is, the higher is the probability that it belongs to the growth group ('Tillväxt i småföretag', 2003). After a while the willingness to grow further may decrease (Burns, 2007)
- Size: It may sound obvious that it is easier for a small company to double its size, but there are likely to be, in all industries and under various circumstances, limits to growth
- Legal form: A limited company with spread ownership seems to be more likely to grow than a proprietorship or a family firm where ownership is restricted.

Strategy
The strategy of the business company may be important for growth. It may concern the following areas (Storey, 1994):

- Product development: A company that wants to grow is rarely relying on only one product
- Market: A company set up to exploit a clearly defined market segment has a higher propensity to grow than a company which is established as a necessity for the founder to be able to support him- or herself financially

- Production technology: Technologies used must be relevant to growth
- Financial basis: To use only internally generated means can be a hindrance to growth, a situation which is not uncommon among family firms
- Recruitment: In order to grow, a company should have the interest and willingness to recruit personnel who have the competency and ability to participate and to work for growth, including overcoming existing obstacles to growth
- Use of advice and assistance from outside: To abandon what could be seen as an exaggerated need for independence when necessary and to take advice and use assistance from outside the firm when necessary can open possibilities for growth. This may, above all, be the case in high-technology companies.

Environment
- Regulations
- Taxes
- Interest rates
- The state of the economy
- Market trends: There may be extraordinary opportunities for possibilities for growth, but also a higher risk of failure, for instance, in volatile areas like IT
- Competition: Strong competition within a market can hamper growth. At the same time it may stimulate even better performance than before
- Localization: If a company that exists to satisfy local demand wants to grow, it must be located in the right area
- Access to labour: Access to qualified people, as well as to other production factors, can influence the growth of a company.

We can only speculate what the above characteristics would look like for a social entrepreneurship operation.

In a survey conducted in Sweden ('Tillväxt i småföretag', 2003) one question was asked concerning obstacles to growth in small business companies. The most common answers were:

- lack of own time (60% of respondents)
- tough competition (39%)
- low profitability (36%)
- shortage of the right sort of people (36%)
- authority rules, approval formalities and the like (35%)

- weak demand (29%)
- shortage of external capital (21%)
- shortage of loans (16%).

It would be interesting to know what the results of a similar study among social entrepreneurial operations would be.

NETWORKING

Successful entrepreneurs are good at networking. This is valid for business entrepreneurs as well as for social entrepreneurs. Some say that Piore and Sabel brought in business networks in entrepreneurship theories in their book of 1984 when they praised the industrial districts in northern Italy as an alternative economic model. They defined industrial districts as geographically concentrated operations that mainly consist of small firms which specialize in specific goods and services (often as part of an end product). Today, there is a more fundamental view on the importance of networks:

> Networks have existed in all economic systems. What is different now is that networks, improved and multiplied by technology, have entered our lives so deeply that 'the network' has become the central metaphor around which our thinking and our economy is organized. If we cannot understand the logic characterizing networks, we cannot exploit the economic change which has now started. (Kelly, 1998, p. 10)
>
> The diversity of networks in business and the economy is mind-boggling. There are policy networks, ownership networks, collaboration networks, network marketing – you name it. It would be impossible to integrate these diverse interactions into a single all-encompassing web. Yet no matter what organizational level we look at, the same robust and universal laws that govern nature's webs seem to greet us. The challenge is for economic and network research alike to put these laws into practice. (Barabási, 2002, p. 217)
>
> Networks is the new sociomorphology and the extension of the logics of network influences to a high extent the way and the results of our production processes, experience, power and culture. (Castells, 1998, p. 519)

We could therefore rightly call our modern society a 'network society'. It is the first time in history that the economic unit has been something other than the individual, for instance as an employee or as a customer, or the collective, such as the business firms or the common sector. Instead, this unit is now the network, where subjects and organizations are connected to each other and are constantly being modified and adapted to each other and to supporting environments and structures (Castells, 1998).

The network society is a more open society. A continuous search across the whole economic, technological and social field is therefore necessary in order for the actors of today to keep in touch with events and not be surprised. Through this search, relationships are built and maintained. 'The network economy is based on technology, but can only be built on relationships. It starts with chips and ends with relations,' (Kelly, 1998, p. 179). Consequently, the study of networks is popular today. However, there is considerable variation in what can be meant by 'network' and 'networking', so competing definitions and perspectives exist.

It is possible to talk about three important parts of a network (Hoang and Antoncic, 2003): the content of the relationships, the governance of these relationships, and the structure or pattern that emerges from the crosscutting ties. These parts are discussed below.

Relationships (between people and between organizations) are viewed as the media through which actors gain access to a variety of resources held by others (Bjerke, 2007). Two such key resources for an entrepreneur are information and advice, which he or she can gain access to through his or her network. Dependence of networks is, however, not restricted to the startup phase. Venturing people continue to rely on networks for various kinds of information, advice and problem-solving, with some contacts providing multiple resources. Relationships can also contain signals or provide the opportunity to justify your reputation as an entrepreneur. In the uncertain and dynamic conditions under which entrepreneurial activity occurs, it is reasonable that resource holders (potential investors and employees) seek information that helps them to gauge the underlying potential of a venture, of which they are or want to be a part. Entrepreneurs seek legitimacy to reduce possible perceived risk by associating with, or by gaining explicit certification from, well-regarded individuals and organizations. To be perceived positively based on your relationships in a network may in turn lead to subsequent beneficial resource exchanges.

The second part of a network that researchers have explored is the distinctive governance mechanisms that are thought to undergird and coordinate network exchange (Bjerke, 2007). Trust between partners is often cited as a critical element that in turn enhances the quality of the resource flows. Network governance can also be characterized by the reliance on 'implicit and open-ended contracts' that are supported by social mechanisms – such as power and influence or the threat of ostracism and loss of reputation – rather than legal support. These elements of network governance can give cost advantages in comparison to coordination through market or bureaucratic mechanisms.

The third part is network structure, defined as the pattern of relationships that are engendered from the direct or indirect ties between actors

(Bjerke, 2007). A general conceptualization guiding the focus on network structure is that differential network positioning has an important impact on resource flows, and hence, on entrepreneurial outcomes.

Conway et al. (2001, p. 355) talk of four key components that should be investigated when studying human networks and human networking (the discussion in this section follows Conway and Jones, 2006, pp. 308–10):

1. Actors: Individuals within the network
2. Links: Relationships between individuals within the network
3. Flow: Exchanges between individuals within the network
4. Mechanisms: Modes of interaction between the individuals within the network.

There is a large number of dimensions that can be used to categorize individuals within a network, from general dimensions such as age, sex, family membership, nationality, ethnicity and education level, to more specific dimensions such as functional background (for instance, finance, marketing or design) or sectorial background. The choice from this breadth of dimensions should be informed by the nature of the network and the purpose behind studying it.

The nature of the links or relationships between the members within the network also varies along a number of dimensions, of which the most relevant are the following (Conway and Jones, 2006, pp. 308–309):

- Formality distinguishes between informal and personal links and formal links that are formulated in a contract, for example
- Intensity is indicated by the frequency of the interaction and the amount of flow or transactions between the two actors during a given time period (Tichy et al., 1979)
- Reciprocity refers to the balance of the flow over time between two actors through a given link. The link is seen as 'asymmetric' or 'unilateral', when the flow is unbalanced (that is, it largely goes only one way), or 'symmetric' or 'bilateral' when the flow is balanced (that is, it mostly goes both ways). Asymmetric links tend to lead to some kind of inequality in power relationships between two actors (Boissevain, 1974)
- Multiplexity signifies the degree to which two actors are linked to each other through several role relationships (for instance, as friend, brother and partner); the greater the number of role relationships there is between two actors, the stronger ties (Tichy et al., 1979). Boissevain (1974, p. 30) argues that: 'There is a tendency for single-stranded relations to become many-stranded if they persist over

time, and for many-stranded relations to be stronger than single-stranded ones, in the sense that one strand role reinforces others'

- Origin refers to the identification of the event that leads to the origin of a link. It intends to incorporate facts such as the context in which the relationship arose and who initiated it
- Motive is when the functional significance of networking does not qualify for providing a convincing explanation of why it happened. When they discuss this issue, Kreiner and Schultz (1993, p. 201) mean that 'one must determine the motives and perspectives of the actors who reproduce such patterns'.

Tichy et al. (1979) distinguish between four types of flows within a network, often named as the 'transaction content' in the network literature:

1. Affect: The exchange of friendship between actors
2. Power: The exchange of power and influence between actors
3. Information: The exchange of ideas, information and know-how between actors
4. Goods: The exchange of goods, money, technology or service between actors.

Individuals may 'exchange' any of these types of transaction content for another, for instance, goods for money or information for friendship, even if in many cases, like in the last one, this can be more implicit than explicit. It is also worth mentioning here that the estimated value of the flow or flows between two actors within the network can vary widely between 'sender/provider' and 'receiver', as well as between other members within the network.

There is a number of ways in which individuals can interact with each other, for instance, talking to each other on the telephone, e-mail, documents or meetings face-to-face. Kelley and Brooks (1991) dichotomize these interaction mechanisms into 'active', which refers to a personal interaction, either face-to-face or on the telephone, and 'passive', which, by and large, refers to documents and other text material where there is no direct relationship between 'provider' and 'receiver' of information. 'Networks do not emerge without considerable endeavour' (Birley et al., 1991, p. 58), and consequently we are not only interested in the mechanisms for the exchange of information, goods and services in a network, but also in those mechanisms and forums through which entrepreneurs build and maintain their networks.

Networks in general may vary along a number of dimensions. The most relevant network dimensions of interest are often (Conway and Jones, 2006, pp. 309–10):

- Size: This dimension simply refers to the number of actors participating within the network (Auster, 1990; Tichy et al., 1979)
- Diversity: This network characteristic often refers to the number of different types of actors within the network (Auster, 1990), which, as mentioned above, can be seen along a number of dimensions like age, sex, education, etc.
- Density: This refers to 'the extensiveness of the ties between elements [actors]' (Aldrich and Whetten, 1981, p. 398), which can be seen as the number of existing links within the network divided by the number of possible 'links' (Rogers and Kincaid, 1981; Tichy et al., 1979). Boussevain (1974, p. 37) claims, however, that 'it must be stressed that network density is simply an index of the potential not the actual flow of information', that is to say, it is a measure of the network structure and not of the network activity. Boussevain (1974, p. 40) also asserts that 'there is obviously a relationship between size and density, for where a network is large the members will have to contribute more relations to attain the same density as a smaller network'. Furthermore, the network density tells us nothing about the internal structure of the network in itself and as Boussevain (ibid.) points out, 'networks with the same density can have very different configurations'
- Openness: In the entrepreneurship literature there is often a distinction made between strong and weak ties. Strong ties are found in cliques and are associated with dense networks, whereas weak ties link people outside the clique and consequently create 'openness' in the network, that is to say, they are boundary-spanning relationships or links spanning 'structural holes' (Burt, 1992)
- Stability: Tichy et al. (1979, p. 508) define this dimension as 'the degree to which a network pattern changes over time'. Auster (1990) develops this further by talking about frequency as well as the magnitude of the changes of members and links within a given network.

One important aspect of networks is that it is possible to separate four levels:

1. Exchange of information
2. Adaption of activities
3. Sharing resources
4. Co-creation.

The further down you go in these levels the more is asked of the members within a network. Networking often stops at the first level.

Networks have been found to assist small entrepreneurial operations in their acquisition of information and advice (Birley, 1985; Carson et al., 1995; Shaw, 1997, 1998), in supplementary acquisition of internal resources (Aldrich and Zimmer, 1986; Hite and Hesterley, 2001; Jarillo, 1989), in their ability to compete (Brown and Butler, 1995; Chell and Baines, 2000; Lechner and Dowling, 2003) and in their development of innovative activities and results (Birley et al., 1991; Conway, 1997; Freel, 2000; Jones et al., 1997; Rothwell, 1991). Gibson (1991, p. 117–18) claims that: 'The more extensive, complex and diverse the web of relationships, the more the entrepreneur is likely to have access to opportunities, the greater the chance of solving problems expeditiously, and ultimately, the greater the chance of success for a new venture.' It may seem like a paradox that at the same time as entrepreneurs are seen as autonomous and independent, they are also 'very dependent on ties of trust and cooperation' (Johannisson and Peterson, 1984, p. 1).

So, 'networks' and 'networking' are important entrepreneurial tools in establishing, developing and improving small business and other operations in society. However, there is a difference between discussing networking as a way to improve on existing operations (a discussion in terms of 'space') and networking as a necessary part of human existence (a discussion in terms of 'place'). Discussions of the first kind often lead to technical issues like what is a good and a bad network, what makes a network more functional, and so on. Typical discussions of networks in terms of 'space' are:

- A more developed network is more valuable to a person who starts an entrepreneurial operation than to somebody who is running an on-going operation
- The advantages of being members in networks are there for large as well as for small entrepreneurial operations, but membership of a network is more important for the survival of a small entrepreneurial operation
- Networks make it possible for small entrepreneurial operations to gain access to resources that are not accessible elsewhere.

Schon (1983) claims that those who want to realize new ideas work informally rather than formally in the beginning and that they do so in networks. There are those who claim that if there were no networking, there would be no venturing. There are even those who want to conceptualize the entrepreneurial process to 'organize oneself through personal networking' (Johannisson, 2000).

Some results that have been found valid for networking by social entrepreneurs are:

- Networks are more important for social entrepreneurs than for business entrepreneurs if for no other reason the former do not offer goods and/or services that can speak for themselves. They constantly need to justify their social entrepreneurial operations
- The differences between strong (emotional) and weak (calculative) ties are not at all so clear or even necessary to separate for social entrepreneurs as for business entrepreneurs
- It is more difficult to be and to replace a champion in social entrepreneurship than it is in a business entrepreneurship context
- Confidence and trust are decisive for social entrepreneurs, simply having contacts is not enough – this can also be the case for business entrepreneurs.

The discussion of networking continues in Chapter Eight, in the context of ICT.

SOCIAL CAPITAL

During the 1990s a new concept of capital, 'social capital', came into general use alongside the established concepts of financial, real and human capital. The idea of social capital came from sociology, not from economics, and it has proven itself to be particularly useful when analysing small firms and entrepreneurship (Westlund and Bolton, 2003, p. 77). The term 'social capital' is commonly attributed to Jacobs (1961). Analysts of social capital are mainly concerned with the significance of relationships as a resource for social action (Nahapiet and Ghoshal, 1998). This reflects the growing concern about the role of social relationships in explaining or understanding business activity. A deeper view is that an actor's embeddedness in social structures endows him or her with social capital (Oinas, 1999; Portes and Sensenbrenner, 1993). In the literature, social capital is defined as the asset that exists in social relations and networks literature (Burt, 1997; Leana and Van Buren, 1999). Social capital can be described as a consequence of how social processes work, where lack of cooperation leads to a decreased flow of information and resources. Furthermore, social capital can reduce transaction costs (Putnam et al., 1993) or as Dosi (1988) puts it, lower the transaction costs by using middlehands that cannot be bought or sold on a market. Social capital can also reduce uncertainty (Fafchamps, 2000). To have access to social capital can be described as a catalyst for a useful social and economic interaction. All in all, social capital offers a way to understand how networks function.

The social capital approach has developed in two ways. Firstly, to demonstrate that the personal network among citizens who start a new business venture allows them to gain access to resources that they cannot raise on their own (Ostgaard and Birley, 1994) and, secondly, to illustrate the influence by social embeddedness and associated dynamism on economic exchange (Portes and Sensenbrenner, 1993).

In other words, networks have an economic as well as a social content. They consist, which has been mentioned above, of weak ties (a 'space' concept) as well as strong ties (a 'place' concept). In the latter case, the term 'embeddedness' is sometimes used. Some important aspects of embeddedness as far as small firms are concerned are:

- The embedded nature of them is not only made up of economic transactions but also of concrete social relationships that are built up by participating actors
- A social relationship between the company's owner/entrepreneur must exist in business contacts before an economic transaction can take place
- A moment of lack of trust, opportunism of a negative kind and disorder is always possible in all business transactions
- It is difficult to discuss a single business activity without considering its predecessor and its follower.

Social capital is, according to Bourdieu and Wacquant (1992, p. 119), 'the sum of the resources, actual or virtual, that accrue to an individual or a group by virtue of possessing a durable network of more or less institutionalized relationships of mutual acquaintance and recognition'. Coleman's (1990) definition is, however, on a different plane than the individual. In his 1990 book (p. 305), he uses the figure below (Figure 4.6) to illustrate the difference between human capital and social capital.

According to Figure 4.6, human capital exists only in the nodes, with the individuals A, B and C. Social capital, on the other hand, is found on the sides of the triangle, that is, in the relationships between the individuals A, B and C. Bourdieu and Wacquant (1992) claim that social capital is provided to individuals when they are part of a network, while Coleman (1990) asserts that social capital exists in the very relationships between people in a network. To Coleman, the differences between human capital and social capital are that the former exists only within people (and is brought along when moving) while the latter exists between people (and cannot be brought along when moving).

Fukyama (1995) defines social capital as: 'The ability of people to work together for a common purpose in groups or organizations.' Leadbeater (1997) adapted this by suggesting a wider meaning to contain building

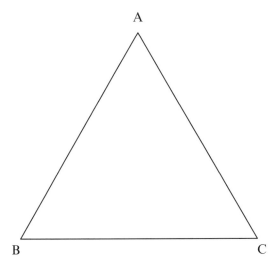

Source: Coleman (1990, p. 305).

Figure 4.6   Differences and relationships between human capital and social capital

something of real value for local communities or contexts. The citizen entrepreneur is using some kind of social capital – relationships, network, trust or cooperation – to get hold of physical and financial capital that can be used to create something of value to the local community. The result of social entrepreneurship can be firms that are not *primarily* run to make a profit, but they can do so, especially when the citizen sector and the common sector are cooperating. One important arena for social entrepreneurship according to some has been to renew governments by becoming more 'professional' in the common sector (Osborne and Gaebler, 1992).

Social capital can be seen as a glue as well as a lubricant (Anderson and Jack, 2002). When it is seen as a glue, it ties people tighter together. When it is seen as a lubricant, it facilitates actions within a network. In the former case social capital may consequently have a binding effect, preventing deviants from acting and thereby having a negative effect on development. Powell and Smith-Doerr (1994, p. 368) state that: Sociologists and anthropologists have long been concerned with how individuals are linked to one another and how these bonds of affiliation serve as both a lubricant for getting things done and a glue that provides order and meaning to social life.

Social capital can also be called 'network capital' (Anderson and Jack,

2002, p. 196). Given that social capital is what ties people together (Putnam et al., 1993), 'a capital' is a reasonable picture of the structural aspects of social capital. As is the case with financial capital it is possible to see social capital as an asset and a necessary part of a structure. It influences the structure and thereby its outcome. Furthermore, as a capital, it is tied to the network and becomes a integrated part of its structure. The earnings of social capital are an asset and can be a lubricant that facilitates the flow of information and resources in a social network (Anderson and Jack, 2002).

Social capital is a productive asset which creates certain specific results which, were social capital not in existence, would be impossible or more difficult (Coleman, 1990). From this perspective, social capital is created within the embeddedness process, that is to say both as a 'result' (a product of network) as well as a 'means' (to facilitate what is going on). The embeddedness that takes place becomes an inevitable part of the social structure. But, as aforementioned, social embeddedness can also have negative consequences because of a group's expectations. Networks can provide a mechanism for trust and legitimacy, but networks can also function to exclude or include – they can consolidate power without spreading it (Flora, 1998).

So social capital can be seen not as a 'thing', but mainly as a process. It is a process that is created in order to facilitate an effective exchange of information and resources – an artefact, which can only be studied from considering its effects.

It is not difficult to think of a close connection between the development of social capital and the corresponding growth of the citizen sector and number of citizen entrepreneurs. The organizations of the citizen sector have been called the 'organizations of the civic society' (Salomon and Anheier, 1997). It is in fact possible to talk about 'civic capital' instead of social capital (Evers, 2001). If social capital is seen as civic capital it points out the role of a wider group of political factors, both in terms of their general role in creating confidence and cooperation, as well as in terms of their building orientation and behaviour of groups and associations in the society. Social capital is then seen both as an indicator of the development of the civic society (built by social as well as political action) and as a way to debate civic engagement with an eye on economic development and governance (Evers, 2001, p. 299).

To summarize, the different kinds *of* capital, that is, assets, upon which man can build a stronger society are (Bridge et al., 2003, pp. 159–60):

- Social capital: This is the social resource upon which people draw in pursuit of their livelihood objectives and which are developed through networks and connectedness, either vertical or horizontal, and that increase people's trust and ability to work together and expand their access. Social capital also encompasses membership of more formalized groups which often entails adherence to mutually agreed or commonly accepted rules, norms and sanctions; and relationships of trust, reciprocity and exchange that facilitate cooperation between citizens

- Human capital: This represents the skills, knowledge, ability to work and good health that together enables people to pursue different livelihood strategies
- Natural capital: This is the term used for the natural resources and resource stocks used for livelihoods. These include the air breathed, the land farmed and the tree used
- Physical capital: This is comprised of the basic infrastructure and producer goods needed to support livelihoods. The infrastructure consists of changes to the physical environment that helps to meet needs, such as affordable transport, secure buildings, adequate water supply, affordable energy and access to information (communications). Producer goods are the tools and equipment that people use to function more productively
- Financial capital: This denotes the financial resources that people use to achieve their livelihood objectives, and which can be exchanged for some of the other 'capitals'.

Westlund and Bolton (2003) see certain differences between social capital and other capital (Table 4.4):

Leville and Nyssens also point out that social capital is a 'public' and not an 'individual' capital:

> Social capital constitutes a resource that may be mobilized to a greater or lesser degree within a production process so as to improve its performance. But it is also an end in itself because it is a 'civic' capital contributing to a democratization process. Social capital is present in groups, networks and the local social fabric. Inasmuch as it is – at least partly – indivisible and thus cannot be appropriated by any single individual social capital constitutes a local quasi) public good. (Laville and Nyssens, 2001, p. 317)

SOCIAL ENTREPRENEURING – WHY AND WITH WHAT EFFECT?

There are many that assert that social entrepreneurs have their roots in the history of local service and development (Grenier, 2009, p. 199). This is

Table 4.4   *Similarities and dissimilarities between social capital and other*
              capital forms

	Similarities	Dissimilarities
Productivity	Social capital is sunk costs that might become obsolete. Social capital can be put to good or bad uses (from society's perspective)	Social capital expresses interests of actors, good or bad from society's perspective. It is not neutral with regard to society's interests
Vintages	Social capital consists of vintages	The vintages of social capital are more comparable to a port wine than to other capital forms. The composition of vintages is decisive. There is no simple correlation between age and decreasing productivity
Accumulation and maintenance	Social capital is worn out if it is not maintained. Social capital is a result of past activities	Social capital is a product of both intentional investments and an unintended by-product of other activities. Accumulation of social capital does not necessarily need deliberate sacrifices for future benefits. Social capital is harder to construct through external interventions
Rights of possession vs. public goods	Access to social capital is never completely public. Access demands connections to a network and/or certain skills	Social capital is *social*, that is, it cannot be individually possessed
Complexity and levels of aggregation	Diversified social capital means less vulnerability to economic structural changes	Social capital is the most diversified, least homogeneous form of capital. Aggregating social capital belonging to different levels meets great methodological difficulties

Source: Westlund and Bolton (2003).

the history that feeds their passion for creating activities of importance to society (Emerson and Twersky, 1996, pp. 2–3).

One question that a social entrepreneur should constantly ask is 'Why am I doing this?' – placing emphasis on 'I' and 'this'. To do something *for* somebody else does neither explain why it is *you* who does it, nor how something came to be characterized as a 'problem' (Boddice, 2009, p. 148).

One unsolved issue in social entrepreneuring (unlike in business entrepreneuring) is how to measure its effect. A number of qualitative and quantitative measures have been suggested recently. The most recognized one is a model for 'social return on investment' (SROI) which was suggested by The Roberts Enterprise Development Foundation (REDF) in the US (Emerson, 1999) and then refined in England by The New Economics Foundation (NEF). These measures have, however, not in any way been generally accepted (REDF has even, according to Nicholls, 2006, stopped using SROI). There are consequently few agreed-upon or even available benchmarks or 'best practices' for the effects of social entrepreneurial operations. The establishment of the effects of social entrepreneurial operations will, therefore, continue to be open for criticism and discussions. One major problem in this context is that a limited and quantitative objective of many social entrepreneurial operations may lead to operational shortsightedness and an inability to focus on more basic social structural issues in their planning and implementation strategies. This may reduce their long-term results as well as their sustainability.

Finally, there are many negative trends in modern society, for instance, lower participation in elections, higher contempt of politicians and decreased involvement in the civic society. Whether social entrepreneurs will be able to counterbalance these negative trends is a very open question.

5. On the importance of social entrepreneuring to local government

LOCAL GOVERNMENTS

The functions of the local government can be viewed differently (Herbert and Thomas, 1997, p. 123). Sharpe (1976) has identified the three major functions of local government as promoting liberty, participation and efficient service provision. Local governments provide liberty by countering a lack of local responsiveness usually associated with overcentralization. Participation in the local is also considered likely to be enhanced by some form of local elections. Finally, local governments are considered most likely to maximize the efficiency of service provision since they can assess local needs better by being close to the point of service delivery.

There have been several stages in development of local governments because urban systems have looked differently over the years (Herbert and Thomas, 1997, pp. 77–9)

- The pre-industrial stage: an urban nucleus
  In the period prior to large-scale industrialization, most cities were small. They normally had populations of less than 50,000 and a rudimentary form of economic, social and political organization. Their transport technology was equally rudimentary. Because of the limitations of transport facilities, governmental influence in cities was restricted to provide urban services for a relatively localized population. Even if the city also provided commercial, religious, social or political functions for a wider hinterland, the frequency of visits by long-distance travellers and the associated functional inter-relationships between the city and this hinterland was still low. The city tended to be a distinct urban nucleus loosely related to a wider rural area and to other cities.
- The industrial stage: urbanized area
  In the early stages of industrialization, particular resources were localized. Some towns could grow in size because of the natural advantages that they possessed. Transport started to become more efficient due to canals being built and railways being constructed.

These provided more efficient means of intercity contact, princi-pally for the transport of industrial materials and finished prod-ucts. This increased the links between towns with complementary industrial structures as well as between industrial towns and market areas. Towns became much larger than their pre-industrial counterparts, although they retained their relatively compact form. Low-status housing gravitated markedly to areas of industrial employment and to new industrial areas. Higher-status residential suburbs tended to develop along the public transport routes radiat-ing outward from the city centres, creating a distinctly tentacular urban form.

● The post-industrial stage
The post-industrial period is characterized by a considerable increase in the speed and efficiency of communications. One special explanation for this was the development of the telephone. Also, the rapid growth in number of motor vehicles changed the emphasis of inter-urban transport to the private car. These changes reduced the constraint of distance on the development of economic and social links both between and within cities. A significant section of the more mobile labour force gravitated to residential areas in more attractive areas at a greater distance from their work. This led to a suburbanization of often large areas of land around major cities. In effect, more dispersed forms of the 'urbanized region' have become more dominant features of the urban system.

It has frequently been asserted that Western urban centres are now being managed, organized and governed in different ways, leading some to pro-claim the emergence of a 'new urban politics' (Cox and Mair, 1988; Kirlin and Marshall, 1988). According to Hubbard and Hall (1998, pp. 1–2), it appears that this new urban politics is distinguished from the old by the ways in which the politics pursued by local governments are being steered away from the traditional activities associated with them. This reorienta-tion of local government is characterized by a shift from the local provision of welfare and services to more outward-orientated policies designed to foster and encourage local growth and economic development. These policies are supported and financed by a diverse array of new agencies and institutions, as public agencies try to promote economic growth. Such cooperation with the private sector has seen local governments taking on entrepreneurial business characteristics – risk-taking, inventiveness, pro-motion and profit motivation – leading many commentators to refer to the emergence of 'entrepreneurial cities' (Gottdiener, 1987; Harvey, 1989; Judd and Ready, 1986; Mollenkopf, 1983).

However, with respect to local government entrepreneurialism, cities are very different from firms (Leitner and Sheppard, 1998, pp. 31–2). Local governments are defined by their territoriality: they are legally fixed in place, with boundaries that can be extended only with difficulty. In contrast, firms' ties to place are contingent, depending in the final instance on considerations of profitability. Furthermore, the political structure of local governments is very different. Firms are institutions governed by their owners, with a hierarchy of authority overlaying intra-firm networks. Local governments also have a hierarchical structure, but their corresponding urban centres are complex communities and networks of public and private institutions and civil society, in which lines of authority are not dictated from above but depend in the final instance on democratic processes – the ability of governing authorities to gain legitimation in the eyes of urban residents. Finally, firms may have relatively straightforward economic goals with profits often as the bottom line. Local states are not primarily responsible for making profit, but are supposed to be concerned for the welfare of their residents.

THE INCREASED INTEREST IN LOCAL GOVERNMENTS

Some reasons for the increasing interest in local governments are:

- The bases of central control of an economy have changed (MacKinnon et al., 2002)
- Small- and medium-sized communities have shown themselves better at managing the modern society in geographically concentrated areas – in spite of globalization in the world (Porter, 1998a)
- Nearness has proven itself to reinforce productivity and innovation (ibid.).

Three developments have influenced local urban centres today, influences that should be seen as possibilities, not as threats (Hall, 2005):

1. Post-industrialization
2. Globalization
3. Migration.

Necessary changes in local governments today are from:

- Services to leadership
- Administration to governance

● Office management to arenas, where venturing citizens ('public entrepreneurs') participate in various action nets.

Learning to be an entrepreneurial city involves, among other things (Painter, 1998, pp. 268–9):

● The acquisition of specific skills, such as those associated with place promotion, auditing, commercial accounting, negotiation with private sector institutions, and the preparation of funding applications
● The development of new self-understandings which might involve, for example, a subordination of the role of 'welfare provider' to that of 'business supporter', or the role of 'bureaucrat' to that of 'strategic manager'
● Acquiescence (rather than active resistance) in the face of centrally imposed requirements to shift to more entrepreneurial practices of governance
● The acceptance of change and of 'challenges' as inevitable or even desirable, in contrast with a previous expectation of stability.

Inspired by Soja (1996), it is possible to talk about three kinds of city places. The first place is the physical aspects of the city, like public spaces, amusement parks, shopping malls, gated communities, as well as shanty towns or other islands of poverty. This place is *perceived*. The second place is rather *con*ceived. It is a product of the creative artist, the artful architect, the utopian urbanist and the philosophical geographer, among others. It is a kind of imaginary city, constituted by an abundance of images and representations (Hubbard and Hall, 1998). The third place is the directly lived place, an enacted city. This third place is the most interesting one in entrepreneurial studies. To use Beyes' (2006, p. 170) words: 'A theatre of entrepreneurship has a lot more to offer than commerce and economic drive.'

A common trend in local government in many countries has been greater activism in promoting local approaches to local conditions (Dupuis et al., 2003). Urban places may phenomenologically be regarded as potential 'directly lived places' – potential sites for reorganizing the established and crafting the new. 'Communities have within themselves the ability to foster entrepreneurship by defining it at the level of every person and every interaction' (Steyaert and Katz, 2004, p. 191), or to phrase it differently, 'crossing research on entrepreneurship and entrepreneurial cities with thoughts on and observations of socially produced places' (Beyes, 2006, p. 255). However, researchers seldom consider the lived culture of entrepreneurial cities or the changing textures and rhythms of everyday life in their work (Hoggart, 1991, p. 184).

Traditionally, one perspective developed in Western industrial societies is that local governments had a strong 'managerial' role in controlling land-use planning and providing local services (Herbert and Thomas, 1997, pp. 124–5). This reflected a liberal-democratic and welfarist tradition associated with a strong Keynesian-type of state control over national economies. Since the mid 1980s, however, with the growth of global competition, the economic sovereignty of the nation-state has declined and most Western governments have had to be more mindful of market forces (more of this in Chapter Six). Most local governments have moved towards a neoliberal mode of operation whereby 'unproductive' public service expenditure has been cut in order to make more capital available for private investment. Also, local government is being replaced by a broader conception of 'local governance' where a kind of combination of common, private and voluntary agencies deliver services once provided by the local government. In this situation, local government becomes only one of many forces affecting the local environment and local service delivery system. Local development in the modern urban centre is increasingly influenced by market forces and quasi-autonomous non-governmental organizations.

In these complex new conditions, relatively little is known empirically about the precise way in which the new forms of local governance are functioning. However, some local governments have been characterized as changing from 'provider' to 'enabler' and the 'managerialism' of the industrial era is being replaced by a post-industrial 'entrepreneurialism' (Davoudi, 1995; Mayer, 1995). Jessop (1996) suggests, for instance, that entrepreneurial governance has become the dominant response to urban problems because this discourse appears particularly attractive to those urban centres being caught in a seeming downward spiral of deindustrialization and decline.

Similarly, the notion of urban entrepreneurialism currently enjoys wide popularity among academics, especially in urban geography, where the examination of urban politics and local socialization forms a logical outgrowth of the locality studies which came to prominence in the 1980s (see Cooke, 1989). A huge interest in the emergence of entrepreneurial forms of urban politics has been displayed by planners, sociologists and cultural theorists, particularly as the reassertion of space in social theory has heightened awareness of the ways in which locality-specific factors mediate more general processes of economic and social change (Soja, 1989).

There appears to be a broad agreement that urban entrepreneurialism is essentially characterized by the proactive promotion of local economic development by local government in alliance with other private sector agencies (Hubbard and Hall, 1998, p. 4). Therefore, it seems that urban entrepreneurialism can be defined through two basic characteristics; firstly, a political prioritization of pro-growth local economic development and, secondly, an associated shift from urban government to urban governance.

The interest in this subject started by drawing attention to the increased involvement of the local state in the proactive encouragement of economic development. In this sense, entrepreneurialism has been described as a distinctive political culture (Graham, 1995). The objectives of entrepreneurial policies are there described as inherently growth oriented: creating jobs, expanding the local tax base, fostering small firm growth and attracting new forms of investment. The aim of such policies is to promote the comparative advantages of the city relative to other cities that may be competing for similar forms of investment.

The current ubiquity of such entrepreneurial policies throughout the advanced capitalist world is now indisputable, and it is possible to conclude that en entrepreneurial attitude has infiltrated even the most recalcitrant and conservative urban centres (Hubbard and Hall, 1998, p. 7). According to Eisenschitz and Gough (1993), what appears to have been crucial in encouraging this widespread adoption of entrepreneurial policies is that they apparently offer something for all local governments, irrespective of political ideology.

> In short, the idea of the internationalization of economic activity, the increased geographical mobility of production and investment, and the rising power of transnational corporations appear to have instilled an edgy insecurity at all levels of the urban hierarchy, with urban governors and representatives feeling obliged to adopt suitable policies to attract capital investment given their perception of an increasingly competitive global economy. (Hubbard and Hall, 1998, p. 7)

The 'generic' entrepreneurial model of governance is reliant on specific boosterist policies. Local governments are allocating increasingly high budgets for the advertising and promotion of their centres as favourable environments for business and leisure (Savitch and Kantor, 1995). The marketing of place seldom restricts itself to presenting the existing virtues of the city, but seeks to redefine and reimage the city, weaving in specific place 'myths' designed to erase the negative iconography of dereliction, decline and labour militancy associated with the industrial place (see Barke and Harrop, 1994; Dunn et al., 1995; Watson, 1991).

In place marketing, like in many other kinds of marketing, it does not make much sense to distinguish between the 'myths' and 'realities' of the urban centre. The images of the place presented in the brochures, adverts, guidebooks and videos come to define the essence of the place as much as the place itself. This is even more evident in the promotion of various prestige projects, described as 'flagships' or 'megaprojects', which are aimed to improve on the perceived success of the rejuvenation of some other places.

These spectacular, large-scale urban projects have attracted attention when discussing entrepreneurial cities. Less substantial, but often highly publicized, some public art has also been fabricated as the entrepreneurial urban landscape is made increasingly playful, blurring the distinctions between entertainment, information and advertising (Hall, 1992; Miles, 1997). Place promotion is sometimes criticized by academics precisely due to a supposed dualism of image and reality implicated by projects of place promotion (see Burgess and Wood, 1988; Watson, 1991).

As image assumes an ever greater importance in the post-industrial economy it is becoming increasingly apparent that in the actual shaping and production of urban centres, it is necessary for them to present positive images of themselves to the outside world. Similarly, programmes of economic development are being driven more and more by image-enhancing initiatives. Narratives of entrepreneurialism often include place promotion.

It is, in this context, important to understand the differences between the processes of selling and marketing urban places. The distinction between 'selling the city' and 'marketing the city' is crucial in understanding the relationship of place promotion to urbanization. In this light, 'the cultural transformation of urban centres into "spectacular" places of (and for) consumption, populated by a harmonious and cosmopolitan citizenry, has sometimes been hypothesized as perhaps the most important element of entrepreneurial forms of local politics' (Hall, 1998, p. 28). However, even if the conscious manipulation of city image is principally designed to make the city more attractive to *external* investors, it is important to realize that it also plays an *internal* role in fostering local support and civic pride, potentially gathering widespread support for entrepreneurial policies (ibid.). Perhaps the manipulation of urban place has become the most important aspect of activities among urban governors and their coalition partners in the modern entrepreneurial era.

This new type of urban policy does not only involve the state of the local place but also a large number of business and citizen actors (Graham, 1995; Leitner, 1990). Inevitably, the new type of speculative projects and initiatives which sometimes are so central to the new type of entrepreneurial policy, are underwritten by actors outside the groups employed by the local government. The rapprochement between political and business communities, as manifest in the bewildering array of partnerships, networks and development corporations, is another reason why it is harder to detect the boundaries between the various sectors of a society. This convergence has resulted in a heightened control by new bourgeoisie and property interests, consisting almost exclusively of business*men* (Peck, 1995; Savage and Warde, 1993). However, this formation of coalitions or partnerships is seen as one of the principal means by which local governors achieve capacity to act.

In conclusion, new urban entrepreneurialism is perceived to be fundamentally different from the other forms of city governance that have preceded it. Many writers seek to stress the shift that has taken the interest among urban governors away from a concern with broad-based welfare and social policies towards the adoption of a more outward-oriented stance designed to foster and encourage local development and economic growth (Hubbard and Hall, 1998, pp. 13–15). However, while urban governors are adopting a more proactive stance and spending more on local economic policies, this does not suggest that there has not been a wholesale abandonment of managerial policies, and that there are important continuities between the two modes, even if they are often depicted as polar opposites.

Savitch and Kantor (1995) argue that a dualistic model of managerialism and entrepreneurialism overshadows the way in which most local governments adopt a mixture of managerial (socially progressive) and entrepreneurial (growth-centred) policies. Furthermore, such ideas may mask the fact that local governments, to a lesser or greater extent, have always pursued entrepreneurial strategies and that they have always been part of local economic development. It is important to stress that there might be dangers in accepting the idea that entrepreneurial governance is distinct from other modes of governance in all respects.

Finally, in the short term, it might be so that the new urban orientation may produce economic growth, neglecting the principles of social justice. 'There is little reason to suppose that the benefits of entrepreneurial policy will be fairly distributed' (Hubbard and Hall, 1998, p. 19).

LOCAL GOVERNMENTS AND VARIOUS KINDS OF ENTREPRENEURS

Local governments are in many ways in the centre of the development of a new entrepreneurial society. Also, they need all sorts of entrepreneurs within their area of interest. For a long time they have tried to promote the immigration of business entrepreneurs in order to create employment and economic growth. Increasingly, however, they need to focus on other types of entrepreneurs as well. First of all, perhaps, they need to act over and above just being employed – not just be and act as if, as we have presented it.

Local government employees' intervention in their own development and employment growth has been called 'municipal-community entre-preneurship' (Dupuis et al., 2003, p. 131). Another, often discussed, type of local entrepreneur central to the 'community' is the 'ordinary' person as entrepreneur (Leadbeater, 1997; Thake and Zadek, 1997), that is, a 'new breed of local activists who believe that energy and organization can improve a community. They can be found organizing street patrols to liberate red-light districts, or running local exchange-trading schemes' (Rowan, 1997, p. T67). But they can also be a prominent member of a local centre who acts entrepreneurially in the sense of attracting external investment, thereby improving on the employment situation, without necessarily starting any business themselves. These people have been called 'community business entrepreneurs' (Vestrum and Borch, 2006, p. 2). Community business entrepreneurship 'entails innovative commu-nity effort as a catalyst for the growth of local employment opportunities' (Dupuis and de Bruin, 2003, p. 115).

Community business entrepreneurs could be defined as the mobiliz-ation of resources in order to create a new activity, institution, enterprise, or an enterprising environment, embedded in an existing social structure, and for the common good of individuals and groups in a specific region (Johannisson and Nilsson, 1989; Paredo and Chrisman, 1990). The com-munity is seen as an aggregation of people within a rural area that are generally accompanied by collective culture/or ethnicity and maybe other shared relational characteristics (Paredo and Chrisman, 2006).

Table 5.1 (adapted from Zerbinati and Souitaris, 2005) presents a summary of the differences between independent business entrepreneurs, corporate entrepreneurs, common sector entrepreneurs (or municipal-community entrepreneurs) and community business entrepreneurs.

Social entrepreneuring thereby becomes a way of re-imagining the role of individuals within communities, where a sense of community has been 'lost' following the embrace of the market and neo-liberalism during the 1980s (Taylor, 2003). Community-based entrepreneurs can play a decisive role for depleted communities (Johnstone and Lionais, 2004).

The term 'depleted community' can be used in order to better under-stand the problems of communities affected by downturns in the local economy. To social entrepreneurs, depleted communities are manifesta-tions of uneven development. However, to Johnstone and Lionais (2004), depleted communities are more than simply locations that lack growth mechanisms – they are also areas to which people retain an attachment:

Table 5.1   Some entrepreneurs of interest to local governments

	Independent business entrepreneur	Corporate business entrepreneur	Common sector entrepreneurs	Community business entrepreneurs
Institutional setting	New business venture	Business venture	Common sector organization	Community
Role and position	Independent business people	Corporate executives	Politicians/ common sector officers	Local public figure/regional developers
Main activity	Create and grow business. Usually invest their own cash, aspiring to create wealth for themselves and their investors	Create values with an innovative project. No financial (but career) risk, but also less potential for creating personal wealth	Create value for citizens by bringing together unique combinations of resources. Career risk and no financial rewards	Facilitate and inspire entrepreneurship and renewal within their community. Limited focus on financial rewards

Source: Adapted from Zerbinati and Sovitaris (2005).

A depleted community, therefore, continues to exist as a social entity because it is shaped by positive social forces as well as by negative economic forces. While the economic signals are for people to move, the ties to community, the emotional bonds and the social benefits of living there create a powerful resistance to leaving. A depleted community, therefore, maintains a strong and active network of social relations. This can be understood in terms of the distinction made in the literature between *space* and *place*. (Johnstone and Lionais, 2004, p. 218)

Johnstone and Lionais (2004) use Hudson (2001), who contrasts 'space' as an economic (capitalistic) evaluation of location based on its capacity for profit with 'place', which is a social evaluation of location based on meaning. It can happen that locations thrive both as spaces for profitable enterprises and as places with a rich social fabric. When this is the case, the location appears to combine the best of economic and social life. Florida (2002) argues, for instance, that certain features of place, such as tolerance to social differences, serve to attract highly creative economic actors who are drivers of wealth creation (Florida, 2002). In such locations there is a synergistic relationship between space and place. Depleted communities do not enjoy this kind of synergy; instead, they suffer from economic stagnation and decline from social problems associated with economic decline (Johnstone and Lionais, 2004, p. 219). Depleted communities may also be expected to have a diminished stock of entrepreneurs especially if, in the past, those communities relied on a limited number of growth mechanisms.

Entrepreneurs working in depleted communities are likely to experience a number of obstacles to development, including venture capital equity gaps (Johnstone and Lionais, 1999, 2000), labour skills gaps (Davis and Hulett, 1999; Massey, 1995a) and a lack of business and financial support institutions (Johnstone and Haddow, 2003), as well as a lack of appropriate institutional thickness (Amin and Thrift, 1994; Hudson, 2000). Because of these obstacles, conventional private sector development in depleted communities is less robust and less likely. As a consequence, depletion could be something of a permanent condition there:

> Redevelopment in depleted communities is not likely to occur through traditional private industry-led mechanisms. If redevelopment occurs at all, it will probably be through less traditional means. This does not imply that the entrepreneurial process is irrelevant; on the contrary, in areas where capitalistic relations are less robust, the entrepreneurial process will, as it is argued here, manifest itself differently. Depleted communities will act as hosts to alternative forms of entrepreneurship that are adapted to their particular circumstances. (Johnstone and Lionais, 2004, p. 220)

Community business entrepreneurs do not look for personal profits. They evaluate wealth in terms of the benefits accruing to their own broader community. Traditional business entrepreneurs aim to provide personal gain and profits for themselves and for the shareholders of their business; community business entrepreneurs aim to create community benefits. Community business entrepreneuring can be distinguished from social entrepreneuring because it is focused on business organizations rather than charities, social ventures and purely social organizations. The process of community business entrepreneuring is neither entrepreneurship in the traditional business sense nor social entrepreneurship as commonly understood in the literature. It employs the tools of the former with the goals of the latter (Johnstone and Lionais, 2004, p. 226).

Although the barriers to development might be the same as those faced by traditional business entrepreneurs (finance gaps, labour skills gaps, lack of business support institutions, etc.), community business enterpreneurs can adapt in a variety of ways to overcome these obstacles. This is due to the fact that communities are not only the location of their entrepreneurial process. Some examples of this from Johnstone and Lionais (2004) are:

- Community business entrepreneurs can accept unconventionally low rates of return from their projects because personal profit is not then an objective
- Community business entrepreneurs may also have a wider choice of organizational forms to employ when doing business
- Once a project is undertaken, community business entrepreneurs have a different set of resources to call upon to achieve their goals. Among these resources is access to volunteers. On top of that, not only do community business entrepreneurs have access to significant volunteer time, but also much of this may come from skilled technicians, professionals and business people
- Another resource available to community business entrepreneurs is access to capital from neo-traditional sources. Community business entrepreneurs can access this by convincing local people, who would normally not invest in private businesses, to invest in their community businesses and organizations
- Similarly, community business entrepreneurs can attract customers who will buy from community-based organizations in preference to other (often non-local) organizations (Kilkenny et al., 1999).

A strong commitment to place enables community business entrepreneurs to marshal a number of financial, professional and labour resources around their projects that would not be available to other, more traditional, business entrepreneurs. That is, community business entrepreneurs use the assets of the community to overcome the obstacles of depletion.

The concepts of space and place have no doubt a bearing on discussing entrepreneurs in the context of local government. Herbert and Thomas (1997, p. 3) present an interesting table (Table 5.2) on this matter.

The rest of this chapter will concentrate on social entrepreneurs in general and public entrepreneurs in particular. 'Social innovation holds the key to our social ills. Social entrepreneurs are the people most able to deliver that innovation' (Leadbeater, 1997, p. 19).

PUBLIC ENTREPRENEURS

To summarize from previous chapters, some social entrepreneurs could be called citizen entrepreneurs and some citizen entrepreneurs could be called public entrepreneurs. The latter are citizen entrepreneurs who come up with social innovations and operate in public places unlike most social enterprisers. So, public entrepreneurs are social entrepreneurs but with some elucidations (compare this with Hjorth, 2009; Hjorth and Bjerke, 2006):

Table 5.2   Cities in space and cities in place

	Cities in Space	City as Place
Traditional	Urban regions and growth	Site and situation
	City and region	Urban morphology
Spatial analysis	Urbanization processes	Social ecology
	Rank-size rules	Natural areas
	Economic base-studies	Social areas
	Classifications	Segregation
	Central place theory	
Behavioural	Urban systems	Residential change
	Urban services	Consumer behaviour
	Labour markets	Housing markets
	Financial services	Images of the city
Relevance	Impacts of urban economies	Urban problems
	Planning urban systems	Area policies
	Control of flow, investments	
Structuralism	Hidden structures	Hidden structures
	Social formations	Problems as manifestations
Humanism	Quality of life	Meaning of place
	Life-worlds	People in the city
New cultural	Post-modern cities	Social construction
		Semiotics of the city

Source: Herbert and Thomas (1997, p. 3).

- The social can be seen as an invention (originating in post-revolutionary France some 200 years ago), meant to make visible the specific problems related to inequality and poverty in a society founded on civil and political inequality (Dean, 1999). Social entrepreneurs are commonly seen as people who are correcting such unsatisfactory states of the society through social enterprising. Public entrepreneurs, on the other hand, are creating *citizenry* through various social innovations, which are things often missing in local communities and thought to be a marginal matter or believed to concern only a few (Hjorth, 2009). Talking about 'public entrepreneuring' means to make some activities in societies more 'public'.

  A public place is a piece of actual, material as well as immaterial, space. It should not be confused with the public realm, that is, state property, or with the public sphere, a notion from political philosophy and translated from the German expression *Öffentlichkeit*. Public places are 'reasonable utopias' because there is nothing impossible in the principle, except for the risk that some citizens might refuse co-presence with others. A public place is a fundamental and fragile expression of urban society. It is a place where what is called 'civilry' is created and 'civilty' is practised.

> I believe that 'the public sphere' is at stake. We urgently need new ideas and tactics for imagining what the public should be today, and for exploring how we can act as citizens in order to enhance individuals' quality of life. My ambition is to contribute to this by elaborating on what I will call a public form of entrepreneurship which can create a new form of sociality in the public realm. The purpose by such a development is to re-establish the social as a force different from the economic rather than being encompassed by it. Entrepreneurship is then re-conceptualized as a sociality-creating force, belonging to society and not primarily to business. I also make use of an analysis of entrepreneurship as distinct from management, the latter being focused on efficient stewardship of existing resources and social control, while the former is animated primarily by creativity, desire, playfulness and the passion for actualizing what could come into being. Public entrepreneurship is a term thus meant to emphasize the creative and playful as central to entrepreneurial activity. (Hjorth, 2009, p. 207)

- Social entrepreneurship is today used primarily when discussing how to 'fix' problems with a withering 'welfare state' (Dreyfus and Rabinow, 1982), including 'reinventing government' (Osborne and Gaebler, 1993). Public entrepreneurs do not try to make the institutions' job better or act as producers offering goods and services in a market, but act as citizens who involve other citizens in developing the social capital in a society in order to passionately increase the inclusiveness and decrease the amount of alienation there
- Citizenship is a composite concept that includes individuals and groups. Discussions of citizenship always have to deal with rights values and social practice in which forms of citizenship are practices (Petersen et al., 1999). Citizenship in today's society is less of an institution and more of an achievement. Citizenship is therefore a matter of identity. Public entrepreneurs are citizen achievers and builders of citizen identity in the community at large or in smaller sub-communities. Phenomenology can come a long way into clarifying the meaning of public entrepreneuring.

Some examples of public entrepreneurial activities are (compare with Thompson, 2002):

- remobilizing depleted social areas
- setting up agencies for support and advice
- re-utilizing buildings and resources for social purposes

- providing 'suitability training'
- generating means for some common good issue
- organizing voluntary operations
- generating or supporting cultural activities that are not commercial
- generating or supporting sports activities that are not commercial.

Public entrepreneuring is often on a small scale and always local. It may even fail if it becomes too big. Also, when the public entrepreneur has gone, the public entrepreneurial activity in question may have problems surviving. This close connection between the public entrepreneur and his or her ambitions means that public entrepreneuring often goes on as a project.

There are many researchers who assert that public entrepreneurs have their roots in a history of local service and development (Grenier, 2009, p. 199). This is the history that feeds their passion for creating activities of importance to society (Emerson and Twersky, 1996, pp. 2–3).

The term 'public entrepreneuring', the way it is used here, was coined in 2006 (Hjoth and Bjerke, 2006). The term may lead to confusion. For instance, 'public' here does not mean that it is a phenomenon associated with what is traditionally called 'the public sector' in the society. It means, instead, entrepreneurial activities, initiated by citizens (not by common sector employees just a few pages back called 'municipal-community entrepreneurs' or 'common sector entrepreneurs', or by 'business entrepreneurs') going on in 'in public places' in the society wherever they may be. Due to this possible confusion it would be proper to here discuss at some length what public entrepreneuring is *not*.

1. Social Entrepreneurship the American Way

Much (if not most) research on social entrepreneurship is done in the US and the American social entrepreneurship discourse, like the American view on entrepreneurship in general, is very dominant, even outside the continent. Social entrepreneurship in the US (as well as elsewhere) is based, of course, on the prevailing social circumstances in place and on the role social entrepreneurs are seen to occupy in society. Catford (1998, p. 97) serves well as an illustration of how the 'problem' is phrased:

> Traditional welfare-state approaches are in decline globally, and in response new ways of creating healthy and sustainable communities are required. This challenges our social, economic and political systems to respond with new, creative, effective environments that support and reward change. From the evidence available, current examples of social entrepreneurship offer exciting new ways of realizing the potential of individuals and communities . . . into the twenty-first century.

The model that is ruling the discussion of 'social entrepreneurship' in the US is one where millionaire CEOs, retiring from their professional careers, or owners who have sold their businesses and made a handsome profit, move into the 'nonprofit sector' and apply their formerly successful business methods to solve social problems. 'Increasingly, entrepreneurially minded nonprofit leaders are bringing the tactics of the private sector to the task of solving social problems. And with good cause: they need the cash' (McLeod, 1997, p. 102). This means to look at solutions of social problems only, or at least primarily, in economic terms – as business solutions. The entrepreneur is here reduced to an economic agent with expertise in business problem-solving, and the social sphere is unproblematically described in terms used by the business sphere: 'Social entrepreneurs have the same core temperament as their industry-creating, business entrepreneur peers but instead use their talent to solve problems on a society-wide scale' (Drayton, 2002, p. 32).

So, descriptions of social entrepreneurs in the US, apart from being individualistic, are most often based on comparing them with business entrepreneurs. Differences between social entrepreneurs and business entrepreneurs, however, are not based on discussing fundamental social orientation or attitudes to the broader society, but centred on matters like long-term versus short-term focus and profit as private means versus profit as means to broaden the business objectives (Thalbuder, 1998; Westlund, 2001). In summary, social entrepreneurs in the US are seen as having a social objective while blending social and commercial methods: 'Social entrepreneurs share many characteristics with commercial entrepreneurs. They have the same focus on vision and opportunity, and the same ability to convince and empower others to help them turn their ideas into reality – but this is coupled with a desire for social justice' (Catford, 1998, p. 96). Schuyler (1998a, p. 1) argues that social entrepreneurs are: 'Individuals who have a vision for social change and who have the financial resources to support their ideas and who exhibit all the skills of successful business people as well as a powerful desire for social change.' Boschee (1998, p. 1) presents social entrepreneurs as: 'Non-profit executives who pay increased attention to market forces without losing sight of their underlying mission.'

Various forms of motivation for social entrepreneurship are identified in the American literature. As an example, Cannon (2000) presents three general types of people who become social entrepreneurs. The first of the three are individuals who have made a lot of money elsewhere, for instance, in business, and who want to give some of it back to society to further social goals. The second type is 'recovering social workers' who are looking for a more effective approach than the existing social support system. The third type is a new breed who have come out of a business school or come from a similar educational line with social entrepreneurship in mind.

As a summary of the above, we can say the following:

- The models are targeting entrepreneurs as individuals
- The models are very rationalistic. If somebody is of the right quality as a person and applies the correct set of activities, he or she will make it as an entrepreneur, social or not
- Entrepreneurs are presented as super-people. Only some people can be entrepreneurs
- Along the same line, entrepreneurship is presented as an extraordinary activity, not an everyday task
- Entrepreneurship should, in the eyes of many scholars, use as much as possible of management and marketing: the more the better. A social entrepreneur is seen as another type of entrepreneur, but he or she will still succeed if they apply formal management and marketing principles.

The social entrepreneurs (public entrepreneurs) we have worked (as researchers) hardly fit this American view at all. Our experience from research in this area (in Sweden) is:

- Social entrepreneurs see themselves as members of a team. They are very humble people and they look at their associates and partners as the major contributors to their success
- They have no formal overall plan for what they are doing and they apply very little 'scientific' management and marketing. Had they had such a plan and had they tried to apply too advanced business tools, they may not even have succeeded. They look at their situations more as taking active responsibility for what they are doing and practising what they preach, rather than telling others what to do or doing market research among 'users'
- They would have felt very uncomfortable had they worked in a formal organization
- They just do what they do naturally. They find it difficult afterwards to explain in any detail what they have been doing and why
- They look at what they are involved in as the most natural thing to do in the societies of today, they are very surprised that not more people are doing what they are doing.

2. The Social Economy (in the EU sense)

A number of statements from the EU indicate that the social economy is given increased attention as a means to create employment (Westlund, 2001, p. 431). The definition of social economy selected by the EU confines it to four types of organizational forms, which are Cooperatives, Mutuals, Associations and Foundations (CMAF). For a long time in Europe, social economy was the same as the national economy, in line with what was meant by social economy in the concept's 'native country', France. It seems to have been used there for the first time in 1830 by Charles Dunoyer in his paper *Nouveau traité d'èconomie sociale* (Bartilsson et al., 2000). Eighteenth-century France was marked by violent class conflicts. Economic thought in France became focused on 'finding a compromise, on restraining the market and crass individualism by launching the peda-gogical and political programme which came to be known as *l'èconomie sociale*' (Trädgårdh, 2000, p. 6). During the nineteenth century the leading social economists there directed their attention towards measures for social peace and reduced class conflicts, often in a conservative, paternal-istic spirit. Profit-sharing was one of the methods advocated. The social economy was regarded as the alternative both to the crude free market economy and to state socialism. As well as cooperation, the social econ-omists worked for the growth of related organizations such as 'mutual' associations of diverse kinds, that is, savings banks, credit banks and edu-cational organizations (ibid.).

Given the historical connotations associated with the term 'social economy', the usefulness of the term is sometimes questionable, at least in some societies. Furthermore, the alternative meaning of social as 'soci-etal' is often lost in some languages, including the Germanic group. Other terms suggested are non-profit sector, not-for-profit sector, solidarity economy, alternative economy and the third system.

We do not find the EU definition for the social economy very useful for public entrepreneuring. Public entrepreneurs are not restricted to any specific organizational form. Furthermore, it is easy to see all four types of organization covered by the EU definition in other sectors of the society than the citizen sector. One could also question whether activities like some cooperatives and savings banks are 'social' activities today.

Finally, we even find it questionable to refer to the situation in which public entrepreneurs are operating as an 'economy', at least in the market sense of the term. The pervasive neo-classical conceptualization of the 'market' often fails appropriately to capture the negotiated and demo-cratic structures of a properly functioning civil society (see, for instance, Spinosa et al., 1997).

3. Social Enterprises

It has been mentioned before that there are two kinds of citizen entrepreneurs, that is, social enterprisers and social innovators (public entrepreneurs). The differences between the two might be worth repeating:

- Public entrepreneurs do not devote themselves to work integration or to providing social and community care services, but to building citizenry
- Public entrepreneuring can hardly be characterized as 'a continuous activity producing goods and/or selling services', which social enterprisers do, according to Defourney (2001)
- Social enterprisers operate mainly in private or semi-sheltered places; public entrepreneurs do not.

4. Corporate Social Responsibility

'Corporate Social Responsibility (CSR)' is fashionable today, but, in our opinion, in several respects often a non-issue. First of all, to be socially responsible as a corporation or as any member of the society is not the same as not being irresponsible. It is, as we see it, to ask of every citizen, group or organization in the society today to behave responsibly. Furthermore, to be socially responsible as a corporation is not the same as, for instance, sponsoring a sport which is not related to one's own business activities, devoting a given percentage of one's profit to build up schools in a poor African village where it is not possible to find one single customer or business partner, or starting a foundation to allocate millions to deserving research. That is *charity* (not to be despised in itself)!

The social entrepreneurs that we have studied, public entrepreneurs, are not involved in corporate social responsibility the way the term is normally understood, nor have they anything to do with charity.

PUBLIC ENTREPRENEURS AND LOCAL GOVERNMENTS

Some different meaning's of the 'entrepreneurial city' are (Painter, 1998, pp. 260–61):

- The city as a setting for entrepreneurial activity: In this definition, the city is seen simply as a container or location for investment and risk-taking activities on the part of the private business. Therefore, if contemporary cities are more entrepreneurial than in the past, this must be simply because the nature of private business has changed (perhaps from a more monopolistic, corporate form to a form which is prepared to accept higher levels of risk for the prospect of very high returns)

- Increased entrepreneurialism among urban residents: In this case entrepreneurial cities would be those in which a large (or at least growing) proportion of residents were becoming entrepreneurs. This might be seen in the establishment of increasing numbers of small- and medium-sized businesses
- A shift from common sector to private sector activity: An entre- preneurial city could be defined as a city in which an (absolutely or relatively) increasing amount of urban economic activity is undertaken by the private sector, either through direct transfers from the common to the private sector, or by competition between the two
- A shift in the values and meanings associated with urban living in favour of business: Here, an entrepreneurial city would be one in which urban life increasingly came to be associated with cultures understood to be somehow entrepreneurial
- A shift in urban politics and governance away from the manage- ment of public services and the provision of local welfare services towards the promotion of economic competitiveness, place market- ing to attract inward investment and support for the development of indigenous private sector firms.

The authors would like to add to this list a preferred meaning of the entrepreneurial city:

- A place where all kinds of entrepreneurial activities can take place and where all parts of the community are seen in entrepreneurial terms.

Looking at the structural aspects of the 'entrepreneurial city', there are two dimensions worth exploring (Jessop, 1998, p. 89). First, institutions and structures that directly support entrepreneurs, existing or potential; and, second, institutions and structures that sustain an entrepreneurial climate. An interesting but difficult question in this regard is how far a general climate conducive to entrepreneurship can be attributed to the form of the urban centre itself as opposed to other localized factors, for example, the presence of well-integrated industrial clusters (Porter, 1990), flexible industrial districts (Piore and Sabel, 1984), and so forth. It may

Table 5.3   Differences between businesses and local communities (from Westerdahl, 2001, p. 40)

Businesses	Local communities
Economical, quantifiable values	Social values which are stressing meaningfulness (which cannot be measured quantitatively)
Clear organizations	Loose connections in networks, which have neither obvious extension nor form
Present standardized economic reports	Participate in bringing up narratives into the open in order to strengthen local identity
Act according to general economic principles	Lean towards what is meaningful in the local context

be hard to separate the effects of an entrepreneurial space/place from the effects of specific entrepreneurial strategies for that space/place since structure and strategy interact and co-evolve.

As aforementioned, there are differences between business situations and local government situations. Some further differences are presented in Table 5.3.

There are four main arenas within which social entrepreneurs can have a potentially critical impact (Grenier, 2009, p. 183). Some of these are valid more for social enterprisers than public entrepreneurs.

1. Community renewal (Brickell, 2000; Moore, 2002; Thake and Zadek, 1997): Social entrepreneurship is said to enhance social capital and build community. Moore (2002) identifies the impetus for social entrepreneurship in the UK as having its origin in community and neighbourhood renewal, in particular urban regeneration, issues that have been policy priorities for many years: 'it is the impetus for local regeneration and renewal that has provided one of the major driving forces of the social entrepreneurship movement' (Moore, 2002, p. 3). 'Community leaders and "social entrepreneurs" were to become the catalysts for overcoming the problems of run-down neighbourhoods' (Newman, 2001, p. 145)
2. Voluntary sector professionalization (Defourney, 2001, 2003; Leadbeater, 1997): Social entrepreneurship is identified in the UK context as essential in the reformation of a sector that is 'slow moving, amateurish, under-resourced and relatively closed to new ideas' (Leadbeater, 1997, p. 50). Defourney argued that there is a 'new entrepreneurial spirit' reflecting an 'underlying movement' which is impacting and reshaping the non-profit sector (Defourney, 2003,

p. 1). In these accounts, social entrepreneurship appears as a kind of modernizing force within the UK voluntary and community sector, providing an impetus for change, new forms of voluntary action, and a professional edge that will take the sector forward to further expand its role as a mainstream provider of social services

3. Welfare reform (Leadbeater, 1997; Mort et al., 2003; Thompson et al., 2000): This is another envisaged social entrepreneurship as a timely response to social welfare concerns and as an answer to the 'crisis of our welfare systems' (Defourney, 2003; see also Dees, 1998; Leadbeater, 1997; Thake and Zadek, 1997). Social entrepreneurship is claimed to 'help empower disadvantaged people and encourage them to take greater responsibility for, and control over, their lives' (Thompson et al., 2000, p. 329), and to counter-depend on welfare systems and charity (Leadbeater, 1997; Mort et al., 2003)

4. Democratic renewal (Favreau, 2000; Moore, 2002; Mulgan, 2006); Moore (2002) argues that globalization and the rapidly changing world have given rise to new philosophical debates, new notions of more socially and environmentally responsible economies, and basic questions such as: what kind of society would we like to live in? 'Social entrepreneurs and the social enterprises they create are one kind of response to a renewed search for the public good' (Moore, 2002). Moore argues that social entrepreneurship is 'producing a new form of citizenship, a new relationship between civil society and the state' (Moore, 2002). Along similar lines Mulgan (2006) describes social entrepreneurship as 'part of the much broader story of democratization: of how people have begun to take control over their own lives, over the economy, and over society' (Mulgan, 2006, p. 94).

Traditionally, local communities' interest in entrepreneurship has been limited to improve and facilitate business entrepreneurs in the own community. But things have changed, as we can see. Some examples of how a local community could act in public places in general are:

- To create awareness:
    - Participate in arranging a public entrepreneuring day
    - Finance various publications in public entrepreneuring issues
    - Institute a prize, 'The local public entrepreneur of the year'
- To participate in building public places more specifically:
    - Physically: offer venues at a low rent; initiate 'middle-age weeks'; arrange cultural exhibitions, music festivals and the like; open an 'entrepreneuring office' accessible for *all* kinds of entrepreneurs, not only in business

- Virtually: Present and discuss public entrepreneurs on the council or community homepage
- Discursively: Start a series of public discussions and lectures on public entrepreneuring
- Emotionally: Participate in discussions about what it means to be a citizen in the local community in question.

Some more specific examples of how local governments could act in public entrepreneurial matters are:

- To visualize a place where the citizens' ideas are received and from where they can be assisted by the local government
- To 'empower' the citizens: to teach citizens how to create
- To encourage employees to be more daring and to break the 'budget pattern'; let them know that they are allowed to make mistakes
- To assist in establishing a fund to be used in public entrepreneuring
- To let the citizens become part of the local government's network
- To arrange a workshop to find out which public entrepreneuring projects can be created, as well as more public entrepreneuring.

One area in which the current literature on the entrepreneurial city might be considered to be lacking is in its failure to consider local variations in entrepreneurial policies (Hubbard and Hall, 1998, pp. 20–22). Many researchers have neglected to focus on this very important aspect of urban governance, that is to say, the way in which their composition, orientation and objectives vary according to local cultural, social and political characteristics.

Like all economic activities, entrepreneuring is socially embedded. Thus, individual entrepreneurs are often socially embedded in networks of interpersonal relations; entrepreneurial firms or organizations are institutionally embedded; and an entrepreneurial society is embedded in a complex web of institutional orders which sustain structural competitiveness and provide an enterprise culture. Entrepreneurial cities in the strong sense are likely to combine all three forms of embeddedness (Jessop, 1998, p. 83).

Many researchers seem to overlook some of the fundamental characteristics of the city in their desire to generalize about the consequences of adopting a stereotypical growth coalition model. This often results in an atemporal and ageographic account of urban politics that fails to relate the trajectory of entrepreneurial governance to (often deeply embedded) 'local structures of feeling' (Williams, 1965).

The essential point being made here is that researchers seldom look at the lived culture of entrepreneurial cities or at the changing textures and rhythms of everyday life as they are affected by (and, of course, affect) entrepreneurial governance:

> One crux in local political cultures is the sense of belonging to a locality; people must identify with the sentiments that its core values imply. Part and parcel of such feelings is the belief that these values are worthy. Such assessments emerge from internal circumstances (e.g. a belief amongst the populace that growth brings jobs for them) (or) from area residents' impression of where their loyalty stands in the national space economy. (Hoggart, 1991, p. 184)

This task of exploring the manner in which entrepreneurial cities are experienced and understood by local populations, and the ways in which this differs from the hyperbole of the city boosters, has as yet received little attention (Hubbard and Hall, 1998, p. 21).

The following list summarizes how a local government may manage complexity in their neighbourhood:

- The postmodern perspective is stressing the unique characters in the local context as a contrast to other contexts (Healey, 1997)
- The society is to an increasing extent created by cultural communication in which people live in parallel, at work, where they live, where they enjoy their spare time (a kind of 'culture of the place') (Öhrström, 2005, p. 54)
- To support territorial nearness and the existence of regional specialization where key technologies (technology here consists of hardware and software as well as of human ware) build the platform for innovative abilities (ibid., p. 63)
- To create relations and coordination between 'reflexive agents' and organizations from all camps (including public entrepreneurs) with a high ability to continuous learning and de-learning (a necessity in a knowledge-based society)
- To think in terms of 'enabling' rather than 'planning' in the traditional sense (Guinchard, 1997). The increasing complexity in the society is asking for more spatial coordination of living, work, service and entrepreneurial activities ('public places'), which in turn presumes strategies interested in a holistic thinking and in coordination between different activities
- Planners who previously had a role as experts to the politicians now become coordinators in a co-acting process – they can no longer deliver the truth but rather become those who moderate different interests and contexts. They become experts of analyses of contexts and on initiating flows, rather than of drawing plans (Öhrström, 2005)

- Politics become local as well as global, run by more or less temporary constellations (ibid.)
- A shift from a linear view on planning as 'government' control to an orientation to be able to influence different networks and partnerships in more or less 'public' places through 'governance' can be seen as a solution to the problem of managing complexity in a local community:

> Urban politics is no longer, if it ever was, a process of hierarchical government in which decisions by local politicians are translated straightforwardly by public bodies into social and economic change. Rather it involves a complex process of negotiation, coalition formation, indirect influence, multi-institution working and public-private partnerships. This diffuse and multi-faceted form of rule has come to be termed 'governance'. (Painter, 1998, p. 261)

According to Jessop (1997), governance is associated with a particular form of rule. Unlike the hierarchical rule provided by local state and the anarchy of the market, he argues that governance involves 'heterarchy', which might be defined as 'rule through diversity'. The change from 'government' to 'governance' also means a shift from an isolated common sector to a model where the business and citizen sectors share responsibility and tasks:

> The new urban entrepreneurialism typically rests on a public-private partnership focusing on investment and economic development with the speculative construction of place rather than amelioration of conditions within a particular territory as its immediate (though by no means exclusive) political and economic goal. (Harvey, 1989, p. 9)

There is simply a smaller and smaller space to place all social activities in that part of society, which is financed by taxes (Öhrström, 2005, p. 53).

Not to forget in today's society:

- Most societies (or part of them) are a result of history. This does not mean that they are best organized and equipped to solve the problems of today and the future
- The units for analysis of the society (or part of it) are not traditional production factors but reflexive human actors (Storper, 1997)
- Innovations cannot be planned to any major degree but are a result of what seem to be random meetings between different 'pictures'.

- Human beings are directed by interpretations and constructed pictures, not by 'reality' as such (if it exists) (Öhrström, 2005, p. 64)
- Successful societies (or part of them) are those who stay away from imitating and copying forces *faster* than they are able to emulate new developments elsewhere (ibid.)
- They cannot successfully be run from above or from the centre. Continuous learning from *all* key actors at *all* levels is needed instead (Storper, 1997).

6. Entrepreneuring and regional development

THE INTEREST IN REGIONAL DEVELOPMENT TODAY

In his book, *New Rules for the New Economy*, Kelly wrote, 'The New Economy operates in a "space" rather than a place, and over time more and more economic transactions will migrate to this new space' (1998, pp. 94–5). He claimed, consequently, that people inhabit places, but, increasingly, the economy inhabits a space.

This myth is very easy to deflate according to Florida (2003). He asserts that people will remain highly concentrated, but opposes Kelly in that 'the economy itself continues to concentrate in specific places' (Florida, 2003, p. 4):

> From the countless interviews, the focus groups I've observed, and the statistical research I've done, it is apparent that place and community are more critical factors than ever before. And it appears that place, rather than being an abstracted 'space' as Kelly suggests, is essential to economic life. The economy itself increasingly takes form around real concentrations of people in real places.

According to Acs (2002, p. 170), two very significant transformations have occurred in our modern political economies in the last few decades of the twentieth century, due to challenges posed by the new socio-economy: a Balkanization of existing economies *and* a concurrent massive devolution in the governance system of both private and public organizations (see Chapter Five).

There are many reasons for the Balkanization of existing economies as a response to globalization. First of all, advanced industrial nations have been forced to specialize in exporting products in which they have 'technological' or 'absolute' advantages. Furthermore, since those industries tend to be found in sub-national regions, this has led to the emergence of a mosaic sub-national geographical agglomeration and regionalization characterized by product-based technological learning systems (Storper, 1992, 1993).

Secondly, globalization has strained nation-states enough for them to strengthen the needs of sub-national regions and communities for roots and anchors in local/regional bonds of ethnicity, language and culture. This has been reinforced by the fact that these regions often have proved to be the source of a robust entrepreneurial culture (Stoffaes, 1987).

Thirdly, nation-states have had to develop a genuine shared community of economic interest at the regional level so that the region-states have become active partners to foreign investors and providers of the requisite infrastructure to leverage regional policies capable of making the region an active participant in the global economy (Ohmae, 1993; *The Economist*, 1994).

Fourthly, as the region-state has emerged, sub-national development blocs have been nurtured by complementarities, interdependencies and externalities via infrastructure, and by networking of economic and business competence in order to transform the meso-economic levels (Dahmén, 1988; de la Mothe and Paquet, 1994b).

Global competitiveness has also led to a massive devolution in the governance systems of both public and private organizations. The reasons for this are several (Acs, 2002, p. 171). First, the search for speed of adjustment has forced corporations to adapt even faster and this has led them to come together in networks capable of taking action in the context of local circumstances. Managers have ceased to be 'drivers of people' and have become 'drivers of learning' (Wriston, 1992). So, a clear development of hierarchical structures to governance of networking structures has taken place.

Secondly, the same thing has been witnessed in the governance of public organizations where the need to do more with less and the growing pressure for more sub-national states to co-operate actively with private organizations to ensure success on the global scene has led governments to devolute power to lower-order public authorities (Osborne and Gaebler, 1992; Paquet, 1994; Rivlins, 1992).

Thirdly, this has led to general praise of bottom-up management (Handy, 1992, 1994; O'Toole and Bennis, 1992). And fourthly, the transformation of the governance of various organizations has not stopped at decentralization and privatization strategies. There has been a growing pressure to allow a maximum open use of all the possibilities of networking. This has led to the proposal to develop virtual enterprises and even governments (Davidow and Malone, 1992; de la Mothe and Paquet, 1994a).

Consequently, there exists today a considerable interest in cluster, regions, regional development and so on, and in the role of entrepreneuring in such contexts. To develop this subject a little bit further:

- During the 1970s, the conditions for economic development in industrialized countries changed dramatically. Previously it had been taken for granted that mass production gave winning advantages. Now this growth model ran into trouble (see, for instance, Nyström, 2002). The industrialized countries could no longer compete with low-cost countries when manufacturing standard products. Companies in the Western world instead had to compete through innovation, flexibility and productivity, which did not turn out to be easy for large companies. Small- and medium-sized firms proved to be better at handling this situation in decentralized systems in geographically limited areas

- In a globalized production and finance economy, countries' central governments have lost control of the flow of investments and labour. At the same time a more knowledge-intensive economy has developed. Regions supporting processes of learning and innovation have been identified as a key source of competitive advantage (MacKinnon et al., 2002)

- Localization has become a competitive factor. Thinking about competition and competitive strategy has previously been dominated by what goes on inside companies. Yet the prominence of clusters suggests that much of the competitive advantage lies outside companies, residing in the locations at which their business units are based (Porter, 1998a). Companies may actually benefit from having more local companies in the same business field as themselves, in spite of the tendency to believe that this will create more local competition, drive up input costs and make it more difficult to retain employees

- Geographic concentration occurs because proximity serves to amplify productivity and innovation (Porter, 1998b). Transaction costs are reduced, the creation and flow of information is improved and local institutions turn out to be more responsive to the specialized needs of companies when there are more of them and peer pressure and competitive pressure are more keenly felt. Paradoxically, the enduring competitive advantages in a global economy are often heavily local, arising from concentrations of highly specialized skills and knowledge, institutions, rivals and sophisticated customers in a particular nation or region. Proximity in geographic, cultural and institutional terms allows special access, special relationships, better information, powerful incentives and other opportunities for advantages in productivity and productivity growth that are difficult to tap from a distance (Porter, 1998b)

- Knowledge is a non-rivalrous production factor which, when used more, will not lead to decreasing returns but can be used by a large number of actors at the same time. Several studies point out the fact that knowledge-intensive production tends to organize itself in clusters (Braunerhjelm et al., 1998).

Let us look at various attempts to account for the development of regional economies and their dependence of entrepreneurship (as entrepreneuring or not). In the spirit of this book, it is convenient to discuss models for explaining regional development as space on the one hand, and interpretations for understanding regional development as place on the other. In this vein, Wigren and Melin (2009) make a distinction between 'competitive ideas' and 'collaborative ideas' for realizing regional innovation systems. The competitive model is based on technocracy, rationality and linearity. Regional development is assumed to be something that can be rationally planned. This can be taken to mean that the process is institutionalized to start with and that there is one best way to proceed. Local knowledge is disregarded and concepts, tolls and processes advocated by the authority are not adjusted to the local context. The interpretations of local actors are not listened to, nor are they involved in a process that they might feel comfortable with. Homogenization, rather than regional diversity and heterogenization, is the result of the competitive model. Regional actors are expected to act in line with what they are expected to do. Decisions are made by a few and the regional dialogue hardly exists.

The collaborative model leaves room for irrationality, ambiguity and non-linearity. Here, regional innovative organizations are seen to share a history, are embedded in the region and share a vision about a regional future. The future is represented by the organizations themselves and their goals as shared by the members of the regional innovation system that provides the basis for defining their roles (Simon, 1991, p. 133):

> For 'success', in terms of regional development and growth, the regional actors and organizations have to collaborate to certain degrees, which requires that each one knows its role in the system and how to fulfil it – and it requires that they have shared representations of the region and its future. The very starting point for such collaboration is the actors' shared history, memories and representations, not subordination and rational planning. (Wigren and Melin, 2009, p. 53)

The collaborative model leaves room for regional learning through collaboration between regional actors. In order for the development and/or change, it is necessary to understand the representations shared by the community members, and if necessary, recreate them. Community members become carriers of the representations. Change and development are dependent on human beings and learning is seen as a social phenomenon. Interpretations and representations created by actors in the region are not forced upon them from above.

MODELS FOR EXPLAINING REGIONAL DEVELOPMENT AS SPACE

Since the earliest days of industrialization similar types of operation have tended to locate in specific places. Groups of firms are established near each other and specific industries are concentrated in certain cities and regions. This is not particularly surprising given the need for proximity to different raw materials and energy sources in the form of coal, timber and water, and transportation. What is new today is that companies locate close to each other because it is valuable in itself. However, until the early 1970s, the existence of 'industrial complexes' (as they were then known) was by and large explained and evaluated primarily on the basis of the cost and availability of capital, labour and physical resources (Isard and Schooler, 1959). However, a dramatic reduction of transportation and communication costs made scholars realize that this approach was inadequate. Economic geographers and regional scientists began to search for alternative models and approaches (Hamilton and Linge, 1979, 1981). Shortly thereafter, the location of economic activity also attracted the interest of scholars from other disciplines (Martin, 1999a). Regional economists began to emphasize the fact that flexible manufacturing systems and forms of network governance would make it possible for firms to capture and to exploit knowledge externalities (same as 'spillovers') (Håkanson, 2003, p. 3). A different vision of labour, it was now commonly argued, enabled firms to better cope with the uncertainty of rapidly changing technologies (ibid.). This facilitated learning and enabled firms in certain regions to maintain and exploit technological advantages that were insensitive to shifts or differences in factor costs (Asheim, 1996; Keeble et al., 1999; Keeble and Wilkinson, 1999; Lawson, 1999; Malmberg and Maskell, 1997; Maskell and Malmberg, 1999a, 1999b; Morgan, 1997; Piore and Sabel, 1984; Porter, 1998b; Pouder and St. John, 1996; Storper, 1992; Storper and Harrison, 1991). We can call this the 'Marshall-based localization as a means of competition'.

Alfred Marshall was the first economist to specifically recognize the mutual advantages that firms could obtain from close proximity to each other, especially if small- and medium-sized enterprises (Hansen, 2001). The idea was that a concentration of firms in close geographical proximity would allow all of them to benefit from large-scale industrial production and technical and organizational innovation beyond the scope of any individual firm. He described these concentrations as 'industrial districts'.

Marshall (1898) focused on factors which determined the localization of industries; factors which are external to individual firms, but advantageous to those firms which are part of the district. Two such factors in his discussion were 'agglomerations' and 'externalizations' (another expression for this latter is 'spillover effects'). Both of these factors depend on decisions made by other firms in the same district. Effects of agglomerations originally discussed by Marshall include (Jonsson and Olander, 2000):

- the creation of a labour pool facilitating the recruitment of personnel
- improvement in the coordination of different steps in the production process
- reduction of stock as firms have quick access to suppliers; and
- more effective and less costly communication channels between business actors.

Later research has added some advantages from industrial districts, for instance, the dissemination of communication and access to ideas are improved, and the geographic concentration of a diverse knowledge base stimulates innovative activities.

As far as knowledge externalities in industrial districts goes there is a much-quoted passage from Marshall:

> When an industry has thus chosen a locality for itself, it is likely to stay there long; so great are the advantages which people following the skilled trade gets from near neighbourhood to one another. The mysteries of the trade become no mysteries; but are as if it were in the air. Good work is rightly appreciated, inventions and improvements in machinery, in processes and the general organization of the business have their merits promptly discussed; if one man starts a new idea, it is taken up by others and combined with suggestions of their own; and thus it becomes the source of further ideas. (Marshall, 1898, p. 271)

It has been pointed out that Marshall's industrial districts do not describe all types of dynamic regional economies, but it seems to be a general opinion that their basic ideas are suitable to many regions in both Europe and the United States (Håkanson, 2003; Storper, 1992). It is not to be forgotten that Marshall also discussed the importance of 'knowledge externalities' in his famous studies.

Today, in a world of databanks and Internet, the role of geographical distance for diffusion of knowledge is not longer so obvious. However, Antonelli (1994) and Audretsch and Feldman (1996), and Jaffe et al.

(1993) among others, discuss the continued importance of 'localized knowledge spillovers'. As one exponent of this view puts it:

> The propensity for innovative activity to cluster spatially will be the greatest in industries where tacit knowledge plays an important role. It is tacit knowledge, as opposed to information, which can only be transmitted informally, and typically demands direct and repeated contacts. (Audretsch, 1998, p. 23)

Renewed interest in the significance of localized economies in industrial districts came strongly in the 1980s, largely due to the work of Piore and Sabel (1984) on the 'third Italy', which was a name they used to distinguish their topic from the old industrial area in north-west Italy and from the less developed area south of Rome. Instead of, as Marshall did, focusing on agglomeration models based on transaction costs, Piore and Sabel stressed flexible production backed up by wider social and institutional support. Similarly, Granovetter (1985) stressed the fact that a social structure and culture only comes about through proximity, and through his concept of embeddedness which points out the importance of collective and institutional grounds for successful coordination.

At about the same time in the 1980s there was another important contribution to the explanation of regional economic growth. Romer (1986) presented a new growth theory and found that the divergence in growth rates may be the result of 'increasing returns to knowledge'.

Porter (1990), in his study on the competitiveness of nations, argues that many successful industries locate within a single town or region to such an extent that it is questionable whether the nation is a relevant unit of economic analysis. Instead, he states that it is more meaningful to look at regional units, where industries are connected in clusters of vertical and horizontal relationships. Porter suggests that successful regions are to operate in so-called 'diamonds' – a much-quoted model. Any equitable history of theories of regional development must include this model (Figure 6.1).

At the points of Porter's diamond are:

- Factor conditions: The situation of the region when it comes to production factors such as skilled labour or advanced infrastructure that are necessary to compete successfully
- Demand conditions: The nature of home demand for the industry's product or service
- Related and supporting industries: The presence or absence in the region of supplier industries and related industries that are internationally competitive.

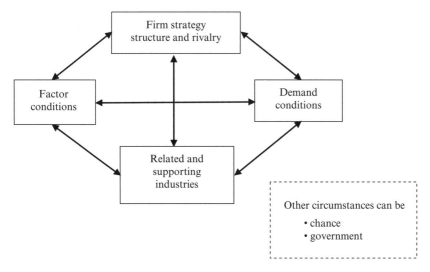

Source: Porter, 1990, p. 127.

Figure 6.1   Regional success pattern

● Firm strategy, structure and rivalry: The conditions in the region governing how companies are created, organized and managed, and the nature of the domestic competition.

Examples of chances that can play a role in regional development according to Porter are:

● pure inventions
● breakthroughs in basic technologies (such as biotechnology, microelectronics)
● discontinuities in input costs, such as the oil crises
● significant shifts in the world's financial markets or exchange rates
● major shifts in market demand globally or regionally
● political decisions in foreign governments
● war.

Porter claims that governments can influence (and be influenced by) each of the four determinants in the diamond, either positively or negatively. However, he asserts that their influence can only be indirect.

Krugman (1991a) has a more active approach. He claims that even if regions have an advantage due to historical circumstances, they can keep their leadership only if they can use agglomeration and spillover effects together with consideration of the importance of transport costs and the size of different markets available. Krugman is the leading representative of what is sometimes called the New Trade Theory (NTT) and a new economics of competitive advantage that has emerged and which assigns a key significance to the role that the internal geography of a nation may play in determining the trading performance of the nation's industries' (Martin and Sunley, 2008, p. 26). Economists, it seems, are discovering geography. Krugman has sought to show how trade is both influenced by and in turn influences the process of geographical industrial specializations within nations (for instance, Krugman, 1991b). Similarly, Porter (1990) argues that the degree of economic clustering of industries within a nation plays an important role in determining the competitive advantage of the nation in question.

Martin and Sunlay (2008, pp. 29–30) assert that the NTT acknowledges the differences among countries as one reason for trade, but it goes beyond the traditional view in four main ways (Krugman, 1990):

1. Trade between nations represents specialization to take advantage of increasing returns to scale rather than to capitalize on inherent differences in national factor endowments. The gains from trade then arise because production costs fall as the scale of output increases
2. Specialization and specific locations of microindustries are seen, to a large degree, as indeterminate and as a historical accident. And whatever pattern exists gets 'locked in' by the cumulative gains from trade. History matters because there is a strong tendency toward 'path dependence' in the patterns of specialization and trade between nations
3. The patterns of demand for, and rewards to, factors of production will depend on the technological conditions of production. Nothing' can be said *a priori* about the development of factor demands
4. The NTT argues that the existence policies will *strategically* create comparative advantage by promoting those export sectors where economies of scale are important sources of rent. Strategic trade policy may enable a nation to shift the pattern of international economic specialization in its own favour (Krugman, 1980). The 'old' models from Ricardo and others saw free trade as the appropriate policy stance (see, for instance, Ricardo, 1817).

The interaction of external economies of scale with transport costs is the key to Krugman's explanation of regional industrial concentration and the formation of regional 'centres' and 'peripheries' (Krugman, 1991b; Krugman and Venables, 1990). With reduction in transport costs, firms will want to concentrate in one site to realize economies of scale both in production and in transport (Martin and Sunley, 2008, p. 30).

Krugman (1993) argues that the large-scale regions are more significant economic units than nation-states. 'It is a strong tendency of both economic activity in general and of particular industries or clusters of industries to concentrate in space' (Krugman, 1993, p. 173).

Rosenberg et al. (1992), as representatives of the NTT, emphasize the importance of high technology for the wealth of nations. High technology is the result of research at tertiary institutes of technology and universities that is transferred to companies through higher education or has been developed by the companies themselves. Rosenberg et al. also emphasize the 'path dependence' in a region's development of a technology, that is, the tendency to continue on the technological path once an industry has invested in it to achieve its competence.

Feldman (1994) introduced the concept of 'regional technological infrastructure', which, in her opinion, contains four classes of factors which are required to complete a commercialization process: agglomeration effects and networks of firms in related industries, concentration of university R&D, concentrations of industrial R&D, and networks of business service firms in close contact with the market.

The available part of our total stock of knowledge in society seems to be correctly classified if it is assumed to have two portions (Acs, 2002): one perfectly accessible part consisting of already established knowledge elements (obtainable via scientific publications, patent applications and so on) and a novel, *tacit* element, accessible only by interactions between actors in an innovation system. The importance of the latter was pointed out in the 1960s by Polanyi (1966), but interest in the phenomenon grew with the discussions of regional development and the like in the 1990s. For example:

> The propensity for innovative activity to cluster spatially will be the greatest in industries where tacit knowledge plays an important role [. . .] it is tacit knowledge, as opposed to information, which can only be transmitted informally, and typically demands direct and repeated contact. (Audretsch, 1998, p. 23)

Coded knowledge and tacit knowledge will be discussed later under 'Interpretations for understanding regional development as place'.

Carlsson (1997) launched the concept of 'technological systems'. He studied the interactions between the actors in a system of competence networks in markets and non-markets. He claims that the approach to public policy based on the theory of market failures is insufficient, since failures in networks, institutions and systems exist as well.

In general there are four types of explanatory models being discussed in relation to regional development:

- Agglomeration theories show that cost reductions may result from shared infrastructure, such as communication and transportation facilities, and access to specialized labour and machinery and the like. In addition, consumer search costs may be reduced and spillover effects may occur as companies learn more quickly about new technologies and market opportunities. Increased returns and positive feedback may also arise as more companies join the region
- Transaction cost theories show that under conditions of uncertainty it may be most efficient to locate near your business partners. Spatial proximity facilitates firms' learning and increases the likelihood that they will react faster to suppliers and customers
- Neoinstitutional theories emphasize cognitive, regulatory and normative frameworks within which firms are located. Geographic closeness fosters a strong local culture that legitimizes homogeneous behaviour in interactions between people and firms:
  1. through pressure exerted on organizations by other organizations
  2. in order to reduce uncertainty
  3. because members in the networks have the same education and backgrounds.
- Resource dependency theories provide an alternative to neoinstitutional theories. They make it possible to explain 'deviant' competitive behaviour in those firms in a region that are able to influence their environment.

  The concept of the cluster has become very prominent during the past decade or so after the relaunching of the concept by Porter. It is possible to trace four, more or less overlapping, perspectives and uses of the cluster concept (Assmo, 2003):
  1. A model for explaining why a region is competitive within a certain industry in comparison to other regions
  2. A perspective from which to describe and structure complex production systems in which actors in different ways form and support a manifold interconnected production structure, often within a more or less geographically concentrated area
  3. A tool for regional planning
  4. A model for social networks, which are thriving through social capital.

But we have many names for the things we love. Instead of clusters, we may talk about industrial districts, local/regional industrial environments, local businesses venturing for global use, competence blocks, learning regions or districts of excellence. Furthermore:

> Clusters are defined as production of similar products and services in a geographically well-defined area. Unlike branch and industry definitions, clusters are usually composed by firms from several branches and are characterized by a differentiated supply of products as well as services. (Braunerhjelm et al., 1998, p. 420; authors' translation)
>
> Cluster is partially replacing the old concepts of sector (for instance, service sector) and branch (for instance, graphic industry). Sector is today too broad and branch classifications are too narrow. A cluster is branch-transgressing. The purpose of thinking and acting in clusters is to start a dynamic interaction between firms in a common strategic knowledge area and interaction between these firms and other actors concerned (educators, research, regional and local community institutions). If we turn to international experiences and research, we can say that cluster is a holistic approach to work with growth, development of regional innovation and profiling, where different actors are working with different part. (NUTEK, 2001, p. 14; authors' translation)
>
> A cluster is a critical mass of companies in a particular field in a particular location, whether it is a country, a state or region, or even a city. Clusters take varying forms depending on their depth and sophistication, but most include a group of companies, suppliers of specialized inputs, components, machinery, and services, and firms in related industries. Clusters also often include firms in downstream (e.g. channel, customer) industries, producers of complementary products, specialized infrastructure providers and other institutions that provide specialized training, education, information, research, and technical support, such as universities, think tanks, vocational training providers, and standard-setting agencies. Finally, many clusters include associations and other collective bodies covering cluster members. (Porter, 1998a, p. 10)

A few comments are worth making in the context of the above quotations:

- Which type of region is relevant when studying the regional anchorage of entrepreneurship depends on which factors are influencing the existence of entrepreneurship in the region. Is it natural conditions, the history of the region or the local culture that are playing the crucial role? (Nilsson, 2002, p. 202)
- Cluster is not purely a high-technology phenomenon. Clusters occur for many types of industry, such as textiles in Georgia, fashion goods in Milan, diamond cutting in Belgium and scientific pens and pencils in Nuremberg. (Cooper and Folta, 2000, p. 348)
- Even if localization in a cluster may be important for all firms, it appears to have particular implications for start-ups and small firms. These are unlikely to have all the resources that they need in-house

and often lack credibility as well as experience. These may be easier to acquire by locating in a cluster. (Cooper and Folta, 2000, p. 349).

Many commentators claim that the business climate is generally more progressive in the US than in Sweden. Still on the subject of regions, Braunerhjelm et al. (1998) saw the following advantages in the American clusters, when comparing biochemical and polymer clusters in Sweden and Ohio:

- established links between researchers, industry and potential financiers exist
- applied research has priority (important basic research is bought)
- supply of venture capital is much broader and more competent in the sense that money is followed by available management and marketing competence
- there is access to a great number of so-called 'business angles', that is, private persons who want to become venture financiers
- mechanisms for introducing new products and/or services on the market are more developed; and
- a clear reward structure exists for successful entrepreneurs.

The driving forces underpinning successful regions are considered by Berggren and Brulin (1985), *Entreprenör* (2003), Johannisson (2002), Mascanzoni and Novotny (2000) and *Metro* (2001). Among their proposals are:

- Access to labour: The more companies there are in the same industry in one place, the greater the chances are of recruiting competent labour
- Locomotive companies: Something like 'hidden champions', these are centres, which coordinate the production of a large number of companies in the region and work at the front of the value-added chain. It is important to keep them!
- Coordination: When companies in the same industry are agglomerating, they start to buy from and sell to each other, develop new ideas and increase the competence in the cluster at large
- Rivalry: If the toughest competitor is located across the street, it seems to stimulate more rivalry than if it is invisible
- Variations: These include other activities of a social and cultural kind in dense local networks
- A demanding home market: This is a market that hones the companies' ability

- Societal services': These include schools, development centres and the like.

Explanations for explaining regional development as space can sometimes present as simplified as the following list of causes (Deiaco and Nordström, 1998):

- long-term developments
- migration
- industrial variety
- regional political ambitions
- university regions.

However, modifications in these models should be made (Amin and Thrift, 2008, pp. 159–65). Firstly, it is inaccurate to refer to the conditions and areas cited by the 'localization thesis' as the only examples of success. That would exclude the reconsolidation of major metropolitan areas such as London, Milan, Frankfurt and Paris as centres of growth. They have acted through their magnet-like pull on finance, management, innovation, business services and infrastructure. There are also some examples of a growing concentration of wealth in certain rural areas characterized by a kind of odd combination of capital intensification in agriculture, the decentralization of office and service industries, and get-togethers of commuters looking for a pleasant lifestyle. These successes have little to do with the logic of flexible specialization or benefits from increased economies of scale.

Secondly, proposing local agglomeration as the symbol for future growth effectively rules out the possibility of transformation and change within the areas of post-Fordist growth just cited.

Thirdly, the localization thesis would mean that the proliferation of localized production complexes is likely to be restricted, as necessary components are not readily transferable to other areas. Local containment of the division of labour requires a gradual build-up that takes time to consolidate and cannot be ruled by traditional instruments of regional policy owing to their ephemeral and composite nature (Amin and Robins, 1990). Furthermore, new growth cannot simply sweep aside local traditions that might resist changes (Glasmeier, 1991).

Fourthly, the idea of a clean break between one production system dominated with one way of doing things and another system with its distinctive structure is too simple to provide a picture of continuity and discontinuity and diversity and contradiction that such change normally suggests (Gertler, 1988; Sayer, 1989; Thrift, 1989).

The growth of giant multinational corporations suggests that the world has become more decentralized and less hierarchically governed at the same time as there have been a number of very considerable problems of integration and coordination (Amin and Thrift, 2008, p. 164). The world economy may have become more decentralized, but not necessarily more decentred. There are still signs of neo-Marshallian nodes acting as collective 'brains', as centres of excellence in a given industry with a number of local networks, knowledge structures and institutions underwriting individual entrepreneurship (Peck, 1991; Todling, 1991; Törnqvist, 1991).

In conclusion, there is a possibility to distinguish other types of industrial districts apart from the Marshallian one and the principle of flexible production found in North Italy according to Markusen (2008, p. 177). Markusen suggests three additional types of industrial districts with quite disparate firm configurations, internal versus external orientation and governance structure. They are a hub-and-spoke industrial district, a satellite platform with an assemblage of unconnected branch plants embedded in external organizational links, and a state-anchored district, focused on one or more common sector institutions.

INTERPRETATIONS FOR UNDERSTANDING REGIONAL DEVELOPMENT AS PLACE

When regional development is seen as place, interpretation of innovation is seen as a social process (Henton et al., 2002):

- it is interactive; it does not occur in a straight line
- it is built on tacit knowledge through interaction and personal experiences
- it takes place in networks based on trust, where key business agents participate
- it works only when it tears down walls
- it combines cooperation and competition; and
- it is place-based.

Saxenian (1994) presented her famous study on a comparison between Silicon Valley (a successful region in the United States) and Route 128 (a less successful region in the United States). She maintains that Silicon Valley has been much more resilient and adaptable than Route 128. Despite similar origins and technologies, the two regions have evolved two different forms of industrial arrangements. Silicon Valley has an industrial system based on regional networks that promote entrepreneuring,

Table 6.1   A comparison between Silicon Valley and Route 128

Silicon Valley	Route 128
A technical culture which crosses over firms and functions	An industrial order which is based on individual firms
Less formal social relationships and cooperative traditions which support experimentations	Relationships between individuals and firms, where secrecy and territorialism rules
Firms organized as loosely coupled engineering teams	Traditional hierarchies within firms
A flexible industrial structure which is organized around the region and its professional and technical networks rather than around individual firms	Distant – even antagonistic – relationships with local institutions A number of independent firms, which lack social and commercial relationships with each other

Source: Saxenian (1994).

collective learning, flexible adjustment and experimenting. Route 128, on the other hand, is dominated by a small number of relatively vertically integrated corporations that by and large keep to themselves. A summary of Saxenian's results can be seen in Table 6.1 (Saxenian, 1994).

Also with this view, clusters are interpreted as rarely appearing out of nowhere. A local pioneer usually provides the spark that sets off the process (*Metro*, 2001):

1.   The pioneer stage: A single individual has a successful business idea
2.   Spinoffs by imitation: The success of the first company simulates others to start similar companies and employees leave to start up their own enterprises
3.   Creating local business networks: The companies start to exchange products and services. Information and knowledge are spread between them
4.   Creating a local culture: When the companies become numerous enough they start to make an impact on the region. Education and infrastructure are adapted to the companies
5.   The region becomes a brand: Sometimes the cluster may become so big that the region itself becomes part of the brand of the companies – for instance, Hollywood.

An example of the intimacy that may exist between different actors in a cluster can be seen in the Italian small business clusters as shown in Figure 6.2.

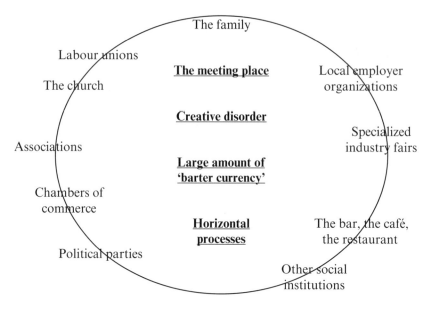

The family

The meeting place

Creative disorder

Large amount of
'barter currency'

Horizontal
processes

Labour unions

The church

Associations

Chambers of
commerce

Political parties

Local employer
organizations

Specialized
industry fairs

The bar, the café,
the restaurant

Other social
institutions

Source: Normann (2001, p. 302).

Figure 6.2   The Italian small business clusters

Many commentators are of the opinion that Silicon Valley is one of the best examples of a successful region. Here are ten of its 'secrets for success' (Bjerke, 2007, p. 213):

1. Failure is tolerated: Having been bankrupt is almost seen as a merit; as a necessary step towards credibility. This attitude may be the region's major strength
2. Unfaithfulness is tolerated: Silicon Valley is not known for traditional loyalty. To jump from one company to another and to exchange secrets is one of the recipes for success
3. Risk seeking: A venture capitalist in Silicon Valley calculates 20 investments the following way: four will go bankrupt, six will lose money, six will go OK, three will go well . . . and one will win the jackpot
4. Reinvestment: The enormous cash flow that is generated in Silicon Valley is, by and large, reinvested
5. Enthusiasm for change: 'Only the paranoid survive' is a traditional slogan (which is associated with Intel's legendary chairman Andy Grove). Cannibalism is the key

6. Support of merit: There are wide opportunities for women and immi-
    grants in Silicon Valley, they say. An understatement! If women and
    immigrants did not go there, they may as well close the place down.
    Generally things are moving so fast that politics is of hardly any
    practical importance – no small thing in itself!
7. Fixation with the product: In Silicon Valley, they always think of the
    latest and coolest products which are loved by the innovators
8. Cooperation: Generations last for months, sometimes weeks. The
    answer: mix the latest with tried and tested borrowed from all and
    sundry
9. Variation: There are lots of things going on all the time – most are
    gone rather quickly
10. Anybody can play: The old American dream has come alive again in
    Silicon Valley. Everybody who lives in the Valley believes that he or
    she can be rich. Maybe this is an exaggeration – but not too much of
    one.

The importance of free and unrestricted movements for the success of
Silicon Valley is confirmed by Saxenian as well:

> It is not simply the concentration of skilled labor, suppliers and informa-
> tion that distinguish the region. A variety of regional institutions – including
> Stanford University, several trade associations and local business organiza-
> tions, and a myriad of specialized consulting, market research, public relations,
> and venture capital firms – provide technical, financial, and networking services
> which the region's enterprises often cannot afford individually. These networks
> defy sectoral barriers: individuals move easily from semiconductor to disk drive
> firms and from computer to network makers. They move from established firms
> to start-ups (or vice versa) and even to market research or consulting firms, and
> from consulting firms back into start-ups. And they continue to meet at trade
> shows, industry conferences, and the scores of seminars, talks, and social activi-
> ties organized by local business organizations and trade associations. In these
> forums, relationships are easily formed and maintained, technical and market
> information is exchanged, business contacts are established, and new enter-
> prises are conceived. This decentralized and fluid environment also promotes
> the diffusion of technological capabilities and understandings. (Saxenian, 1994,
> pp. 96–7)

A successful region in Sweden is Gnosjö. According to Johansson (2001),
some central concepts for the Gnosjö spirit are:

- It is concentrated to three clusters – metal, plastics and machinery
  – which together account for more than 40% of employment there
- There is cooperation as well as competition

- Many companies are suppliers to large industries in the country, such as cars and manufacturers and engineering, which sometimes means that the companies compete for the same order
- Cooperation means buying from, borrowing from or using each other as sub-suppliers
- Everybody is positive towards the development of business networks, which are created by business connections and personal relationships
- It is based on well-developed social capital with a very positive attitude towards business venturing.

If we compare Silicon Valley and Gnosjö, we can state the following 11 points (Johannisson, 2002, pp. 139–43):

1. Role in the global economy: The technological innovations of Silicon Valley have strongly contributed to a changing global society, above all within information technology. Gnosjö has proven its role as a successful centre for industrial development but not on a global level.
2. Key resources: In Silicon Valley the key resource is knowledge capital at a high level. The educational level in Gnosjö is, on average, lower, but it is compensated with a kind of confidence capital (social capital) for creating and spreading knowledge
3. Organization of competence: In Silicon Valley, as in Gnosjö, the competence has been organized locally and regionally. In Silicon Valley you can get access to this competence, if you have an idea to test. In Gnosjö the local knowledge bank is opened if you can demonstrate your solidarity
4. Focus of learning processes: What you can learn in Silicon Valley is high technology, above all information technology. In Gnosjö the technical development is not that high, but equally fast. There, learning is dominated by what could be described as 'ingenuity' and 'shrewdness'
5. Geographic mobility, industrial dynamism and social variation: Silicon Valley is characterized by high mobility between firms and across the borders of the region. In Gnosjö the opposite is the case, although social mobility can relate to a way of life between being employed and becoming your own boss
6. Attractiveness: Silicon Valley offers nature, climate and a spirit of creativity and freedom. Gnosjö has long been admired for its vital small business venturing and its, by and large, total lack of unemployment
7. Infrastructure of networks: In Silicon Valley and in Gnosjö networking between firms and other actors plays a decisive role in the

development of the region. In Silicon Valley this is run by what we could call 'individual calculative ambitions'. In Gnosjö networking mirrors a more collective capital

8. Dominant institutions: As far as formal structures are concerned, economic institutions dominate in Silicon Valley, while the social networks in Gnosjö have been generated by and continue to generate formal institutions such as free churches, sports organizations and business associations. The basic systems of the informal institutions also differ

9. Entrepreneuring: Dense, regional environments generally generate different forms of partnership. Team entrepreneuring is common in Silicon Valley. Gnosjö can be characterized as a kind of collective entrepreneuring process, that is, business venturing in a wide sense, which is less tied to individual firms

10. Identity: Silicon Valley rests on the 'American dream' and its entrepreneurial values. In Gnosjö they want to show that they can do what is impossible in other parts of the country

11. Variation: Variation is big in both Silicon Valley and Gnosjö although the information and communication industries dominate in Silicon Valley and plastics and engineering dominate in Gnosjö.

According to Normann (2001) the crucial question is how to become a good home for value creation activities. He presents a list of desiderata for successful regions (pp. 313–14):

- They should be nerve centres to some locomotive companies
- There should be clusters of different kinds and sizes around these internationally competitive locomotive companies
- They should be the home of some highly competitive knowledge-intensive service companies, since these now lead the development of an economy
- Physical and informational infrastructures should be of a high standard
- There should be a high quality of life for 'global knowledge entrepreneurs', including areas such as health care, culture, ecology and nature
- There should probably be a high proportion of people from unconventional business circles, such as entrepreneurial immigrants and women, involved with business innovation and new start-ups
- There should be several meeting places for exchanging tacit knowledge, both within industry clusters and across various areas of society including between industry, culture and politics

- People move from one context to another at the same time as they change the way in which they organize themselves
- There should be a high degree of reconfigurability
- There should be a high level of quality of the 'strategic conversation' and probably an informal but effective 'strategic management coalition' between actors from all areas of society
- There should be experiments going on to break taboos and boundaries with regard to traditionally structured areas such as welfare services
- There should be a high degree of externalization of support functions for city services in infrastructure, education, health care and so on, as well as a certain level of 'outsourcing' of such services to international players
- The area should be recognized as one in which aesthetic and cultural issues are particularly high priorities and there should be a range of people from around the world visiting for this reason.

Listed below are some 'buts' added to common proposals as to content in successful regions:

- They should be guided by a vision, *but* this should not be pronounced as *one* vision and it should be shared by the people, who live and work in the region
- Key actors should be involved in the development, *but* they should be there with their brain (understanding) and heart (wishing) as well as their stomach (daring) and feet (acting)
- There should be lots of networks, *but* they should overlap and intersect with each other, not consist only of friends and colleagues
- There should be locomotive companies, *but* they should be admired and talked about with pride
- There should be lots of entrepreneuring, *but* within all sectors of society, not only among business firms
- There are many proposals for what should be contained in a successful region, *but* timing is very important. The situation should rather be compared with baking a soufflé than baking a sponge cake (Nilsson, 2002, p. 204).

A NECESSARY CHOICE OR POSSIBILITIES FOR COMBINING SPACE AND PLACE?

Choosing the approach to look at regional development can be a result of a strict view on the differences between explaining and understanding, and triggered by the answers to five critical questions to the view of looking at regional development as building a more progressive place:

1. What is an industrial region?
2. How important is entrepreneuring to an industrial region?
3. Is it possible to successfully build an industrial region from the top, down?
4. Is it possible to successfully pick the geese that will lay the golden eggs to be part of the industrial region?
5. How can visions, networks, ideals and systems be humanized in an industrial region?

What is an Industrial Region?

This is a fundamental question separating the view of behaving in a successful region as a space and acting in the same quality region as a place. Industrial districts have almost exclusively been studied and treated as objective phenomena, on the assumption that it is possible to identify the crucial parameters that are necessary to succeed and then work (hard) to apply them (Acs, 2002). Human abilities such as will-power, passion and empathy have hardly been considered at all. Social capital is assumed to be produced by formal institutions, which generate trust and absorb uncertainty (Hjorth and Johannisson, 2002).

When looking at a region as a space, and when applying mainstream regional economics, a phenomenon as an 'industrial region' is taken as an objective fact – as a thing. The person studying a region has, therefore, the right to define what his or her study area is and what it contains. Such a view also claims that what is happening when specific senior actors get together is that industrial regions are constructed rationally using plans, decisions and coordinated action.

An alternative view – and a view that is associated with looking at a region as a place – is, for instance, social constructionism (compare with Alberti, 2003). The question is then what drives the regional process. Is it actors translating ideas (Czarniawska and Sevón, 1996) or institutional agents pursuing institutional interests? The simplest answer would be both, but their co-presence seems to be creating a third driving fact – a collective intention, the agglomeration of personalized skills of stakeholders. An industrial region then gradually comes into existence through repeated discussions and materializes as names and labels come to be given to those events and activities that take place and by endorsing supportive organizations with the name of the region (Berg, 2001). In that way, you are 'invoking' (ibid.) and you 'make sense of' the region (Berger and Luckmann,

1967; Smircich and Stubbart, 1985; Weick, 1979, 1995). The region then becomes a cognitive fact but not an objective one (Burrell and Morgan, 1979; Pfeffer, 1981; Weick, 1979).

Even more interesting to phenomenologists is to go one step deeper and look at how language (not just cognition or social constructionism) is building up a 'region'. It is based on the belief that all knowledge is context-dependent. With this view, a region (industrial or not) is built up as an 'epistemic community' more than anything else and its defining knowledge is formed through the pursuit of common practice in the region (Håkanson, 2003). Among the fundamental errors when studying regions in competition is the common usage of the concept 'tacit knowledge' as the notion that whereas tacit knowledge is difficult both to imitate and to replicate, the converse is true for articulated knowledge. These ideas have gained widespread acceptance because they fit nicely with the widespread 'resource-based view'. In its crudest form, it suggests that knowledge can be dichotomized into 'tacit and easily imitated' knowledge (Almeida and Kogut, 1999, p. 907).

The prominence that this line of reasoning has come to enjoy is curious for several reasons. First, it implicitly equates 'articulation' with 'codification', that is, when knowledge is articulated, it follows that it is codified into fixed, standardized and easily replicable forms. In reality, codification is a time- and resource-consuming activity, the potential benefits of which are often unclear (Murtha et al., 2001). Second, it assumes that once knowledge is articulated, it is difficult (if not impossible) to protect its dissemination:

> Since tacit knowledge is assumed to be more or less inimitable, the logic of the argument requires that a potential imitator, although mastering all other aspects of the skill or activity in question, does not share, cannot draw on or even create whatever tacit understanding may be involved in its execution. In reality, the employees of firms in the same industry tend to share much of the tacit knowledge that their practice requires. This puts them in a situation where they may sometimes imitate one another's advances by simple trial and error, without necessarily having access to codified descriptions of these advances. (Håkanson, 2003, pp. 8–9)

The fact is that 'tacit knowledge' is *not* a very important element to understand differences in competiveness between regions, nor is it needed to explain the existence of local knowledge externalities. The more interesting focus is to answer questions regarding the size, location and communication pattern of epistemic communities, where tacit as well as explicit knowledge is transferred and retained.

How Important is Entrepreneuring to an Industrial Region?

As we see it, entrepreneuring is crucial for the success of the industrial region. Nothing happens if nobody acts. Entrepreneuring is, after all, about coming up with things that the environment can use.

However, in successful industrial regions we should consider entrepreneuring in all varieties that exist in the modern society. It appears (or should appear) in all sectors of society, that is, in the common, business and citizen sectors:

> The outstanding features of successful industrial regions are the concentration of specialized and complementary epistemic communities, on the one hand, and a high level of innovation and entrepreneurship – within existing firms but especially in the form of new business [and other new entrepreneurial activities], on the other. (Håkanson, 2003, p. 20)

Is it Possible to Successfully Build an Industrial Region from the Top, Down?

Economic geography normally looks at possibilities to find general principles for what should be contained in a progressive region. Cultural geography asserts that a more realistic alternative is to discover the unique, organic conditions existing in an industrial region and then to support and participate in dialogues in creative and constructive networks, where key actors move forward together. Industrial regions (and clusters) are extremely difficult (or impossible) to create from the outside or from the top, down. Existing regions have a history and have taken time to develop, from within and the bottom, up.

Is it Possible to Successfully Pick the Geese that will Lay the Golden Egg to be Part of the Industrial Region

Too many power-holders in incubators, industrial villages and local community institutions believe they can decide beforehand which types of industries and business firms should be included in their region ('they shall belong to the future' and 'they shall have a growth potential' are common requests), and also that they can pick out those that will be most successful. This contrasts with everything we think we know about how innovation works. Innovative processes cannot be planned to any major degree, they behave in a random, almost arbitrary way and they are practically unpredictable. The task is rather to do your best in an industrial region to create even more turbulence, even more variety, to 'let a thousand flowers bloom'. Participating actors then have the best conditions in which gradually to build something that is meaningful and sustainable.

How can Visions, Networks, Ideals and Systems be Humanized in an Industrial Region?

People interpret their belonging (or lack of belonging) in an industrial region in different ways, which may seem coherent and meaningful only to themselves (people are 'embedded' in their social context). There are, according to the cultural geographers, several problems associated with the dominant, super-rational view on how to develop successful industrial regions (Hjorth and Johannisson, 2002):

- There is a need for a gradualist approach, based on hermeneutics, social constructionism and/or phenomenology
- You should listen to local 'storytellers'
- You need a local 'world-view'
- You should study local history
- You should take part in fostering a meaningful local epistemic community, thereby strengthening a local collective identity.

One may ask whether it is necessary to choose between an economic geography and a cultural geography, that is, between space and place. There are other views on the subject. Bathelt and Glückler assert that 'the debate is somewhat misdirected for it tries to separate those economic and social aspects that are inseparable' (2008, p. 74). So, they claim that economic geography cannot be either economized or culturalized. They are dimensions of the same empirical reality which should be studied in a dialogue rather than based on a reductionist prioritization (Stark, 2000). Bathelt and Glückler (2008) suggest that we should use what they call a 'relational perspective'. This leads to specific ideas about:

- conception of space
- object of knowledge (or research object); and
- conception of action.

A relational perspective is based on 'a relationship between space and economy which is contrary to that of regional science' (Bathelt and Glückler, 2008, p. 79). The latter looks at space as a container which confines and determines economic behaviour. Also, space is supposed to be possible to discuss without referring to what is going on in it. In contrast, a relational perspective assumes that economic action transforms the localized situation and provides institutional conditions for future action. Like Storper and Walker (1989), this perspective emphasizes that the economic actors themselves produce their own regional environments. And economic action can only be understood if the particular economic and social context of that action is analysed (Bahrenberg, 1987). Economic action can never be treated as a separate research object isolated from those economic and social structures and relations where they take place.

Furthermore, Bathelt and Glückler (2008, pp. 79–80) assert that 'economic actors and their action and interaction should be at the core of theoretical framework of economic geography and not space and spatial categories'. They suggest that the conception of space should be a perspective (Glückler, 1999), that is, to use space as a basis for asking particular questions but not as a primary objective of knowledge.

So, the relational perspective contends that economic action and interaction are the central objects of knowledge in the analysis, not space-economy, spatial systems or spatial categories. Economic action is seen as being embedded in structures of social (and economic) relations and contextualized as a context-specific process. Research in relational economic geography should focus on processes, such as institutional learning, creative interaction, economic innovation and inter-organization, and investigate these through a geographical lens rather than uncovering spatial regularities and structures (Bathelt and Glückler, 2008, p. 81).

Regional science normally employs, as does neoclassical economics, an atomistic view of economic agents. In contrast, a relational perspective emphasizes contextuality of all human action, being embedded in structures of on-going social relations (Grabher, 1993; Granovetter, 1985). To summarize, economic action is seen in a regional perspective as a process, situated in time and place (Bathelt and Glückler, 2002a, 2002b; Giddens, 1990; Glückler, 2001; Martin, 1994, 1999b; Philo, 1989; Sunley, 1996).

Hudson (2008, p. 102) is of a similar opinion to Bathelt and Glückler (2008):

> There is an as yet unresolved – and maybe irresolvable – debate as to the character of the relationships between culture and economy, with important differences within as well as between the advocates of culture/cultural economy and those of economy/political economy. Recognizing this, and so at the risk of some oversimplification, I want to suggest that the recent debates in economic geography can be represented in terms of a dialogue between the proponents of political economy and those of cultural economy. However, rather than

seeing these as complementary alternatives, I want to argue that they are most appropriately seen as complementary perspectives from which we can seek to understand more fully and in more subtle and nuanced ways economies and their geographies.

But there are more scholars that are of the opinion not to see space and place as alternatives or to look at a given space as a static fact when researching regions, for instance:

- Paasi (2008, pp. 385–6) claims that 'regional identity' has become a popular subject and has in turn created a new wave of regionalism, not the least because of the developments in Europe (Keating, 1998). Various regional authorities have started campaigns to try to make their regions into 'products' to be sold on the market in order to attract tourists, skilled professionals and investment capital. Regional identity is sometimes connected to such concepts as social capital or learning regions, trust and solidarity (Keating, 2001; MacLeod, 1998). However, ordinary people and their regional identities have often remained marginal to such efforts by regional actors and the meanings of regional identity are still vague, even what Sayer (1992, pp. 138–9) refers to as a 'chaotic conception'. According to Paasi (2008), the view of region as taken for granted and looking at regional identity as something that people already have or that people are struggling for may hide social, ethnic and cultural conflicts of kinds that exist in most states and may lead to social exclusion, both outside and inside a region and in external relations. Discussion of the institutional and symbolic links between identity and bounded spaces is therefore of crucial importance to any study of regional identity
- Coe et al. (2008, p. 200) argue that it is the interacting effects between territorialized relational networks and global production networks within the context of changing regional governance structures that contribute to regional development, not inherent facts of regional advantages
- Dicken and Malmberg (2008, p. 264) assert that existing regional concepts differ 'in the way they incorporate the spatial or territorial dimension, in the definition of the system and in the analysis of its working'. Some of them are primarily functional, like industrial networks (Håkansson, 1989), commodity chains (Gereffi, 1994) or industrial clusters (Porter, 1990). In these cases, the system is defined by various types of manifest relations between actors and firms who make up the system. In general, these approaches are

weak in specifying the role of space and territory. There are other approaches, of a territorial type – such as industry agglomerations (Malmberg and Maskell, 1997), industrial districts (Becattini, 1990), innovative milieus (Maillat, 1998), national innovative systems (Lundvall, 1992) or learning regions (Asheim, 1996) – which elaborate more carefully the spatial aspects of the system. For analytical convenience regional systems are defined as functional *or* territorial (we would say as a space *or* a place), although, of course, all regional systems are both functional *and* territorial (Dicken and Malmberg, 2008, p. 266).

7. Entrepreneurial action and environment

Green, eco-friendly, carbon neutral – these are amongst the top buzzwords of today. In all aspects of life we hear a lot about saving the environment and reducing carbon emissions, but what does that mean in relation to entrepreneuring practice? With more and more companies transforming all or part of their businesses into 'green' ventures, the question 'What does greening mean in an entrepreneurial context?' arises. In the growing movement toward green businesses, the role of the entrepreneur still remains little studied. Therefore, entrepreneurs accepting responsibility for the impacts they have on air, land, water and fellow humans is the issue to be discussed in this chapter. The chapter will discuss what it means to be green in entrepreneurial thinking by outlining some of the previous studies and identifying some key issues. The chapter then moves on to a discussion of extended responsibilities: that of corporate social responsibility (CSR) when it is taken seriously. Finally, the phenomenology of green- and CSR-oriented entrepreneuring practice in time, timing, space and place will be discussed.

The concepts of green entrepreneuring, environmental entrepreneurs and, more recently, ecoentrepreneuring are relatively new ones. Entrepreneurs create and extract value from various situations and by including environmental and social concerns extend the obligations. Consequently, green- and socially oriented entrepreneurs are including concerns for the natural environment and fellow humans in their activities – in the local community surrounding the operation as well as at distance somewhere else and later. Studies linking green associations into entrepreneurial actions have only been in wide use since the early 1990s, when Bennett (1991), Berle (1991) and Blue (1990) began to employ the terms 'environmental entrepreneur', 'green entrepreneur', 'ecoentrepreneur' and their derivation 'ecopreneur' (for an overview, see Schaper, 2010). More recently these concepts have been examined by, for instance, Andersen (1998), Anderson and Leal (1997), Cohen and Winn (2007), Dean and McMullen (2007), Dixon and Clifford (2007), Hostager et al. (1998), Isaak (1998), Keogh and Polonsky (1998), Kyrö (2001), Larson (2000), Linnanen (2002), Pastakia (2002), Schaltegger (2002), Schaper (2002, 2010), Seelos and Mair (2005), Walley and Taylor (2002).

Attempts to shed light on this complex issue by creating typologies and categories of green entrepreneurs have been made by, for example, Isaak (2002), Kyrö (2001), Linnanen (2002), Schaltegger (2002), Walley and Taylor (2002). In Walley and Taylor's (2002) study, the differing internal motivations and external structural forces that influence green entrepreneurs are put into four categories: innovative entrepreneurs, ad hoc enviropreneurs, ethical mavericks and visionary champions. Their motivations range from more or less narrow business concerns, all the way to a desire to change the capitalist system.

In a similar vein, Isaak (2002) differentiates between types of green businesses – either 'green' businesses that did not start out with environmental concerns but make innovations along the way, and on the other hand 'green-green businesses', which are thoroughly green from their inception.

For Gerlach (2002), ecopreneurs are individual innovators who see their business as embracing environmental values as a core component of their identity and as aiding in their competitive advantage in the marketplace (see also Schaper, 2010). Anderson and Leal (1997, p. 3) define ecopreneurship as 'entrepreneurs using business tools to preserve open space, develop wildlife habitat, save endangered species and generally improve environmental quality'. Andersen (1998, p. 135) says that 'entrepreneurs create and extract value from a given situation and that environmentalists also find themselves deeply embedded in social ideas of value'. Schuyler's (1998b, p. 3) more generic definition, on the other hand, states that 'the term ecopreneurs has been coined for entrepreneurs whose business efforts are not only driven by profit, but also by a concern for the environment'. From the ongoing debate about green entrepreneurship it becomes clear that the strategies adopted differ between traditional entrepreneurs on one hand, and green and social entrepreneurs on the other. A well-known distinction is that traditional entrepreneurs are considered to generate social value as a by-product of economic value whereas social and green entrepreneurs give social value top priority (Dixon and Clifford, 2007; Keogh and Polonsky, 1998; Vyakarnam et al., 1997).

From the explicit dual concern about both economic and environmental values, the green entrepreneur's intentionality and belief system in terms of values and aspirations are also regarded as important motivators (for example, Dixon and Clifford, 2007; Keogh and Polonsky, 1998), which is also noted by Schaper (2010, pp. 8–9):

> Ecopreneurs vary dramatically in the significance they place on this goal. For some business ventures, such altruistic goals are more important than financial return or commercial viability; for others, it assumes equal ranking with

traditional measures of economic and commercial success; and, for others still, it is only a secondary factor after business feasibility. But by including an aspect of intentionality, we can separate green entrepreneurs from 'accidental ecopreneurs' – business ventures whose firms operate in an environmentally friendly manner, but do so more as an unanticipated by-product of other business processes than because of a deliberate focus on this issue. Beyond this, however, it becomes much harder to identify and define environmental entrepreneurship. Ecopreneurs do not fit a mould – they come in many different forms and engage in a wide variety of business activities – and thus far it has not been possible to identify a 'typical' profile. Only the entrepreneur's behaviour – their goals, what they actually do in their business and the outcomes they produce – can safely be used to set them apart.

Underlying assumptions about driving forces also relate to discussions about the business segments in which green entrepreneurs are operating. Linnanen (2002, pp. 72–74), for example, classifies environmental businesses into four different segments. Each has a distinctive character, and their emergence has been influenced by a different combination of drivers. Three main drivers for environmental business and technology can be identified as follows:

1. The geographical area of influence, ranging from local, to regional, to global. The balance has shifted from local point-source pollution, such as waste-water treatment, to global and more complex issues, such as climate change
2. Reason for market emergence, either by regulation or by voluntary decisions of market actors. Besides the traditional command-and-control approach of regulations, market-based instruments and voluntary actions have become increasingly important
3. Degree of enforcement, varying from high to low, which differs from country to country and from one law to another.

On the premises of the above drivers, Linnanen (2002, pp.72–74) then proposes the following four segments that can be identified among environmental businesses:

1. Nature-oriented enterprises: These are concerned with wildlife habitat preservation, eco-tourism and other close-to-nature concepts that utilize economic and human resources to improve, or at least sustain, the state of the environment. In their purest form these enterprises might consist of a sustainable use of natural resources, perhaps in ventures operated by people with alternative lifestyles. Nature-oriented entrepreneurs are a growing breed in the travel and hospitality industry. Resorts and hotels are increasingly

creating energy and conservation programmes where restaurateurs are implementing recycling plans. Other forms of ecoentrepreneurs are transforming traditional business models with increasingly green technologies

2. Producers of environmental technology: The production of such technology is driven by legislative pressure on communities or industrial enterprises to reduce their environmental load on water, air and soil. This segment can be exemplified by businesses operating in so-called 'clean technologies', which use environmental science to conserve the natural environment and resources; for example, recycling, water purification, sewage treatment, removal of pollutants and contaminants, solid waste management, energy conservation and renewable energy systems

3. Providers of environmental management services: These aim to advise corporations to utilize environmental systems and services as a source of competitive edge. This segment includes services provided for environmental management systems, consulting and accounting services. The promotion and implementation of well-known standardized environmental management systems are examples of this category. In increasing numbers, even smaller companies around the world are choosing to publish reports pertaining to their environmental, social and economic policies, practices and performance (for example, ISO 14001). These reports serve multiple purposes: they provide companies with a management tool to enhance the quality of their operations through continuous improvement while strengthening public accountability, and at the same time address the needs and expectations of external stakeholders (for example, investors, customers, NGOs, communities, academics) for environmental, social and economic information

4. Producers of environmentally friendly products: Such products as these are differentiated from existing products by their better environmental performance over the product life cycle. Environmental products are a thriving category in green entrepreneuring. From attracting only small portions of the population, many start-ups have identified the increasing demand for organic food and green travel services, although still being a somewhat contested and small segment of the industries. Green entrepreneurs can be better positioned to take advantage of these niche opportunities and be more responsive to customer feedback.

Linnanen (2002, p. 73), finally, summarizes the drivers of these four environmental business segments as follows:

Table 7.1   Drivers of eco-business sectors

Segment	Driver: Geographical influences	Driver: Reason for market emergence	Driver: Degree of enforcement
Nature-oriented enterprises	Local	Market	Low
Environmental technology	Local and regional	Regulation	High
Environmental management services	Global	Regulation and market	Low
Environmental products	Global	Market	Low

Source: Linnanen (2002, p. 73).

EXTENDED COMMITMENTS – CSR AND ENTREPRENEURING

Since Rachel Carson's book *Silent Spring* was published in 1962, environmental management concerns have developed in sophistication. From filters, high chimneys, sewage treatment works, and other reactive end-of-the-pipe solutions forced by external legal frameworks in the 1960s and the 1970s, via the introduction of standardized environmental management systems in the 1990s, towards increased attention on proactive operations driven by ideas that internalize environmental aspects into the very core idea of the operation. Particularly, the United Nation's convened report of the World Commission on Environment and Development (WCED; aka the 'Brundtland Report') in 1987, the 1992 Earth Summit in Rio de Janeiro, and the subsequent Local Agenda 21s, were high on the agenda until the late 1990s.

After a few years of declining attention in the public debate, environmental concerns are again on the rise, and public opinion is moving as well. Recent debates about such issues as global warming and increased greenhouse gases (mostly carbon dioxide) have again contributed to an increased general interest in human-related environmental change and impact. The multifaceted complexity of environmental issues in society, for instance, environmental management in organizations, are increasingly being recognized as an integration of not only financial and environmental issues, but also of social, and sometimes also cultural, responsibility.

From a company viewpoint, the well-known 1987 WCED definition of sustainable development – a development that 'meets the needs of the present without compromising the ability of future generations to meet their own needs' – clearly resonates with the present-day concept of CSR (a concept less discussed in relation to entrepreneurs). A rationale for such an extension of the environmental focus to include social factors is also aptly noted by Charles Secrett, former director of Friends of the Earth in the UK:

> [T]here are no environmental solutions to environmental problems, except over geological time scales. There are only economic, social and political solutions because the causes of environmental degradation are economic, social and political by nature. (Mehra and Jørgensen, 1997, p. 23)

Consequently, the concept of CSR remains linked to the concept of sustainable development – particularly the early public documents on sustainable development (for example, WCED, 1987) resonate in the contemporary debate about CSR. It must therefore always be remembered that the concept of sustainable development is a framework in which not only environmental, but also economic and social indicators, are interlinked. Ideally, an organization (or a society) that is ecologically, economically and socially sustainable – in the spirit of the 1987 WCED report – may be understood as one that continuously increases shareholder and stakeholder value while simultaneously decreasing the energy and material intensity of the products and services it provides.

CSR: A PLETHORA OF CONCEPTS

Nowadays, the concept of CSR is increasingly found in texts dealing with environmental and social matters of business activities, as well as in programme explanations and scientific investigations. In public debate, on the other hand, the concept remains vague and open-ended, posing as many questions as answers, for example, when stating that enterprises should make decisions based not only on financial factors such as profits or dividends, but also based on the immediate and long-term social and environmental consequences of their activities (Wikipedia, 29 May 2007). In a similar broad vein, McWilliams and Siegel (2001, p. 117) define CSR as 'actions that appear to further some social good, beyond the interests of the firm and that which is required by law'. Concerning the problem of defining and narrowing down the concept of CSR, a great deal of scientific material has been written (for a historical overview, see Frederick, 2006).

The concept of CSR is immured in an aura of high ideals; obligations to consider the interests of customers, employees, shareholders, communities and ecological considerations in (all) business ventures are becoming increasingly stressed and generally accepted (at least in lip service). Consequently, CSR has become a buzzword in recent years, travelling from the conscious NGOs, through the corporate boardrooms and smaller business managers, and right down into consumer consciousness. The ease with which this worship of CSR rolls off one's tongue has much to do with the attention given to the concept in recent years. Increasingly being a concept explicitly embracing economic, environmental, social and cultural factors, the concept of CSR has been 'pummelled and massaged to suit countless agendas' (*The Guardian*, 8 November 2006). The concept of CSR is therefore also subject to much debate and criticism. Matten and Moon (2008, p. 405), for example, note that the concept of CSR is 'nationally contingent, essentially contested, and dynamic', while Devinney (2009) argues that the notion of CSR is potentially an oxymoron because of the naturally conflicted nature of the corporation.

While CSR has gained considerable academic, corporate and media attention, fewer scholars have yet addressed the role of CSR in the entrepreneuring discourse. The above discussion of CSR is most commonly associated with the need of multinational corporations (MNCs) to protect their reputations and their brand image. The term 'corporate' in CSR simply gives the impression that it is the domain of big business. Still, the concept of CSR can also be associated with small- and medium-sized enterprises (SMEs) and their need to uphold a reputation within a smaller network of contacts. Such aspects of sustainable manufacturing and consumption have implications for SMEs as well as for entrepreneurial action. Still, research on CSR in SMEs and entrepreneurship has only recently attracted interest from academics (for example, Fassin, 2008; Quinn, 1997; Spence, 1999; Spence and Rutherford, 2003; Thompson and Smith, 1991; Vyakarnam et al., 1997).

The concept of CSR is thus less emphasized in entrepreneurial studies. One impediment for implementing CSR in entrepreneurial situations is the increased workload it generates. In general, entrepreneurial processes are characterized by less formal structures and looser control systems, less documentation and fewer procedural hurdles, and a lack of specialized staff with time to focus on controlling and reporting.

There are, however, some general arguments for CSR implementation, which can also be addressed in an entrepreneurial context:

- CSR as a question of managing risks and recognizing opportunities: The risk management approach tends to involve reactive or proactive stances to local and legal requirements, compliance with current regulation and standards, both domestically and internationally, and focuses on reducing the risks in current operations and the risk of sanctions or lack of business for failing to meet minimum standards. A more proactive approach is to see CSR as opportunity management to access new markets and increase efficiency

- CSR as a question of improving brand reputation and employer branding: The importance of public reputation is becoming more important. Reputation plays an increasing role in keeping organizations honest and forcing them to take definitive actions. Potential customers as well as competitors, journalists and 'watchdogs' typically use online sources to find information about a company. Because of this increased transparency and access to information, 'traditional branding' – whether through mission statements, marketing or affiliations – can easily be verified and evaluated.

UNDERSTANDING GREENNESS AND CSR IN ENTREPRENEURING

Green- and CSR-oriented entrepreneuring embrace operations that differ in terms of time, timing, space and place. Local initiatives, such as resorts and municipal projects, are characterized by immobility (of place) and planning horizons, sometimes extending decades ahead. The temporal aspects of such entrepreneuring can therefore range from environmental initiatives having biological life cycles of decades and centuries, industrial product life cycles of some 10–20 years, material life cycles of a few years, to present-day social concerns. Similarly, the spatial aspects of green entrepreneuring initiatives are ranging from immobile places and natural habitats, to dependencies upon favourable entrepreneurial climate, all the way to flexible operations that are capable of changing production lines on a daily basis.

Green and CSR entrepreneuring initiatives might also be triggered for different reasons, for example, when more profound external situations trigger a change in direction, or less dramatic conditions when enthusiasts attract attention to start new projects. Some entrepreneurs might also launch environmental responsibilities largely as a consequence of pressure from legislation, governmental agencies, local pressure groups or NGOs.

In terms of the time, timing, space and place notions discussed in the previous chapters of this book, the discussion about green and CSR entrepreneuring in this chapter is a reflection of humans who are extending their entrepreneurial initiatives towards a closer association between economic, environmental and social values. In most cases, such incorporation of economic and environmental concerns reflects a time conception based on the exact quantification of *chronos'* clock-time, which enhances routinization and standardization. Still, other forms of timely initiatives at a certain place can also be found among green- and CSR-oriented entrepreneurs. Enthusiasts and dedicated teams of entrepreneurs who are launching new initiatives are quite frequently driven by a 'kairic' feeling for the right moment to act. Likewise, any moments of truth, when judicious decisions are taken from a choice of alternatives, can be characterized as 'kairic'. Starting a green or a social initiative could be a question of vital business importance, an identification of a niche opportunity, or any situation when judicious decisions beyond the mainstream and the rule of the textbooks are taken.

Similarly, the two spatial conceptions of place and space (*topos* and *chora*), can be recognized in the green- and CSR-oriented entrepreneurial initiatives. The environmental programmes can be intended for a certain place (*topos*) within the boundaries of a resort, a municipality or within an organization, which at the same time could be focused on abstract and distant places and spaces – by addressing workers' conditions in distant production units, a concern for the ecosystem, the ozone layer or global warming.

Some of the particular characteristics of green- and CSR-oriented entrepreneuring, which differentiate them from most other (traditional) entrepreneurs, are the following:

- Green- and CSR-oriented entrepreneurs tend to have an extended focus in the first place on which the business depends, rather than adding greenness and social concerns onto a existing business initiative
- Financial incentives and opportunities are used as tools for implementing 'good behaviour', rather than seeking high profit from being a green- and CSR-oriented entrepreneur
- Competence in environmental and CSR issues is available from the start, rather than being obtained later
- The role of being green and CSR oriented in the entrepreneurial idea is seen as an integral part of the day-to-day operations; rather than being reduced to a policy-level document.

Green- and CSR-oriented entrepreneuring engagements also tend to be strong on issues related to the local neighbourhood and on the global (visionary) level. Engagement is strong on questions of green products, recycling, local environment and social justice, as well as on a global level. In the spatio-temporal conceptions used in this book, the care of the *topos'* local environment – where the entrepreneur is located or the distant location where the production takes place – creates most attention. Consequently, goals and specific objectives of green- and CSR-oriented entrepreneuring are quite frequently limited in scope but broad in intention.

It must be noted, however, that CSR and greenness comes with an opportunity cost: the alternatives that the resources, time and effort could have been used for, if they have not been used to extend responsibility obligations. This is particularly burdensome for a small actor, such as an individual entrepreneur. Some of the reasons why small firms and entrepreneurs find extended environmental and social obligations problematic are (see Worthington and Britton, 2009, pp. 218–19):

- Small actors have limited resources and cannot spread costs over larger units
- Lack of human and material resources for implementing improved responsibility practices
- Small actors are less visible for legislators and monitors, which means that they can avoid some (obligatory or voluntary) commitments.

The triple bottom-line approach – of including financial, environmental and social factors – is hardly the key towards realizing sustainable development. At best, a triple bottom-line approach serves as a step towards less unsustainable developments (in time and space). The singular bottom line still counts in business operations, and it is financial. From a business point of view, 'sound finances' remain a prerequisite for running a company over time. There is a potential that triple bottom-line thinking – of including economic, environmental and social responsibilities – can be seen to be diverting attention limiting resources and time from what is perceived to be core business. Managing more than one bottom line can be perceived as simply creating more work.

Still, entrepreneurs who are addressing a triple bottom-line approach are considering interests beyond their own. They are trying to find a place where they can make a difference, depending on the values they like to reflect in their new ventures. These entrepreneurs start with what is available to them and look at what they can achieve using those resources. In such a relational network, over time and space, responsibilities taken go beyond a motivation of pure self-interest. Attempts for preserving a place for coming generations, or improving today's situation elsewhere, are based on a relational understanding of one's needs and the needs of others. By identifying one's relation to someone, or something, which could be distant in time and space, is not only self-centred. Therefore, a willingness to accept responsibility for behaviour and its consequences (that go beyond legal requirements and self-interest) is a basic characterization of green- and CSR-oriented businesses, regardless of the size of the operation.

8. Entrepreneuring and ICT-based networking

This book has already mentioned that the interconnected, web-enabled world of the twenty-first century has seen dramatic changes in the way people network with each other. The global network economy has few boundaries, which is both fascinating and intimidating. The ceaseless flow of information that people avidly try to absorb means that the understanding of the human's implacement gets easily lost in an increasing focus on the Internet's virtual space. However, whilst information and communication technology can work to everyone's advantage, society still (in most cases) deals in human relationships – which take place at, and from, different places.

It is undeniably true that economic and technical development is, almost without exception, encouraged by increased speed. To juxtapose time with clock-time and speed is, however, problematic if one deals with other human beings (animals and nature) instead of technical devices only.

The focus on increased speed has become extremely important in today's modern firms, and for technology-led industry speed is the essence of usability – speed is everything. Companies compete with one another by trying to offer faster solutions, where faster in many cases is intended to be equivalent to better. Humanity is submerged in a culture of fast messages that proclaim we must always try to be even faster. Nowadays, when someone is asked how long time it takes to do something, they are actually being asked how fast it can be done. The valorization of speed is clearly supported by information and communication technology (ICT)-based networking, and entrepreneurs are not outside this tendency. In the practice of entrepreneuring people are continuously placed in a position where they need to make judgements about others (or be judged themselves). This needs to be done so that decisions can be made about all sorts of functional necessities for business operations and society.

Contemporary networking methods based on ICTs frequently lack the experience of what Hallowell (1999) calls 'the human moment' – the encounter where people share the same place in a meaningful moment of conversation. How then can meaningful relations be created in ICT-based entrepreneuring without face-to-face contact? In traditional networks social relations emanate from connections and dealings between persons or groups. To create and uphold trustful social relations in electronic networks is somewhat different in that a direct counterpart might be more unknown and distant.

This chapter explores how the rise of increasingly sophisticated ICT-based networks influence entrepreneurial communication and cooperation. The first section discusses the opportunities and threats emanating from the increased use of ICT in entrepreneurial processes. This is followed by a section on the central aspects of control and trust in ICT-supported entrepreneuring. The discussion then concludes with an examination of some alternative directions for entrepreneuring in ICT network settings.

NEW FORMS OF SOCIAL CAPITAL BUILDING

Nowadays, social networking sites are becoming central aspects of business and social interaction, and information sharing. Entrepreneurs increasingly use different forms of social networks to complement their own resources and to discuss aspects of establishing a business, as well as to find support and knowledge through social channels (see Aldrich and Zimmer, 1986). These connections within and between social networks create social capital, which can be summarized as 'resources that are potentially available from one's social ties'. In Burt's words (2002, p. 202), 'social capital is a metaphor about advantage'. People can invest time and other resources in the strengthening of social ties and networks – the contacts that lead to successful outcomes are their social capital. Ruef (2010, p. 201) explains the development in the following way:

> To many observers, a focus on entrepreneurial groups – or, more colloquially, venture 'founding teams' – is a thoroughly modern pre-occupation. It was only in the late 1980s and early 1990s that scholars in business management and policy began to question the image of the heroic individual found in traditional treatments of entrepreneurship.

However, Ruef (ibid.) also makes it clear 'that the historical evidence and frameworks that can be deployed to study entrepreneurial groups are far less recent than literature might seem to suggest'.

Consequently, entrepreneurship scholars have quite recently started to pay attention to the ancient interplay of human networking and social capital building (see Anderson and Miller, 2003; Bosma et al., 2004; Brüderl and Preisendörfer, 1998; Davidsson and Honig, 2003; Madsen et al., 2008; Mosey and Wright, 2007; Renzulli et al., 2000; Rooks et al., 2009). In this focus on entrepreneuring and social capital, Madsen et al.

(2008, p. 73) investigate how the make-up of financial, human and social capital impacts on entrepreneurial action – they find social capital to be important, but also the 'most elusive and least consensual of the three forms of capital included in the research framework'.

Uzzi (1997) finds that entrepreneurial firms benefit most when there is a balance between bonding social capital – which enhances cooperation between network partners – and bridging social capital, which provides non-redundant information. Entrepreneurs benefit from social networks by the enlarging information and resource networks, and by positioning themselves within valuable social networks (Blau, 1977; Burt, 1992; Granovetter, 1973). For a survey of the literature on entrepreneurship in a spatio-temporal network context, see Nijkamp, (2003). However, many of the referenced articles on entrepreneuring and networks are based on an implicit understanding of concrete and physical place-connectedness and embeddedness. Li (2008, pp. 273–4), for instance, suggests that:

> Networks are characterised with regional embeddedness. Knowledge spill-over, interfirm relationships, utilisation of shared resources, a well-developed local skills base and the evolution of the region through tacit and explicit knowledge exchange, are typical features of regional networks. These features also provide the basis for a social and economic 'connectivity' that underlines the operation of firms in networks.

What, then, has time, timing, space and place to do with an analysis of social capital and entrepreneuring in network organizations? The understanding of time, timing, space and place becomes, in fact, a central aspect of networking today. In ICT network organizations, the boundary between the physical here and now, and the virtual there and now is erased by the computer's interface. If our counterpart is distant – and perhaps more or less unknown – to us, how can we then trust and rely on the people fulfilling their promises and delivering the services and goods agreed upon? The issue of trust is therefore an important aspect of social capital, in which ICT network settings have clear spatio-temporal implications. It is insufficient, however, to consider these implications through only a singular aspect of spatio-temporality, that is to say, through either clock-time or abstract space.

In financial and manufacturing machine network interactions, the valued-added (clock) time processes remain a question of (physical or recently virtual) compatibility. In human-machine network interactions, the question of compatibility becomes a question of finding user-friendly interfaces that are controlled by clocks at a specific place (compare this with situated interactions). In human ICT networking, however, the sense of time, timing, space and place cannot be reduced to functional (and inhuman) momentary spaces of entering commands and monitoring execution, as in making finance transactions and controlling task operations. Instead, ICT-based entrepreneurial networking tries to mimic the instantaneous impression of real time and real place – the here and now. It remains to be seen how this increasingly sophisticated and intertwined interaction with machines mimicking humans will influence views of, for instance, trust and 'kairic' timely situations. But at a minimum, it provides a cautionary reminder that concepts traditionally associated with human behaviour cannot be taken for granted in increasingly sophisticated ICT-based networking.

The online world of ICT-based network organizations differs from the physical organizational setting in ways that have implications relevant to entrepreneuring. In particular, the loss of face-to-face dynamics obscures the physical dimensions of character and personality, the nature of relationships, and the institutional character normally relied upon to form decisions about trust and cooperation. Different forms of ICT-based networking have recently created sophisticated systems of human cooperation in global virtual networks. Such a form of global virtual organizational development places strong demands for trustworthiness among the participants because spontaneous physical interaction between the actors, as in an office setting, is no longer possible in virtual communication (see Monge and Contractor, 2001). From this question of trust, especially in global and virtual settings, follows further questions of wisdom and judgement in actions undertaken – trust and other forms of social capital do not only emanate from rules and regulations, but also from action in concrete and timely situations. To uphold a trust relationship in a virtual ICT-based entrepreneurial network – in which interaction is frequently with persons unknown, unseen or distant – a timely form of discernment must be called for.

To summarize, the key difference between trust in entrepreneurial networks based on physical proximity, and trust in virtual network forms of entrepreneuring is that whereas the former has a clear site-consciousness, the latter is not bound to either flows of physical goods and services between proximate human beings or to any particular place. Certainly, ICT-based network organizations are ruled by rational and decontextualized clock-time (*chronos*) as well. But the virtual form in an ICT-based network organization still gives new possibilities to break the iron law of clock time, watch and ward, and the time-wasting friction of distance. But this nonetheless presupposes delicate forms of trust at a distance, beyond the physical proximity of more traditional entrepreneurial networks.

THE POSSIBILITIES OF ICT-BASED ENTREPRENEURING

ICT is a diverse set of technological tools and resources at the very heart of every organized venture. ICT also plays an increasingly central role as an interface in a growing number of business endeavours, thus particularly replacing traditional face-to-face interaction between proximate humans. Overall, this use of ICT resources enhances the potential for efficiency in terms of reducing costly time-consuming friction, supports innovation and extends the diversity of options in work organization. Benefits of ICT-based entrepreneurial networks are, for example, that it impacts positively on swift information sharing among the participants in an entrepreneurial network, and that effective exploitation of ICT management systems leads to increased cooperative planning and implementation between actors that would otherwise not have met one another.

ICT plays a key role today in spawning new ideas, methods, processes, products and organizational change. The relation between ICT and value creation, in terms of the generation and spreading of new ideas, methods and processes is of central importance for entrepreneurs and society in general. ICT allows for the interconnectedness between varying actors and organizations and is often the primary source for new venture creation.

Two relatively new forms of ICT-based cooperation are 'open source' and 'social networking'. Open source-based entrepreneuring is about starting up new ventures in a more or less open and transparent environment on interactive communities. Fruitfully developing such relationships is based on trust, and (more or less) freely giving advice and referrals based on the law of reciprocity. Members who participate in open source ventures give and take ideas, and engage expertise and people. Unlike traditional venture capital entrepreneuring, or incubator entrepreneur relationships and seed projects, open source projects do not always insist on financial investment, or 'first look' rights with the companies who join the project. Backing up open source projects is instead the result from a mutual interest between project members as opposed to traditional contractual rights. Open source projects, such as in software development (for example, Linux) thus rely on the belief that people are inherently fair, likely to support one another and give back to the source rather than to steal ideas. Interaction and learning from others are more valuable than confidentiality and secrecy. An additional aspect to open source entrepreneuring beyond sharing and idea exchanges, is the role of open source projects as impetus to entrepreneuring. The dissemination of open source information shortens development and time-to-market cycles. Consequently, the basis of value creation migrates from back-end product development towards front-end cooperation and customer development.

Social networking and online communities have thus supported new forms of entrepreneuring, for example, open source cooperation. Social networking provides new modes of participation, also in business operations. ICT-based social networking can actually be an effective way for new members to participate. More recently, mobile devices (for example, smartphones) have provided essential participation options.

Still, ICT-based entrepreneuring, such as open source projects, is of course not a panacea for improved efficiency in new business ventures. The introduction of ICT-based networking in entrepreneurial ventures also illustrates important aspects of control and trust.

PROBLEMS OF ICT-BASED ENTREPRENEURING

From its etymological origin in Old Norse, 'trust' has been associated with questions of making and breaking cooperative relations in human face-to-face interaction and in errands to companies and authorities (see, Shamir and Lapidot, 2003). In doing so, the implicit assumption is that the contact is between two or more human counterparts. Therefore, traditional forms of trust, based on personal acquaintance, are both timely and local. However, the introduction and growing ubiquity of ICT-based networking – in entrepreneuring and elsewhere – will increasingly call into question the assumption that a human counterpart in the communication process is actually present. Advancements in the use of ICT-based systems have blurred the already less-than-clear relationship between humans and machines (see Collins and Kusch, 1999; Goldberg et al., 2000; Latour, 1996). This has implications for me understanding of trust in different forms of networks. The difficulty is that the growing ICT-based entrepreneurial networking has a very sparse institutional structure, and trust regulation is particularly negligible. Therefore, we increasingly have to (quickly) trust counterparts who are not only unknown but distant, and may be beyond the reach of effective control and legal systems.

Over time, some of our trustful counterparts in ICT-based entrepreneurial networks will therefore become only remotely associated with direct face-to-face interaction. Still, in many instances, Internet-based social networking is improving life, giving a richer experience and an extended world-view, as well as opening up the world for new forms of collaboration.

Central in the discussion of ICT-based entrepreneurial networking concerns are issues of trust and control – issues that are somewhat problematic and in need of some further elaboration.

THE LIMITS TO CONTROL AND TRUST IN ICT NETWORKING

Trust is one of the major defining elements of social capital, and the relationship between trust and control in organizations has become accentuated by the introduction of new forms of cooperation, for example, by the use of ICT. Trust and control are central elements of risk reduction. New organizational forms and new business development practices lead to changes in the relation between trust and control in organizations. Matters of trust and control in networks are of interest in studies of entrepreneuring – particularly, the nexus of trust and control in network forms of entrepreneuring remains a pressing issue. In the case of ICT-based networks in entrepreneurial situations, many assumptions of trust and control may be challenged, which also means that questions of coordination, control and trust become central issues.

The complex nature of trust in human interaction has generated a vast literature from various disciplines (and this paragraph is based on Rämö, 2004, 2007). By way of a basic working definition, it can be postulated that trust involves aspects of wisdom and judgement by the person who trusts the other's ability to reciprocate implicitly promised actions. Such a suspension of disbelief between actors does not develop instantaneously. It is most likely developed through action between parties in contractual or non-contractual relations that gradually becomes implicit and trustful. Trust, on the analysis proposed by Baier (1986), involves elements of judgement and discretionary power beyond instrumental specifications (for example, beyond contracts). In many ways, Baier's analysis corresponds with Luhmann's (1979) in that they both acknowledge that trust reduces complication and enhances the effectiveness of agency. Almost all accounts of trust revolve around situations of reducing risk and uncertainty in ways that contracts cannot – either as implicit background factors of human action or as explicit forms of risk-reduction. Based upon Granovetter's (1985) classic argument that economic behaviour is 'embedded' in informal social and trustful relationships, many socially oriented management scholars have stressed the importance of embeddedness in social network relations (Brass et al., 1998; Gössling, 2005; Uzzi, 1997). Moreover, there are some examples in the literature of both 'swift trust' and high initial trust levels based on 'hidden' favourable factors that question the need for long-term cooperation for creating trust (McKnight et al., 1998; Meyerson et al., 1996).

One of the main discussions in the network literature concerns issues of trust and control – and this relationship has been shown as problematic. Typically, control and trust may be seen as alternatives (see Knights et al., 2001). However, Colletti et al. (2005), find that a strong control system could enhance the level of trust, hence being complementary. In contrary to both, Tomkins (2001) argues that seeing control systems as either substitutive or complementary both mean a static view ignoring the very process of building trust. Dekker (2004) found that issues of trust certainly influenced interaction and concurred with Tomkins (2001) that the major value of contracting may not be in ex-post control, but in the process of setting goals and methods to enable mutual planning and cooperation. The balance between trust and control in coordination of networks is therefore much debated and the tensions between centralized control and decentralized trust are thus accentuated by the different understandings of time, timing, space and place. New organizational forms and new cooperative practices lead to changes in the relation between trust and control in organizations, which is a trend supported by various forms of network-based cooperation.

The understanding of trust and control as a dichotomy is problematic. Firstly because trust and control are intertwined in all forms of organized action – in traditional forms of organizing as well as in ICT-based cooperation. Bijlsma-Frankema and Costa (2005), for example, call it the 'trust-control nexus'. The relations between trust and new organizational forms have been elaborated by, for example, Creed and Miles (1996, p. 26) in their discussion of the relative importance of trust for the owner-managed entrepreneurial form, the vertically integrated functional form, the diversified divisionalized form, the mixed matrix form and the network form. Boltanski and Chiapello (2005) find that on the one hand there is a requirement to be mobile and to adapt to new opportunities for connections, but on the other hand, there is a requirement to be reliable – someone who can be trusted.

The literature on the notion of control suggests that there are two basic approaches. Eisenhardt (1985), for instance, discusses the external measurement-based control and internal values-based control, in which the measurement approach can either focus on the behaviour of employees (behaviour control) or on the outcome of those behaviours (outcome control).

The basis of formal control is increasingly being questioned by the introduction of new forms of cooperation. The speeding up of markets, continuous change, flexibility and virtuality of organizational forms means that the forms of cooperation are becoming looser, more distant and based on lateral relationships and collaboration over the Internet. ICT-based network forms of entrepreneuring and inter-organizational entrepreneurial alliances are examples of this. These forms of cooperation mean that the possibilities and/or capabilities to control and enforcing contracts are reduced, and instead trust becomes increasingly important in lubricating cooperation. Trustful relationship-building is becoming important when embeddedness in shared and proximate cultures is weakening.

The network is important when it comes to acquiring knowledge, complementary means, and legitimacy. The structure of networks varies from a loose collection of ties to close-knit groups of co-working entrepreneurs. However, networks with strong ties run the risk of overembeddedness, that is, of stifling economic performance (Granovetter, 1985; Uzzi, 1996). From an entrepreneurial point of view, there is also the danger of being blind to new developments or being 'locked-in' (Johannisson, 2000). Weak ties, on the other hand, are based on a group of persons whose working connections are more infrequent or irregular. From such loose and non-affective contacts follows diversity and access to various sources of new information and new contacts. These weak ties bridge disparate segments of a social network and may offer new options (Burt, 1992; Granovetter, 1973).

Hoang and Antoncic's (2003) examination of network-based research in entrepreneuring finds that networks are viewed as the media through which actors gain access to a variety of resources held by other actors, and that entrepreneurs seek legitimacy to reduce this perceived risk by associating with, or by gaining explicit certification from, well-regarded individuals and organizations.

Action and communication based on right and timely moments to act judiciously in unique situations are encouraged virtues in entrepreneuring. However, such timely judgement-based decisions cannot be depicted by using clocks only; impromptu situations do occur irrespective of the clock. In a similar fashion, attention to the spatial aspects of 'traditional' entrepreneurial networks has gone from models inherited from economics, as exchange, distribution and allocation in 'abstract' geometrical extensions, towards nuanced and contextual understanding of space and place in entrepreneurial relationship-building.

In entrepreneurial settings, there are different dimensions of performance. A simplistic picture of this is that entrepreneurs not only have to manage and improve what already exists and is already known (that is, efficiency), but they also have to be keenly aware and attentive of possible threats and opportunities (that is, effectiveness). The latter is an example of action in a concrete, timely and opportune situation, quite frequently regardless of clock-time, checklists and regulations.

9. Summary and conclusions

SUMMARY

This book opened in the Introduction by presenting the four themes that run through the whole book and it ended by providing the ambition of this book and its outline. Chapter One discusses these four themes in further detail. The first theme, the conceptual quartet of time, timing, space and place have been applied as analytical categories in order to find out what it means, really, to discuss entrepreneurial thinking and economic action along those categories. Unlike everyday use of the four terms, we have not taken them for granted but used them in order to gain insight into entrepreneurial imagination and into some situations of related economic action.

Another set of analytical concepts discussed in the book is behaviour and action. We found that the two concepts stand for different orientations in modelling and/or interpreting human activities, and we have become convinced that action is more adequate than behaviour when discussing entrepreneurship today than what is behaviour.

A third fundamental duality taken from science in general in order to apply it to our subject of interest is explaining and understanding. We found not only applications of both in our subject, but also that they lead to distinct differences in approaching and comprehending this subject.

A fourth and final theme investigated in this book is our philosophical orientation to phenomenology, that is, ascertaining the subjective nature of 'lived experience' and how this is based on the subjective meaning that people attribute to explaining or understanding this experience.

Chapter One continued by discussing the consequences to entrepreneurial thinking and related economic action using the two basic alternatives of objective and subjective time (what we came to talk about as '*chronos*-time' or '*kairos*-timing') on one hand and space (*chora*) or place (*topos*) on the other hand, after having presented the development of these four concepts in the philosophical and scientific history of humankind. This led, among things, to us preferring to use the term 'entrepreneuring' to 'entrepreneurship'.

Chapter Two started by providing the picture of the development of the academic subject of entrepreneurship in its 300 years of existence. We claimed that it is possible today to separate two views on entrepreneurship. We referred to them as the American view and the Scandinavian view. The American view looks at entrepreneurship as basically an economic phenomenon aimed at satisfying demands by creating something new. This view relies heavily on concepts like 'market', 'growth' and 'opportunity recognition'. The Scandinavian view looks at entrepreneurship as belonging to the whole society, not only to its economy, aiming at satisfying demands and/or needs. The term 'entrepreneuring' belongs here. The American view seems to be more space based and the Scandinavian view more place based. The American view dominates almost everywhere.

Chapter Two continued to outline in more detail the consequences of looking at the world in terms of behaviour and action, with an explaining or an understanding ambition and as a phenomenologist. Looking at human activities as 'behaviour' means in its pure form classic behaviourism, where only observable stimuli and responses are of interest. Development of classic behaviourism has included not observable (but measurable) cognitive aspects as well, but no account is made of how these aspects come about. 'Action', on the other hand, is seen as reflecting and intentional activity, which is radically different from behaviour.

Some theories called Actor Network Theories have become quite popular in some camps. We presented these in Chapter Two but did not find these extreme empirical and material-semiotic actor approaches very useful in our case.

The discussion of the development in the history of science of 'explaining' and 'understanding' came next in Chapter Two. Not all scientists recognize the differences between the two, but we claim that human activities as action belong to the second category. Based on the categories of explaining and understanding our next step was to present different 'schools' researching the topic. We provided several examples of both and noted their differences.

Chapter Two ended by presenting the way we look at and use phenomenology in more detail. This section started with outlining three possible levels to approach time, timing, space and place. The two non-phenomenological levels are the descriptive approach and the social constructionist approach, in addition to the phenomenological focus presented in this book.

Chapter Three was devoted to our modern society and the kinds of entrepreneuring that occur there. We outlined some characteristics of our modern society in order to provide a picture of a genuinely new society or, at least, a society which contains genuinely new aspects. As 'managing opportunities' is so central to the American view and not to the Scandinavian view, a whole section was allocated to discuss that subject. We contrasted that with entrepreneuring as improving our own situation and living. Next we discussed different sectors, situations and contexts in the society where entrepreneuring occurs. We made a distinction between the common sector, the market sector and the citizen sector and found several differences in entrepreneuring in the three, especially when comparing business entrepreneuring and social entrepreneuring.

Chapter Four discussed social entrepreneuring. We made a distinction between public entrepreneuring, which is part of citizen entrepreneuring, which in turn is part of social entrepreneuring. We saw public entrepreneuring as what is done by social innovators in public places unlike social enterprisers who operate in more or less sheltered places.

Chapter Four continued by comparing the start and development of business entrepreneurial efforts and social entrepreneurial efforts. The chapter ended by discussing two aspects of distinct relevance to entrepreneuring, that is, (social-based) networking and social capital.

Chapter Five related social entrepreneuring to local governments. They have come in a different light, considering developments such as post-industrialization, globalization and migration. This has forced local governments to rely more on governance. A large section of Chapter Five was devoted to clarifying what public entrepreneurs are *not*.

Chapter Six went up one step, geographically wise, and presented research on entrepreneuring and regional development. This research was presented in two groups, one coming up with explanatory models based on space and another coming up with understanding-oriented interpretations based on place. The chapter ended by asking five critical questions which separate the two groups.

Chapter Seven discussed what it means to be green or eco-friendly in entrepreneurial thinking by presenting some research made in the matter (it turned out to be quite little), by identifying some key issues and by providing a more extensive discussion of the role of corporate social responsibility (CSR) here.

Chapter Seven extended the discussion about entrepreneuring and networking by concentrating on the latter when based on information and communication technology (ICT). Apart from what had earlier been discussed about entrepreneuring and networking some new issues came to light here, namely, speed, control and trust.

SOME CONCLUSIONS

- We think we have gained some further insight into and have moved the subject of entrepreneurial thinking a little further by applying the analytical categories of time, timing, space and place.
- Using the concepts of time, timing, space and place we have asked questions that would not otherwise have been asked, and discussed the world of entrepreneurial thinking and economic action somewhat differently than how it is normally.
- We have found reasons to be stricter when discussing entrepreneurship and similar activities in terms of either behaviour or action and consequently want to associate the entrepreneurship of today as more of the latter.
- We have seen distinct differences in explaining human activities versus understanding them.
- We are now convinced that research in any subject, including the one presented in this book, gains from the clarification of which philosophy of science it is based on. We have found phenomenology a very promising base, even if very little research on entrepreneurial thinking and economic action has been done using phenomenology (although practice-based research has become widespread).
- We have found many differences in explaining or understanding entrepreneurial thinking in terms of time or timing on one hand and in terms of space or place on the other.
- With our focus, it is seen to be better to talk about the active form of 'entrepreneuring' rather than the more static 'entrepreneurship'.
- We have identified two views on how entrepreneurship is seen today – the American view and the Scandinavian view. There are several distinct differences between the two. The American view looks more space-based and the Scandinavian view more place-based.
- Behaviour and explanation look at the entrepreneurial world as full of circumstances; action and understanding look at that world as meaningful.
- Entrepreneurs don't simply exist, they act 'as if'.
- There are examples of schools trying to explain entrepreneurship and there are examples of schools trying to understand it. We found that *understanding* human activity is more adequate in our case than only trying to explain it.
- There are differences between the various approaches to time, timing, space and place. Unlike the descriptive approach and the constructionistic approach, the phenomenologist approach, which we adopt in a Heideggerian way, concerns information about how

perception and action in the world is guided directly by our lived experience which in turn, unlike the other two approaches, is not guided by constructed and abstracted mental models.

- Our modern society is genuinely new enough to justify the name 'entrepreneuring society', 'innovating society' or 'networking society'.
- 'Opportunity' is a term that can be understood in many ways. It should not to be taken for granted that opportunities 'exist' to be discovered.
- As entrepreneurship researchers have problems identifying entrepreneuring with any specific personal traits or specific set of activities, we propose to discuss the phenomenon as it goes on in different sectors, situations and contexts in society.
- We know very little about entrepreneuring in the common sector, but it is clear that we need to develop a new terminology to study this. As far as entrepreneuring in the market sector is concerned, it is clear that it is here that the American view rules almost uncontested. Citizen entrepreneuring is such a new and interesting field that much of the future of entrepreneuring research should be devoted to it.
- There is reason to make a distinction between social entrepreneuring, citizen entrepreneuring and public entrepreneuring.
- Public entrepreneuring by social innovators is not a new phenomenon, but it is much less researched than its importance in society suggests.
- It is not possible to directly use our knowledge of the start and development of business entrepreneurial efforts to social entrepreneurial efforts. Much remains to be researched here.
- Networking and social capital are highly relevant topics to social entrepreneuring.
- Social entrepreneuring in general and public entrepreneuring in particular are very relevant and important to local governments, but often ignored and neglected.
- There has been an increased interest in the entrepreneurship literature in common sector government as well as in regional development. Research on the former is, however, much younger than research on the latter.
- Local governments are forced today to change into more learning, more leadership, more entrepreneuring and more governance.
- One interesting new aspect as far as entrepreneuring and local government is concerned is how the latter can operate in public places, where public entrepreneurs are already building citizenry and sociality.

- There is a definite difference between explaining entrepreneuring and regional development by models compared to understanding it by interpretations.
- There is a large range of variations behind green entrepreneuring, all the way from a narrow business concern to an ambition to change the capitalist system.
- There is also a huge number of areas where green entrepreneuring may be relevant.
- Corporate social responsibility (CSR) is associated with a plethora of concepts, although not frequently studied in entrepreneurship.
- There are relationships between green entrepreneuring and CSR on one hand and time, timing, space and place on the other.
- The understanding of time, timing, space and place becomes a central aspect of networking today, ICT based or not.
- Some important aspects of ICT-based networking include speed, control and trust.
- There are possibilities and problems as well as limits in ICT networking.

So, after this long and winding journey, why have we bothered? Perhaps the concepts of time and timing as well as space and place have already found their general meaning. Time as a denomination of sequential relations that any event has to any other in an indefinite and continuous duration. Space, on the other hand, signifies a denomination of the unlimited great three-dimensional realm or expanse in which all material objects are located and all events occur. In short: it is time that is measured with a clock and space with a ruler. Is that what human endeavours in time and place are all about? As argued in this book, it is far from that simple. Instead, symbolic practices derive their meaning in social life only through the structure of social relations within which they come into play; in this case, in an interplay between time, timing, space, place and entrepreneuring.

References

Ackerman, P.L. and L.G. Humpreys (1990), 'Individual differences theory in industrial and organizational psychology', in M.D. Dunnette and L.M. Hough (eds), *Handbook of Industrial and Organizational Psychology*, vol 1, 2nd edn, Palo Alto, CA: Consulting Psychology Press.

Acs, Z.J. (2002), *Innovation and the Growth of Cities*, Cheltenham, UK and Northampton, MA, USA: Edward Elgar.

Adam, B. (2004), *Time*, Cambridge and Malden, MA: Polity Press Ltd.

Agnew, J. (1987), *The United States in the World Economy*, Cambridge: Cambridge University Press.

Alberti, F. (2003), 'What makes it an industrial district? A cognitive perspective', paper presented at Uddevalla Symposium 2003, 12-14 June.

Aldrich, H.E. and D. Whetten (1981), 'Organization-sets, action-sets, and networks: making the most of simplicity', in P. Nystrom and W. Starbuck (eds), *Handbook of Organizational Design*, vol 1, New York: Oxford University Press.

Aldrich, H.E. and C. Zimmer (1986), 'Entrepreneurship through social networks', in D.L. Sexton and R.W. Wilson (eds), *The Art and Science of Entrepreneurship*, Cambridge, MA: Ballinger.

Allen, K.R. (2010), *New Venture Creation*, 5th edn, Florence, KY: South-Western.

Almeida, P. and B. Kogut (1999), 'Localization of knowledge and the mobility of engineers in regional networks', *Management Science*, **45**, 905–17.

Altman, I. and S.M. Low (eds) (1992), *Place Attachment*, New York and London: Plenum Press.

Alvord, S., D. Brown and C. Letts (2002), 'Social entrepreneurship and social transformation: an exploratory study', Hauser Center for Nonprofit Organizations working paper no. 15, available from Social Science Research Network Electronic Paper Collection.

Amenta, E. and M. Young (1999), 'Making an impact: conceptual and methodological implications of the collective goods criterion', in M. Gingli, D. McAdam and C. Tilly (eds), *How Social Movements Matter*, Minneapolis, MN: University of Minnesota Press.

Amenta, E. and N. Caren (2004), 'The legislative, organizational, and beneficiary consequences of state-oriented challengers', in D. Snow, S. Soule and H. Kriesi (eds), *The Blackwell Companion to Social Movements*, Oxford: Blackwell.

Amin, A. and K. Robins (1990), 'The re-emergence of regional economies? The mythical geography of flexible accumulation', *Environment and Planning D: Society and Space*, **8** (1), 7–34.

Amin, A. and N. Thrift (1994), 'Living in the global', in A. Amin and N. Thrift (eds), *Globalization, Institutions and Regional Development in Europe*, Oxford: Oxford University Press.

Amin, A. and N. Thrift (2008), 'Neo-Marshallian nodes in global networks', in R. Martin (ed.), *Economy: Critical Essays in Human Geography*, Aldershot and Burlington, VT: Ashgate, reprinted in *International Journal of Urban and Regional Research* (1992), **16**, 571–87.

Amin, A., A. Cameron and R. Hudson (2002), *Placing the Social Economy*, London: Routledge.

Amit, R., L. Glosten and E. Muller (1993), 'Challenges to theory development in entrepreneurship research', *Journal of Management Studies*, **30** (5), 815–34.

Andersen, A.R. (1998), 'Cultivating the garden of Eden: environmental entrepreneuring', *Journal of Organizational Change Management*, **11** (2), 135–44.

Anderson, A.R. and S.L. Jack (2002), 'The articulation of social capital in entrepreneurial networks: a glue or a lubricant?', *Entrepreneurship and Regional Development*, July–Sept, 193–210.

Anderson, A.R. and C.J. Miller (2003), '"Class matters": human and social capital in the entrepreneurial process', *Journal of Socio-Economics*, **32** (1), 17–36.

Anderson, B.B. and G.J. Dees (2006), 'Rhetoric, reality, and research: building a solid foundation for the practice of social entrepreneurship', in A. Nicholls (ed.), *Social Entrepreneurship: New Models of Sustainable Social Change*, Oxford: Oxford University Press.

Anderson, K. (1991), *Vancouver's Chinatown: Racial Discourse in Canada, 1875–1980*, Montreal, QC: McGill-Queen's University Press.

Anderson, R.B., B. Honig and A.M. Peredo (2006), 'Communities in the global economy: where social and indigenous entrepreneurship meet', in C. Steyaert and D. Hjorth (eds), *Entrepreneurship as Social Change*, Cheltenham, UK and Northampton, MA, USA: Edward Elgar.

Anderson, T.L. and D.R. Leal (1997), *Enviro-Capitalists: Doing Good While Doing Well*, Boston: Rowman & Littlefield.

Antonelli, C. (1994), 'Technology districts, localized spillovers and productivity growth: the Italian evidence on technological externalities in core regions', *International Review of Applied Economics*, **8**, 18–30.

Apel, K.-O. (1984), *Understanding and Explanation*, Cambridge, MA: The MIT Press.

Arbnor, I., S.-E. Borglund and T. Liljedahl (1980), *Osynligt ockuperad* [*Invisibly Occupied*], Malmö: Liber.

Arbnor, I. and B. Bjerke (2009), *Methodology for Creating Business Knowledge*, 3rd edn, London: Sage Publications Ltd.

Arendt, H. (1958), *The Human Condition*, Chicago, IL: University of Chicago Press.

Aristotle (1996), *Physics*, translated by Robin Waterfield, New York: Oxford University Press.

Asheim, B.T. (1996), 'Industrial districts and "learning regions": a condition for prosperity', *European Planning Studies*, **4**, 379–401.

Assmo, P. (2003), 'Creative clusters. Ideas and realities for cluster growth', paper, University of Trollhättan/Uddevalla.

Audretsch, D.B. (1998), 'Agglomeration and the location of innovative activity', *Oxford Review of Economic Policy*, **14**, 18–29.

Audretsch, D.B. and M.P. Feldman (1996), 'R&D spillovers and the geography of innovation and production', *American Economic Review*, **86**, 630–40.

Audretsch, D.B. and R. Thurik (1999), 'Capitalism and democracy in the 21st century: from the managed to the entrepreneurial economy', *Journal of Evolutionary Economics*, **10**, 17–34.

Auster, E. (1990), 'The interorganizational environment: network theory, tools, and applications', in F. Williams and D. Gibson (eds), *Technology Transfer: A Communication Perspective*, London: Sage.

Austin, J.E. (2006), 'Three avenues for social entrepreneurship research', in J. Mair, J. Robinson and K. Hockerts (2006) (eds), *Social Entrepreneurship*, Basingstoke and New York: Palgrave Macmillan.

Austin, J.E., H. Stevenson and J. Wei-Skillern (2006), 'Social entrepreneurship and commercial entrepreneurship: Same, different, or both', *Entrepreneurship Theory and Practice*, **30** (1), 1–22.

Bachelard, G. (1964), *The Poetics of Space*, New York: Orion.

Bahrenberg, G. (1987), 'Über die Unmöglichkeit von Geographie als "Raumwissenschaft". Gemeinsamkeiten in der Konstituierung von Geographie bei A. Hettner and D. Bartels' ['On the impossibility of Geography as a science of "space". Commonalities in the consequences of Geography as seen by A. Hettner and D. Bartels'] in G. Bahrenberg, J. Deiters, M. Fischer, W. Gaebe, G. Hard and G. Löffner (eds), *Geographie des Menchen. Dietrich Bartels zum Gedenken* [Human Geography. In Memory of Dietrich Bartels], Bremen, Germany: Bremer Beiträge zur Geographie und Raumplanung.

Baier, A. (1986), 'Trust and antitrust', *Ethics*, **96**, 231–60.

Banks, J. (1972), *The Sociology of Social Movements*, London: Macmillan.

Barabási, A.-L. (2002), *Linked. The New Science of Networks*, New York: Perseus Publishing.

Barke, M. and K. Harrop (1994), 'Selling the industrial town: identity, image and illusion', in J.R. Gold and S.V. Ward (eds), *Place Promotion: The Use of Publicity and Marketing to Sell Towns and Regions*, Chichester: John Wiley & Sons.

BarNir, A. and K. Smith (2002), 'Interfirm alliances in the small business: the role of social networks', *Journal of Small Business Management*, **40** (3), 219–32.

Baron, R.A. (1998), 'Cognitive mechanisms in entrepreneurship: why and when entrepreneurs think differently than other people', *Journal of Business Venturing*, **12**, 275–94.

Baron, R.A. and S.A. Shane (2008), *Entrepreneurship. A Process Perspective*, 2nd edn, Mason, OH: Thomson Higher Education.

Barringer, B.R. and R.D. Ireland (2006), *Entrepreneurship. Successfully Launching New Ventures*, Upper Saddle River, NJ: Pearson Education, Inc.

Bartilsson, S., G. Gillberg, H.-E. Hermansson and P. Olofsson (2000), *Arbete i egen regi. Från arbetsmarknadsprojekt till social ekonomi* [*Working on One's Own. From Labour Market Projects to Social Economy*], Göteborg, Sweden: Daidalos.

Bathelt, H. and J. Glückler (2002a), *Wirtschaftsgeographie. Ökonomische Beziehungen in räumlicher Perspektive* [*Business Geography. Economic Relations in a Space Perspective*], Stuttgart, Germany: UTB – Ulmer.

Bathelt, H. and J. Glückler (2002b), 'Wirtschaftsgeographie in relationaler Perspektive: Das Argument der zweiten Transition' ['Business geography in a relational perspective: the argument of the second transition'], *Geographische Zeitschrift*, **90**, 20–39.

Bathelt, H. and J. Glückler (2008), 'Toward a relational economic geography', in R. Martin (ed.), *Economy. Critical Essays in Human Geography*, Aldershot and Burlington, VT: Ashgate, reprinted in *Journal of Economic Geography*, 2003, **3**, 117–44.

Bartunek, J.M. and R.A. Necochea (2000), 'Old insights and new times: Kairos, Inca cosmology, and their contributions to contemporary managerial inquiry', *Journal of Management Inquiry*, **9**, 103–13.

Becattini, G. (1990), 'The Marshallian industrial district as a socio-economic notion', in F. Pyke, G. Becattini and W. Sengenberger (eds), *Industrial Districts and Inter-Firm Cooperation in Italy*, Geneva: International Institute for Labour Studies.

Benner, M. (2002), 'Time and the new economy', in I. Holmberg,

M. Salzer-Mörling and L. Strannegård (eds), *Stuck in the Future? Tracing the 'New Economy'*, Stockholm: Bookhouse Publishing.

Bennett, S.J. (1991), *Ecopreneuring: The Complete Guide to Small Business Opportunities from the Environmental Revolution*, New York: John Wiley & Sons.

Berg, P.O. (2001), 'The summoning of the Øresund region", in B. Czarniawska and R. Solli (eds), *Organizing Metropolitan Space and Discourse*, Solna, Sweden: Liber.

Berger, P.L. and T. Luckmann (1967), *The Social Construction of Reality*, London: Allen Lane.

Berggren, C. and G. Brulin (1985), *Från myt till människa* [*From Myth to Man*], Stockholm: FA-rådet.

Berglund, H. (2007), 'Researching entrepreneurship as lived experience', in H. Neergaard and J.P. Ulhøi (eds), *Handbook of Qualitative Research Methods in Entrepreneurship*, Cheltenham, UK and Northampton, MA, USA: Edward Elgar.

Berglund, K. and A.W. Johansson (2008), *Arenor för entreprenörskap* [*Arenas for Entrepreneurship*], Stockholm: Stiftelsen för Småföretagsforskning.

Berle, G. (1991), *The Green Entrepreneur: Business Opportunities That Can Save the Earth and Make You Money*, Blue Ridge Summit, PA: Liberty Hall Press.

Berman Brown, R. and R. Herring (1998), 'The circles of time: an exploratory study in measuring temporal perceptions within organizations', *Journal of Managerial Psychology*, **13**, 580–602.

Berry, W. (1980), *A Part*, Boston, MA: Harcourt Brace.

Beyes, T. (2006), 'City of enterprise, city as prey? On urban entrepreneurial spaces', in C. Steyaert and D. Hjorth (eds), *Entrepreneurship as Social Change*, Cheltenham, UK and Northampton, MA, USA: Edward Elgar.

Bhaskar, R. (1998), *The Possibility of Naturalism. A Philosophical Critique of the Contemporary Human Sciences*, London: Routledge.

Bill, F., A. Jansson and L. Olaison (2010), 'The spectacle of entrepreneurship: a duality of flamboyance and activity', in F. Bill, B. Bjerke and A.W. Johansson (eds), *(De)mobilizing the Entrepreneurship Discourse. Exploring Entrepreneurial Thinking and Action*, Cheltenham, UK and Northampton, MA, USA: Edward Elgar.

Birch, D. (1979), *The Job Generation Process*, Cambridge, MA: MIT Program on Neighborhood and Regional Change.

Birley, S. (1985), 'The role of networks in the entrepreneurial process', *Journal of Business Venturing*, **1**, 107–17.

Birley, S., S. Cromie and A. Myers (1991), 'Entrepreneurial networks:

their emergence in Ireland and overseas', *International Small Business Journal*, **9** (4), 56–74.

Bijlsma-Frankema, K. and A.C. Costa (2005), 'Understanding the trust-control nexus', *International Sociology*, **20** (3), 259–82.

Bjerke, B. (1989), *Att skapa nya affärer* [*To Create New Business Ventures*], Lund, Sweden: Studentlitteratur.

Bjerke, B. (1999), *Business Leadership and Culture*, Cheltenham, UK and Northampton, MA, USA: Edward Elgar.

Bjerke, B. (2007), *Understanding Entrepreneurship*, Cheltenham, UK and Northampton, MA, USA: Edward Elgar.

Bjerke, B. (2010), 'Entrepreneurship, space and place', in F. Bill, B. Bjerke and A.W. Johansson (eds), *(De)mobilizing the Entrepreneurship Discourse. Exploring Entrepreneurial Thinking and Action*, Cheltenham, UK and Northampton, MA, USA: Edward Elgar.

Bjerke, B. and C. Hultman (2002), *Entrepreneurial Marketing*, Cheltenham, UK and Northampton, MA, USA: Edward Elgar.

Blau, P.M. (1977), 'A macrosociological theory of social structure', *American Journal of Sociology*, **83** (1), 26–54.

Blue, J. (1990), *Ecopreneuring: Managing for Results*, London: Scott Foresman.

Blundel, R.K. and D. Smith (2001), *Business Networking: SMEs and Inter-Firm Collaboration, a Review of the Research Literature with Implication for Policy*, report to Small Business Services PP03/01, Sheffield: Department of Trade and Industry, Small Business Service.

Boddice, R. (2009), 'Forgotten antecedents: entrepreneurship, ideology and history', in R. Ziegler (ed), *An Introduction to Social Entrepreneurship*, Cheltenham, UK and Northampton, MA, USA: Edward Elgar.

Boissevain, J. (1974), *Friends of Friends: Networks, Manipulations and Coalitions*, Oxford: Basil Blackwell.

Boli, J. (1991), 'Sweden: is there a viable third sector?', in R. Wutknow (ed), *Between States Perspectives*, Princeton, NJ: Princeton University Press.

Boltanski, L. and E. Chiapello (2005), *The New Spirit of Capitalism*, London: Verso.

Bornstein, D. (2004), *How to Change the World. Social Entrepreneurs and the Power of New Ideas*, Oxford: Oxford University Press.

Borzaga, C. and J. Defourney (eds) (2001a), *The Emergence of Social Enterprise*, Abingdon and New York: Routledge.

Borzaga, C. and J. Defourney (2001b), 'Conclusions', in C. Borzaga and J. Defourney (eds) (2001), *The Emergence of Social Enterprise*, Abingdon and New York: Routledge.

Boschee, J. (1998), 'What does it take to be a social entrepreneur?', accessed February 2008 at: www.socialentrepreneurs.org./whatdoes. html.

Bosma, N., M. van Praag, R. Thurik, and G. de Wit (2004), 'The value of human and social capital investments for the business performance of start-ups', *Small Business Economics*, **23** (3), 227–36.

Bosma, N. and R. Harding (2007), *Global Entrepreneurship Monitor*, 2006, summary results, Babson College, Babson Park, MA and London Business School, London.

Bottomore, T. and R. Nisbet (eds) (1979), *A History of Sociological Analysis*, London: Heinemann.

Bourdieu, P. (1977), *Outline of a Theory of Practice*, Cambridge: Cambridge University Press.

Bourdieu, P. (1990), *The Logic of Practice*, Cambridge: Polity Press.

Bourdieu, P. (1998), *Practical Reason*, Cambridge: Polity Press.

Bourdieu, P. (2000), *Pascalian Meditations*, translated by R. Nice, Cambridge: Polity Press.

Bourdieu, P. and L.J.D. Wacquant (1992), *An Invitation to Reflexive Sociology*, Chicago, IL: University of Chicago Press.

Boutaiba, S. (2004), 'A moment in time', in D. Hjorth and C. Steyaert (eds), *The Politics and Aesthetics of Entrepreneurship*, Cheltenham, UK and Northampton, MA, USA: Edward Elgar.

Boyd, N. and G.S. Vozikis (1994), 'The influence of self-efficacy on the development of entrepreneurial intentions and actions', *Entrepreneurship Theory and Action*, Summer, 63–77.

Brass, D.J., K.D. Butterfield and B.C. Skaggs (1998), 'Relationships and unethical behavior: a social network perspective', *Academy of Management Review*, **1**, 14–31.

Braudel, F. (1993), *A History of Civilizations*, New York: Penguin Books.

Braunerhjelm, P., B. Carlsson and D. Johansson (1998), 'Industriella kluster, tillväxt och ekonomisk politik' ['Industrial clusters, growth and economic policy'], *Ekonomisk Debatt*, **26** (4), 419–30.

Brenner, N. (1997), 'Global, fragmented, hierarchical: Henri Lefebvre's geographies of globalization', *Public Culture*, **10** (1), 135–67.

Brickell, P. (2000), *People Before Structures: Engaging Communities Effectively in Regeneration*, London: Demos.

Bridge, S., K. O'Neill and S. Cromie (2003), *Understanding Enterprise, Entrepreneurship and Small Business*, 2nd edn, New York: Palgrave Macmillan.

Brinckerhoff, P.C. (2000), *Social Entrepreneurship: The Art of Mission-Based Venture Development*, New York: John Wiley & Sons.

Brooks, A.C. (2009), *Social Entrepreneurship: A Modern Approach to*

Social Venture Creation, Upper Saddle River, NJ: Pearson Education, Inc.

Brown, B. and J.E. Butler (1995), 'Competitors as allies: a study of the entrepreneurial networks in the US wine industry', *Journal of Small Business Management*, **33** (3), 57–66.

Brown. J.S. and P. Duguid (2002), 'Local knowledge: innovation in the networked age', *Management Learning*, **33** (4), 427–37.

Brüderl, J. and P. Preisendörfer (1998), 'Network support and the success of newly founded businesses', *Small Business Economics*, **10** (3), 213–25.

Burgess, J. and P. Wood (1988), 'Decoding Docklands: place advertising and the decision-making strategies of the small firm', in J. Eyles and D.M. Smith (eds), *Qualitative Method in Human Geography*, Cambridge: Polity Press.

Burns, P. (2007), *Entrepreneurship and Small Business*, 2nd edn, London: Palgrave Macmillan.

Burrell, G. and G. Morgan (1979), *Sociological Paradigms and Organizational Analysis*, London: Heinemann.

Burt, R.S. (1992), *Structural Holes. The Social Structure of Competition*, Harvard, MA: Harvard University Press.

Burt, R.S. (1997), 'The contingent value of social capital', *Administrative Science Quarterly*, **42**, 339–65.

Burt, R.S. (2002), 'The social capital of structural holes', in M. Guillen, R. Collins, P. England and M. Meyer (eds), *New Directions in Economic Sociology*, New York: Russell Sage.

Buttimer, A. and D. Seamon (1980) (eds), *The Human Experience of Space and Place*, New York: St. Martin's Press.

Cannon, C. (2000), 'The attributes of citizens: virtue, manners and the activity of citizenship', *National Journal*, 16 June, 1898–904.

Cantillon, R. (1755 [1955]), *Essai sur la nature du commerce en general* [*Essay on the Nature of Commerce in General*], London: Fletcher Gyles.

Carlsson, B. (1997), *Technological Systems and Industrial Dynamics*, Norwell, MA: Kluwer Academic Publishers.

Carson, D., S. Cromie, P. McGowan and J. Hill (1995), *Marketing and Entrepreneurship in SMEs*, Hemel Hempstead: Prentice-Hall International (UK) Ltd.

Carson, R. (1962), *Silent Spring*, Boston, MA: Houghton Mifflin.

Casey, E.S. (1993), *Getting Back into Place. Toward a Renewed Understanding of the Place-World*, Bloomington, IN: Indiana University Press.

Casey, E.S. (1998), *The Fate of Place: A Philosophical History*, Berkeley, CA: University of California Press.

Castells, M. (1998), *The Rise of the Network Society*, Oxford: Blackwell Publishers.

Catford, J. (1998), 'Social entrepreneurs are vital for health promotion – but they need supportive environments too', editorial, *Health Promotion International*, **13**, 95–8.

Chell, E. and S. Baines (2000), 'Networking, entrepreneurship and micro-business behaviour', *Entrepreneurship and Regional Development*, **12**, 195–215.

Cho, A.H. (2006), 'Politics, values and social entrepreneurship: a critical appraisal', in J. Mair, J. Robinson and K. Hockerts (eds), *Social Entrepreneurship*, London and New York: Palgrave Macmillan.

Clayton, D.W. (2000), *Islands of Truth: The Imperial Fashioning of Vancouver Island*, Vancouver, BC: UBC Press.

Coe, N.M., M. Hess, H.W. Yeung, P. Dicken and J. Henderson (2008), '"Globalizing" regional development: a global production networks perspective', in R. Martin (ed.), *Economy: Critical Essays in Human Geography*, Aldershot and Burlington, VT: Ashgate, reprinted in *Transactions of the Institute of British Geographers*, 2004, **29**, 468–84.

Cohen, B. and M.I. Winn (2007), 'Market imperfections, opportunity and sustainable entrepreneurship', *Journal of Business Venturing*, **22** (1), 29–49.

Cohen, S., W. Eimicke and M. Salazar (1999), 'Public ethics and public entrepreneurship', paper presented at the Annual Research Meeting of the Association of Public Policy Analysis and Management, Washington, DC, Nov. 4–6, 1–22.

Coleman, J.S. (1990), *Foundations of Social Theory*, Cambridge, MA: Harvard University Press.

Colletti, A.L., K.L Sedatole and K.L. Towry (2005), 'The effect of control systems on trust and cooperation in collaborative environments', *The Accounting Review*, **80** (2), 477–500.

Collins, H. and M. Kusch (1999), *The Shape of Actions: What Humans and Machines can Do*, Cambridge, MA: The MIT Press.

Conway, S. (1997), 'Informal networks of relationships in successful small firm innovation', in D. Jones-Evans and M. Klofsten (eds), *Technology, Innovation and Enterprise: the European Experience*, Basingstoke: Macmillan.

Conway, S., O. Jones and F. Steward (2001), 'Realising the potential of the social network perspective in innovation studies', in O. Jones, S. Conway and F. Steward (eds), *Social Interaction and Organisational Change: Aston Perspectives on Innovation Networks*, London: Imperial College Press.

Conway, S. and O. Jones (2006), 'Networking and the small business', in

S. Carter and D. Jones-Evans (eds), 2nd edn, *Enterprise and Small Business. Principles, Practice and Policy*, Harlow: Pearson Education.

Cooke, P. (1989), 'Locality, economic restructuring and world development', in P. Cooke (ed), *Localities: The Changing Face of Urban Britain*, London: Unwin Hyman.

Cooke, P. and D. Schwartz (eds) (2007), *Creative Regions: Technology, Culture and Knowledge Entrepreneurship*, London: Routledge.

Cooper, A. and T. Folta (2000), 'Entrepreneurship and high-technology clusters', in D.L. Sexton and H. Landström (eds), *Handbook of Entrepreneurship*, Oxford: Blackwell Publishers Ltd.

Cope, J. (2005), 'Researching entrepreneurship through phenomenological inquiry: philosophical and methodological issues', *International Small Business Journal*, **23** (2), 163–89.

Coulter, M. (2001), *Entrepreneurship in Action*, Upper Saddle River, NJ: Prentice Hall.

Cox, K.R. and A. Mair (1988), 'Locality and community in the politics of local economic development', *Annals of the Association of American Geographers*, **78**, 307–25.

Coyle, D. (1997), *The Weightless World*, Oxford: Capstone Publishing.

Creed, W.E.D. and R.E. Miles, (1996), 'Trust in organizations: a conceptual framework linking organizational forms, managerial philosophies, and the opportunity cost of control', in R.M. Kramer and T.R. Tyler (eds), *Trust in Organizations: Frontiers of Theory and Research*, London: Sage.

Cresswell, T. (2004), *Place: A Short Introduction*, Oxford: Blackwell.

Cronon, W. (1992), 'Kennecott journey: the paths out of town', in W. Cronon, W. Miles and J. Gitlin (eds), *Under an Open Sky*, New York: Norton.

Cunningham, J.B. and J. Lischeron (1991), 'Defining entrepreneurship', *Journal of Small Business Management*, **29** (1), 43–51.

Curran, J. and R.A. Blackburn (1991), *Paths of Enterprise*, London: Routledge.

Curry, M.R. (2002), 'Discursive displacement and the seminal ambiguity of space and place', in L. Lievrouw and S. Livingstone (eds), *Handbook in New Media*, London: Sage Publications.

Czarniawska, B. and G. Sevón (eds) (1996), *Translating Organizational Change*, Berlin: Walter de Gruyter.

Dahmén, E. (1988), 'Development blocks in industrial economies', *Scandinavian Economic History Review*, **36**, 3–14.

Dart, R. (2004), 'The legitimacy of social enterprise', *Non-profit Management & Leadership*, **14** (4), 411–24.

Davidow, W.H. and M.S. Malone (1992), *The Virtual Corporation:*

Structuring and Revitalizing the Corporation for the 21st Century, New York: HarperCollins Publishers.

Davidsson, P. and B. Honig (2003), 'The role of social and human capital among nascent Entrepreneurs', *Journal of Business Venturing*, **18** (3), 301–31.

Davis, C. and L. Hulett (1999), 'Skills needs in the resource-based sectors in Atlantic Canada', report presented at Skills Development in the Knowledge-Based Economy, Moncton, NB, June.

Davoudi, S. (1995), 'Dilemmas of urban governance', in P. Healey et al. (eds), *Managing Cities: The New Urban Context*, Chichester: John Wiley & Sons.

Dean, M. (1999), *Governmentality – Power and Rule in Modern Society*, London: Sage.

Dean, T.J. and J.S. McMullen (2007), 'Toward a theory of sustainable entrepreneurship: reducing environmental degradation through entre-preneurial action', *Journal of Business Venturing*, **22** (1), 50–76.

de Bruin, A. (2003), 'State entrepreneurship', in A. de Bruin and A. Dupuis (eds), *Entrepreneurship: New Perspectives in a Global Age*, Aldershot: Ashgate.

de Carolis, M. (1996), 'Toward a phenomenology of opportunities', in P. Virno and M. Hardt (eds), *Radical Thought in Italy*, Minneapolis, MN: University of Minnesota Press.

de Certeau (1984), *The Practice of Everyday Life*, Berkeley, CA: University of California Press.

Dees, J.G. (1998), *The Meaning of Social Entrepreneurship*, accessed February 2007 at: http://faculty.fuqua.duke.edu/centers/case/files/dees-SE.pdf.

Dees, J.G., J. Emerson and P. Economy (2001), *Enterprising Nonprofits: A Toolkit for Social Entrepreneurs*, New York: John Wiley & Sons.

Dees, J.G., J. Emerson and P. Economy (2002), *Strategic Tools for Social Entrepreneurs*, New York: John Wiley & Sons.

Dees, J.G. and B.B. Anderson (2006), 'Framing a theory of social entrepreneurship: building on two schools of practice and thought', in R. Mosher-Williams (ed.), *Research on Social Entrepreneurship: Understanding and Contributing to an Emerging Field*, ARNOVA occa-sional paper series, **1** (2), Indianapolis; IN: ARNOVA.

Defourney, J. (2001), 'Introduction. From third sector to social enter-prise', in C. Borzaga and J. Defourney (eds), *The Emergence of Social Enterprise*, Abingdon and New York: Routledge.

Defourney, J. (2003), 'A new entrepreneurship in the social economy', accessed September 2006 at: www.emes.net/en/recherche/emes/analyse.php.

Deiaco, E. and L. Nordström (1998), 'Blomstrande näringsliv och dyna-miska regioner' ['Flourishing industry and dynamic regions'], in J.-E.

Nilsson, *Blomstrande näringsliv [Flourishing Industry]*, Stockholm: Royal Swedish Academy of Engineering Sciences.

Dekker, H. (2004), 'Control of inter-organizational relationships: evidence on appropriation concerns and coordination requirements', *Accounting, Organizations and Society*, **1**, 27–49.

de La Mothe, J. and G. Paquet (1994a), 'The dispersive revolution', *Optimum*, **25** (1), 42–8.

de La Mothe, J. and G. Paquet (1994b), 'The shock of the news: a techno-economic paradigm for small economies', in M. Stevenson (ed.), *The Entry into New Economic Communities: Swedish and Canadian Perspectives on the European Economic Community and North American Free Trade Accord*, Toronto, ON: Swedish-Canadian Academic Foundation.

De Leeuw, E. (1999), 'Healthy cities: urban social entrepreneurship for health', *Health Promotion International*, **14** (3), 261–9.

Deleuze, G. and F. Guattari (1980), *A Thousand Plateaus – Capitalism and Schizophrenia*, London: The Athlone Press.

Delmar, F. (2000), 'The psychology of the entrepreneur', in S. Carter and D. Jones-Evans (eds), *Enterprise and Small Business. Principles, Practice and Policy*, Upper Saddle River, NJ: Prentice Hall.

Delmar, F. and P. Davidsson (2000), 'Where do they come from? Prevalence and characteristics of nascent entrepreneurs', *Entrepreneurship and Regional Development*, **12**, 1–23.

Dennis, C. (2000), 'Networking for marketing advantage', *Management Decision*, **38** (4), 287–92.

Derrida, J. (1981), *Dissemination*, Chicago, IL: Chicago University Press.

Devinney, T.M. (2009), 'Is the socially responsible corporation a myth? The good, the bad, and the ugly of corporate social responsibility', *Academy of Management Perspectives*, **23** (2), 44–56.

Dey, P. (2006), 'The rhetoric of social entrepreneurship: paralogy and new language games in academic discourse', in C. Steyaert and D. Hjorth (eds), *Entrepreneurship as Social Change*, Cheltenham, UK and Northampton, MA, USA: Edward Elgar.

Dicken, P. and A. Malmberg (2008), 'Firms in territories: a relational perspective', in R. Martin (ed.), *Economy: Critical Essays in Human Geography*, Aldershot and Burlington, VT: Ashgate, reprinted in *Economic Geography*, 2001, **77**, 345–63.

Dixon, S.E.A. and A. Clifford (2007) 'Ecopreneurship – a new approach to managing the triple bottom line', *Journal of Organizational Change Management*, **20** (3), 326–45.

Dollinger, M.C. (2003), *Entrepreneurship. Strategies and Resources*, 3rd edn, Upper Saddle River, NJ: Prentice Hall.

Dosi, G. (1988), 'Sources, procedures and microeconomic effects of innovation', *Journal of Economic Literature*, **36**, 1126–71.

Dourish, P. (2004), *Where the Action Is: The Foundation of Embodied Interaction*, Cambridge, MA and London: The MIT Press.

Drayton, W. (2002), 'The citizen sector: becoming as competitive and entrepreneurial as business', *California Management Journal*, **12** (1), 29–43.

Dreyfus, H. (1989), 'Alternative philosophical conceptualizations of psychopatology', in H.A. Durfee and F.T. Rodier (eds), *Phenomenology and Beyond: The Self and its Language*, Dordrecht, The Netherlands: Kluwer Academic Publishers.

Dreyfus, H. (1991), *Being-in-the-World: A Commentary on Heidegger's Being and Time*, Cambridge, MA: The MIT Press.

Dreyfus, H. and P. Rabinow (eds) (1982), *Michel Foucault – Beyond Structuralism and Hermeneutics*, London: Harvester Wheatsheaf.

Dreyfus, H. and S. Dreyfus (2005), 'Expertise in real world contexts', *Organization Studies*, **26** (5), 779–92.

Droysen, J.G. (1858 [1897]), *Grundrisse der Historik*, reprinted in E.B. Andrews translation *Outline of the Principles of History*, Boston: Ginn & Co.

Drucker, P. (1969), *The Age of Discontinuity: Guidelines to our Changing Society*, London: Heinemann.

Drucker, P. (1985), *Innovation and Entrepreneurship*, London: Heinemann.

Dunn, K.M., P.M. McGuirk and H.P.M. Winchester (1995), 'Place-making: the social construction of Newcastle', *Australian Geographical Studies*, **33**, 149–66.

Dupuis, A. and A. de Bruin (2003), 'Community entrepreneurship', in A. de Bruin and A. Dupuis (eds), *Entrepreneurship: New Perspectives in a Global Age*, Aldershot: Ashgate.

Dupuis, A., A. de Bruin and R.D. Cremer (2003), 'Municipal-community entrepreneurship', in A. de Bruin and A. Dupuis (eds), *Entrepreneurship: New Perspectives in a Global Age*, Aldershot: Ashgate.

The Economist (1994), 'Canada: welcome to Cascadia', **331**, (7864), 52.

The Economist (2000), 'The new economy: untangling e-conomics', 23 September.

The Economist (2001), 'The next society: a survey of the near future', 3 November.

Edwards, S. (2002), 'Social enterprise: changing the landscape of welfare provision in the United Kingdom and Ontario, Canada', paper presented at ISTR Conference, Cape Town, South Africa, July.

Eisenhardt, K.M. (1985), 'Control: organizational and economic approaches', *Management Science*, **31** (2), 134–48.

Eisenschitz, A. and J. Gough (1993), *The Politics of Local Economic Development*, London: Macmillan.

Ekman, R. and J. Hultman (2007), 'Produktgörandet av platser' ['Manufacturing places'], in R. Ekman and J. Hultman (eds), *Plats som produkt* [*Place as a Product*], Lund, Sweden: Studentlitteratur.

Emerson, J. (1999), 'Social return on investment: exploring aspects of social creation', Roberts Enterprise Development Foundation *Box Set, 2*, Chapter 8, San Francisco: REDF.

Emerson, J. and F. Twersky (1996), *New Social Entrepreneurs: The Success, Challenges and Lessons of Non-Profit Enterprise Creation*, San Francisco, CA: Roberts Enterprise Development Foundation.

Entreprenör, (2003), 'Kluster – vår tids företagsmagneter' ['Clusters – the business magnets of our time'], **1–2**, pp. 30–34.

Entrikin, J.N. (1991), *The Betweenness of Place. Towards a Geography of Modernity*, Baltimore, MD: The Johns Hopkins University Press.

Eriksson, K. and M. Ådahl (2000), 'Finns det en ny ekonomi och kommer den till Europa?' ['Is there a new economy and will it come to Europe?'], *Penning-och valutapolitik*, **1**, Stockholm: Bank of Sweden.

Evers, A. (2001), 'The significance of social capital in the multiple goal and resources structure of social enterprises', in C. Borzaga and J. Defourney (eds), *The Emergence of Social Enterprise*, Abingdon and New York: Routledge.

Fafchamps, M. (2000), 'Ethnicity and credit in African manufacturing', *Journal of Development Economics*, **61**, 205–35.

Fassin, Y. (2008), 'SMEs and the fallacy of formalising CSR', *Business Ethics: A European Review*, **17** (4), 364–78.

Favreau, L. (2000), 'The social economy and globalisation: an overview', in J. Defourney, P. Develtere and B. Foneneau (eds), *Social Economy North and South*, Leuven, Belgium: Katholieke Universiteit Leuven and Universite de Liege.

Fay, B. (1996), *Contemporary Philosophy of Social Science*, Oxford: Blackwell Publishers.

Feldman, M. (1994), *The Geography of Innovation*, Norwell, MA: Kluwer Academic Publishers.

Ferguson, M. (1980), *The Acquarian Conspiracy*, Los Angeles, CA: Jeremy P. Tarcher.

Flora, J.L. (1998), 'Social capital and communities of place', *Rural Sociology*, **63**, 481–506.

Florida, R. (2002), *The Rise of the Creative Class*, New York: Basic Books.

Florida, R. (2003), 'Cities and the venture class', *City & Community*, **2** (1), March, 3–19.

Forbes, D.P. (2005), 'Are some entrepreneurs more overconfident than others?', *Journal of Business Venturing*, **20**, 623–40.

Forest, B. (1995), 'West Hollywood as symbol: the significance of place in the construction of a gay identity', *Environment and Planning D: Society and Space*, **13** (2), 133–57.

Foucault, M. (1980), 'The eye: conversation with J.-P. Barou and M. Perrot', in C. Gordon (ed.), *Power/Knowledge: Selected Interviews and Other Writings, 1972–1977, by Michel Foucault*, Hemel Hempstead: Harvester Press.

Foucault, M. (2008), 'Of other spaces', in C. Lévy (ed.), *The City. Critical Essays in Human Geography*, Aldershot and Burlington, VT: Ashgate, reprinted in *Diacritics*, 1986, **16**, 22–7.

Frederick, W.C. (2006), *Corporation, Be Good! The Story of Corporate Social Responsibility*, Indianapolis, IN: Dog Ear Publishing.

Freel, M. (2000), 'External linkages and product innovation in small manufacturing firms', *Entrepreneurship and Regional Development*, **12**, 245–66.

Friedman, R. (2005), *The World is Flat: The Globalized World in the Twenty-First Century*, London: Penguin.

Fujita, M., P. Krugman and A.J. Venables (2001), *The Spatial Economy – Cities, Regions and International Trade*, Cambridge, MA: The MIT Press.

Fukyama, F. (1995), *Trust: The Social Virtues and the Creation of Prosperity*, London: Penguin.

Gadamer, H.G. (1997), *Sanning och metod* [*Wahrheit und Methode*, 1960] [*Truth and Method*], Göteborg, Sweden: Daidalos.

Gaglio, C.M. (1997), 'Opportunity recognition: review, critique and suggested research directions', in J. Katz and R.H. Brockhaus (eds), *Advances in Entrepreneurship, Firm Emergence and Growth*, Greenwich, CT: JAI Press.

Gaglio, C.M. and J.A. Katz (2001), 'The psychological basis of opportunity identification: entrepreneurial alertness', *Small Business Economics*, **16**, 95–111.

Garfinkel, H. (1967), *Studies in Ethnomethodology*, Cambridge: Polity Press.

Gartner, W.B. (1988), 'Who is the entrepreneur? Is the wrong question', *American Journal of Small Business*, **12** (4), 11–32.

Gartner, W.B., B.J. Bird and J.A. Starr (1992), 'Acting as if: differentiating entrepreneurial from organizational behavior', *Entrepreneurship Theory and Practice*, **16**, 13–30.

Gawell, M., B. Johannisson and M. Lundqvist (2009) (eds), *Samhällets entreprenörer* [*The Society's Entrepreneurs*], Stockholm: KK-stiftelsen.

Geertz, C. (1973), *The Interpretation of Cultures*, New York: Basic Books.

Gereffi, G. (1994), 'The organization of buyer-driven global commodity chains: how US retailers shape overseas production networks', in G. Gereffi and M. Korzeniewicz (eds), *Commodity Chains and Global Competition*, Westport, CT: Praeger.

Gerlach, A. (2002), 'Sustainable entrepreneurship and innovation', unpublished paper, Centre for Sustainable Management (CSM), University of Luneburg, Germany.

Gertler, M. (1988), 'The limits of flexibility: comments on the post-Fordist vision of production and its geography', *Transactions of the Institute of British Geographers*, **13**, 419–32.

Gibson, D. (1991), *Technology Companies and Global Markets: Programs, Policies and Strategies to Accelerate Innovation and Entrepreneurship*, Lanham, MD: Rowman and Littlefield.

Giddens, A. (1984), *The Constitution of Society*, Cambridge: Polity Press.

Giddens, A. (1990), *The Consequences of Modernity*, Cambridge: Polity Press.

Giddens, A. (1991), *Modernity and Self-identity: Self and Society in the Late Modern Age*, Cambridge: Polity Press.

Glasmeier, A. (1991), 'Technological discontinuities and flexible production networks: the case of Switzerland and the world watch industry', mimeo, Department of Geography, University of Texas at Austin.

Glückler, J. (1999), *Neue Wege geographischen Denkens? Eine Kritik gegenwärtiger Raumkonzepte und ihrer Forschungsprogramme in der Geographie* [*A New Road for Geographical Thinking? One Critique of the Present Space Concept and Its Research Programme in Geography*], Frankfurt and Main: Verlag Neue Wissenschaft.

Glückler, J. (2001), 'Zur Bedeutung von Embeddedness in der Wirtschaftsgeographie' [On the meaning of embeddedness in business geography'], *Geographische Zeitschrift*, **89**, 211–26.

Goffman, E. (1959), *The Presentation of Self in Everyday Life*, Harmondsworth: Penguin Books.

Goldberg, K., R.F. Malina and D. Penrose (2000), *The Robot in the Garden: Telerobotics and Telepistemology in the Age of the Internet*, Cambridge, The MIT Press.

Gössling, T. (2004), 'Proximity, trust and morality in networks', *European Planning Studies*, **5**, 675–89.

Gottdiener, M. (1987), *The Decline in Urban Politics*, Beverly Hills, CA: Sage.

Grabher, G. (1993), 'Rediscovering the social in the economics of interfirm relations', in G. Grabher (ed.), *The Embedded Fir: On the Socioeconomics of Industrial Networks*, London and New York: Routledge.

Graham, S. (1995), 'The city economy', in P. Healey, S. Cameron, S. Davoudi, S. Graham and A. Madani-Pour (eds), *Managing Cities: The New Urban Context*, Chichester: John Wiley & Sons.

Granovetter, M. (1973), 'The strength of weak ties', *American Journal of Sociology*, **78** (6), 1360–80.

Granovetter, M. (1985), 'Economic action and social structure: the problem of embeddedness', *American Journal of Sociology*, **91**, 481–510.

Grenier, P. (2009), 'Social entrepreneurship in the UK: from rhetoric to reality?', in R. Ziegler (ed.), *An Introduction to Social Entrepreneurship*, Cheltenham, UK and Northampton, MA, USA: Edward Elgar.

Guinchard, C.G. (1997), (ed.), *Swedish Planning: Towards Sustainable Development*, Gävle, Sweden: Swedish Society for Town and Country Planning.

Habermas, J. (1984), *The Theory of Communicative Action*, Cambridge: Polity Press.

Hacking, I. (1983), *Representing and Intervening: Introductory Topics in the Philosophy of Natural Science*, Cambridge: Cambridge University Press.

Håkansson, H. (1989), *Corporate Technological Behavior – Co-operation and Networks*, London: Routledge.

Håkanson, L. (2003), 'Epistemic communities and cluster dynamics: on the role of knowledge in industrial districts', paper, Copenhagen Business School.

Hall, E.T. (1959), *The Silent Language*, New York: Doubleday.

Hall, T. (1992), 'Art and image: public art as symbol in urban regeneration', University of Birmingham School of Geography working paper no. 61.

Hall, T. (1998), 'Introduction', in T. Hall and P. Hubbard (eds), *The Entrepreneurial City*, Chichester: John Wiley & Sons.

Hall, T. (2005), *Urban Geography*, 3rd edn, London: Routledge.

Hall, T. and P. Hubbard (1998) (eds), *The Entrepreneurial City*, Chichester: John Wiley & Sons.

Hallowell, E.M. (1999), 'The human moment at work', *Harvard Business Review*, January–February, 58–66.

Hamilton, F.E.I. and G.J.R. Linge (eds) (1979), *Spatial Analysis, Industry and the Industrial Environment, Volume 1: Industrial Systems*, Chichester: John Wiley & Sons.

Hamilton, F.E.I. and G.J.R. Linge (eds) (1981), *Spatial Analysis, Industry and the Industrial Environment, Volume 2: International Industrial Systems*, Chichester: John Wiley & Sons.

Handy, C. (1992), 'Balancing corporate power: a new federalist paper', *Harvard Business Review*, **70** (6), 59–72.

Handy, C. (1994), *The Age of Paradox*, Boston, MA: Harvard Business School Press.

Hansen, N. (2001), 'Knowledge workers, communication, and spatial diffusion', in B. Johansson, C. Karlsson and R.R. Stough (eds), *Theories of Endogenous Regional Growth*, New York: Springer-Verlag.

Hardt, M. (2002), *Gilles Deleuze. An Apprenticeship to Philosophy*, Minneapolis, MN: University of Minnesota Press.

Harvey, D. (1989), 'From managerialism to entrepreneurialism: the transformance of governance to late capitalism', *Geografiska Annaler*, 71B, 3–17.

Healey, P. (1997), *Collaborative Planning – Shaping Places in Fragmented Societies*, Basingstoke and London: MacMillan Press.

Heidegger, M. (1927/1962), *Being and Time*, San Francisco, CA: Harper & Row.

Henton, D., J. Melville and K. Walesh (1997), *Grassroots Leaders for a New Economy. How Civic Entrepreneurs are Building Prosperous Communities*, San Francisco, CA: Jossey-Bass.

Henton, D., J. Melville and K. Walesh (2002), 'Collaboration and innovation: the state of American regions', *Industry & Higher Education,* **16** (1), February, 9–17.

Herbert, D.T. and C.J. Thomas (1997), *Cities in Space. City as Place*, 3rd edn, London: David Fulton Publishers.

Hindova, V., D. Barry and D.J. Ketchen, Jr. (2009), 'Entrepreneurship as emancipation', *Academy of Management Review,* **34** (3), 477–91.

Hite, J. and W. Hesterley (2001), 'The evolution of firm networks: from emergence to early growth of the firm', *Strategic Management Journal*, **22** (3), 275–86.

Hjorth, D. (2001), Rewriting Entrepreneurship. Enterprise Discourse and Entrepreneurship in the Case of Re-organising ES, doctoral thesis, Växjö, Sweden: Växjö University Press.

Hjorth, D. (2004), 'Creating space for play/invention – concepts of space and organizational entrepreneurship', *Entrepreneurship and Regional Development*, **16**, 413–32.

Hjorth, D. (2007), 'Lessons from Iago: narrating the event of entrepreneurship', *Journal of Business Venturing*, **22**, 712–32.

Hjorth, D. (2009), 'Entrepreneurship, sociality and art: re-imagining the public', in R. Ziegler (ed.), *An Introduction to Social Entrepreneurship*, Cheltenham, UK and Northampton, MA, USA: Edward Elgar.

Hjorth, D. and B. Bjerke (2006), 'Public entrepreneurship: moving from social/consumer to public/citizen', in C. Steyaert and D. Hjorth (eds),

Entrepreneurship as Social Change, Cheltenham, UK and Northampton, MA, USA: Edward Elgar.

Hjorth, D. and B. Johannisson (2002), 'Conceptualising the opening phase of regional development as the enactment of a "collective identity"', paper presented at Second Conference of the International Entrepreneurship Forum 'Entrepreneurship & Regional Development', Beijing, September 5–7.

Hjorth, D. and C. Steyaert (2003), 'Entrepreneurship beyond (a new) economy: creative swarms and pathological zones', in C. Steyaert and D. Hjorth (eds), *New Movements in Entrepreneurship*, Cheltenham, UK and Northampton, MA, USA: Edward Elgar.

Hjorth, D. and C. Steyaert (2004) (eds), *Narrative and Discursive Approaches in Entrepreneurship*, Cheltenham, UK and Northampton, MA, USA: Edward Elgar.

Hoang, H. and B. Antoncic (2003), 'Network-based research in entrepreneurship. A critical Review', *Journal of Business Venturing*, **18**, 165–87.

Hoggart, K. (1991), *People, Power and Place: Perspectives on Anglo-American Politics*, London: Routledge.

Holmberg, I., M. Salzer-Mörling and L. Strannegård (eds) (2002), *Stuck in the Future? Tracing the 'New Economy'*, Stockholm: Bookhouse Publishing.

Hostager, T.J., T.C. Neil, R.L. Decker and R.D. Lorentz (1998), 'Seeing environmental opportunities: effects of intrapreneurial ability, efficacy, motivation and desirability', *Journal of Organizational Change Management*, **11** (1), 11–25.

Hubbard, P. and T. Hall (1998), 'The entrepreneurial city and the "new urban politics"', in T. Hall and P. Hubbard (eds), *The Entrepreneurial City*, Chichester: John Wiley & Sons.

Hudson, R. (2000), *Production, Places and Environment: Changing Perspectives in Economic Geography*, Harlow: Prentice Hall.

Hudson, R. (2001), *Producing Places*, London: Guildford Press.

Hudson, R. (2008), 'Conceptualizing economies and their geographies: spaces, flows and circuits', in R. Martin (ed.), *Economy: Critical Essays in Human Geography*, Aldershot and Burlington, VA: Ashgate, reprinted in *Progress in Human Geography*, 2004, **28**, 447–71.

Husserl, E. (1931), *Ideas: General Introduction to Pure Phenomenology*, London: George Allen Unwin.

Husserl, E. (1964), *The Idea of Phenomenology*, The Hague: Martinus Nijhoff.

Ireland, R.D., M.A. Hitt and D.G. Sirmon (2003), 'A model of strategic management', *Journal of Management*, **29**, 963–89.

Irigaray, L. (1993), 'Place, interval: a reading of Aristotle, *Physics* IV', in L. Irigaray, *An Ethics of Sexual Difference*, Ithaca, NY: Cornell University Press.

Isaak, R. (1998), *Green Logic: Ecopreneurship, Theory and Ethics*, Sheffield: Greenleaf.

Isaak, R. (2002), *The Making of the Ecopreneurs*, Sheffield: Greenleaf.

Isard, W. and E.W. Schooler (1959), 'Industrial complex analysis, agglomeration economics and regional development', *Journal of Regional Science*, **1**, 16–32.

Jacobs, J. (1961), *The Death and Life of Great American Cities*, New York: Random House.

Jaffe, A., M. Trajtenberg and R. Henderson (1993), 'Geographic localization of knowledge spillovers', *Quarterly Journal of Economics*, **108**, 577–98.

James, E. (1989), 'The private provision of social service: a comparison of Sweden and Holland', in E. James (ed.), *The Nonprofit Sector in International Perspective*, Oxford: Oxford University Press.

Jammer, M. (1982), *Concepts of Space. The History of Theories of Space in Physics*, 3rd edn, New York: Dover Publications, Inc.

Jaques, E. (1982), *The Form of Time*, New York: Crane Russak.

Jarillo, J. (1989), 'Entrepreneurship and growth: the strategic use of external resources', *Journal of Business Venturing*, **4** (2), 133–47.

Järvenpää, S.L. and D.E. Leidner (1999), 'Communication and trust in global virtual Teams', *Organization Science*, **6**, 791–815.

Jedlowski, P. and C. Leccardi (2003), *Sociologia della vita quotidiana* [*Sociology of Everyday Life*], Bologna, Italy: Il Mulino.

Jessop, B. (1994), 'Post-Fordism and the state', in A. Amin (ed.), *Post-Fordism*, Oxford: Blackwell.

Jessop, B. (1996), 'The entrepreneurial city: re-imaging localities, re-designing economic governance or re-structuring capital', paper presented at the Annual Conference of the Institute of British Geographers, University of Strathclyde.

Jessop, B. (1997), 'The governance of complexity of governance: preliminary remarks on some problems and limits of economic guidance', in A. Amin and J. Hausner (eds), *Beyond Markets and Hierarchy: Third Way Approaches to Transformation*, Cheltenham, UK and Lyme, NH, USA: Edward Elgar.

Jessop, B. (1998), 'The narrative of enterprise and the enterprise of narrative: place marketing and the entrepreneurial city', in T. Hall and P. Hubbard (eds), *The Entrepreneurial City*, Chichester: John Wiley & Sons.

Johannisson, B. (1990), 'Community entrepreneurship – cases and conceptualization', *Entrepreneurship and Regional Development*, **2**, 71–88.

Johannisson, B. (2000), 'Networking and entrepreneurial growth', in

D.L. Sexton and H. Landström (eds), *The Blackwell Handbook of Entrepreneurship*, Oxford: Blackwell.

Johannisson, B. (2002), 'Entreprenörskapets regional organisering – bortom storskalighet och teknologi' [The regional organizing of entrepreneurship – beyond economy scale and technology], in P. Aronsson and B. Johannisson (eds), *Entreprenörskapets dynamic och regionala förankring* [The Dynamics and Regional Connection of Entrepreneurship], Växjö, Sweden: Växjö University Press.

Johannisson, B. (2005), *Entreprenörskapets väsen* [The Essence of Entrepreneurship], Lund, Sweden: Studentlitteratur.

Johannisson, B. (2009), 'Towards a practice theory of entrepreneuring', *Small Business Economics*, Online edition, accessed 15 February 2010.

Johannisson, B. and A. Nilsson (1989), 'Community entrepreneurs: networking for local development', *Entrepreneurship and Regional Development*, **1**, 3–19.

Johannisson, B. and R. Peterson (1984), 'The personal networks of entrepreneurs', paper presented at the Third Canadian Conference of the International Council for Small Business, Toronto, 23–5 May.

Johansson, A.W. (2004), 'Narrating the entrepreneur', *International Small Business Journal*, **22** (3), 273–93.

Johansson, I. (2001), 'Nätverk och Gnosjöanda' [Network and the Spirit of Gnosjö], in M.-L. von Bergmann-Winberg and W. Skoglund (eds), *Lokalt utvecklingsarbete och entreprenörskap i Gnosjö, Åseda och Bispgården* [*Local Development Work and Entrepreneurship in Gnosjö, Åseda and Bispgården*], seminar at Bispgården, Sweden, 22 November.

Johnstone, H. and R. Haddow (2003), 'Industrial decline and high technology renewal in Cape Breton: exploring the limits of the possible', in D. Wolfe (ed), *Clusters Old and New: The Transition to a Knowledge Economy in Canada's Regions*, Kingston, QC: McGill-Queen's University Press.

Johnstone, H. and D. Lionais (1999), 'Identifying equity gaps in a depleted local economy', paper presented at the Canadian Council for Entrepreneurship and Small Business Annual Conference, Banff, Alberta, Canada, November.

Johnstone, H. and D. Lionais (2000), 'Using Pareto distributions to better characterize equity gaps and improve estimates of informal venture capital', paper presented at the Frontiers of Entrepreneurship Research Conference 2000, Kauffman Center for Entrepreneurship Leadership, Babson College, Wellesley, MA.

Johnstone, H. and D. Lionais (2004), 'Depleted communities and community business entrepreneurship: revaluing space through place', *Entrepreneurship and Regional Development*, **16**, May, 217–33.

Jones, C. and A. Spicer (2009), *Unmasking the Entrepreneur*, Cheltenham, UK and Northampton, MA, USA: Edward Elgar.

Jones, O., C. Carduso and M. Beckinsale (1997), 'Mature SMEs and technological innovation: entrepreneurial networks in the UK and Portugal', *International Journal of Innovation Management*, **1** (3), 201–27.

Jonsson, O. and L.-O. Olander (2000), 'Production and innovation networks – a regional matter', paper presented at Uddevalla Symposium 2000, June 15–17.

Jonung, L. (2000), 'Den nya ekonomin i ett historiskt perspektiv utifrån debatten och litteraturen' ['The new economy in a historical perspective in the public debate and in the literature'], *Ekonomisk Debatt*, **28** (6), 561–6.

Judd, D. and R.L. Ready (1986), 'Entrepreneurial cities and the new politics of economic development', in G.E. Peterson and C.W. Lewis (eds), *Reagan and the Cities*, Washington, DC: Urban Institute Press.

Keating, M. (1998), *The New Regionalism in Western Europe*, Cheltenham, UK and Lyme, NH, USA: Edward Elgar.

Keating, M. (2001), 'Rethinking the region: cultural, institutional and economic development in Catalonia and Galicia', *European Urban and Regional Studies*, **8**, 217–34.

Keeble, D. and F. Wilkinson (1999), 'Collective learning and knowledge development in the evolution of regional clusters of high technology SMEs in Europe', *Regional Studies*, **33**, 295–303.

Keeble, D., C. Lawson, B. Moore and F. Wilkinson (1999), 'Collective learning processes, networking and "institutional thickness" in the Cambridge region', *Regional Studies*, **33**, 319–32.

Kelley, M. and H. Brooks (1991), 'External learning opportunities and the diffusion of process innovations to small firms: the case of programmable automation', *Technological Forecasting and Social Change*, **39**, 103–25.

Kelly, K. (1998), *New Rules for the New Economy*, New York: Viking.

Keogh, P.D. and M.J. Polonsky (1998), 'Environmental commitment: a basis for environmental entrepreneurship?', *Journal of Organizational Change Management*, **11** (1), 38–49.

Kilkenny, M., L. Nalbarte and T. Besser (1999), 'Reciprocated community support and small town-small business sector', *Entrepreneurship and Regional Development*, **11**, 231–46.

Kinneavy, J.L. (1986), 'Kairos: a neglected concept in classical rhetoric', in J.D. Moss (ed), *Rhetoric and Praxis*, Washington, DC: Catholic University of America Press.

Kinneavy, J.L and C.R. Eskin (1994), '*Kairos* in Aristotle's *Rhetoric*', *Written Communication*, **11** (1), 131–42.

Kirkeby, O.F. (1998), *Management Philosophy: A Radical-Normative Perspective*, Berlin: Springer.

Kirlin, J.J. and D.R. Marshall (1988), 'Urban governance and the new politics of entrepreneurship', in M. McGeary and I. Lynn (eds), *Urban Change and Poverty*, Washington, DC: National Academic Press.

Kirzner, I.M. (1973), *Competition and Entrepreneurship*, Chicago, IL: University of Chicago Press.

Kirzner, I.M. (1979), *Perception, Opportunity, and Profit*, Chicago, IL: University of Chicago Press.

Knights, D., F. Noble, T. Vurdubakis and H. Willmott (2001), 'Chasing shadows: control, virtuality and the production of trust', *Organization Studies*, **22** (2), 311–36.

Knorr-Cetina, K. (1981), *The Manufacture of Knowledge: An Essay on The Constructivist and Contextual Nature of Science*, Oxford: Pergamon Press.

Kreiner, K. and M. Schultz (1993), 'Informal collaboration in R&D: the formation of networks across organizations', *Organization Studies*, **14** (2), 189–209.

Krugman, P. (1980), 'Scale economies, product differentiation and the pattern of trade', *American Economic Review*, **70**, 950–59.

Krugman, P. (1990), *Rethinking International Trade*, Cambridge, MA: The MIT Press.

Krugman, P. (1991a), *Geography and Trade*, Leuven, Belgium: Leuven University Press.

Krugman, P. (1991b), 'Increasing returns and economic geography', *Journal of Political Economy*, **99**, 14–31.

Krugman, P. (1993), 'The current case for industrial policy', in D. Salvatore (ed.), *Protectionism and World Welfare*, Cambridge: Cambridge University Press.

Krugman, P. and A. Venables (1990), 'Integration and the competitiveness of peripheral industry', in C. Bliss and J. Braga de Macedo (eds), *Unity with Diversity in the European Community*, Cambridge: Cambridge University Press.

Kuhn, T. (1962), *The Structure of Scientific Revolution*, Chicago, IL: University of Chicago Press.

Küpers, W. (2005), 'Phenomenology of embodied implicit and narrative knowing', *Journal of Knowledge Management*, **9** (6), 114–33.

Kuratko, D.F. and R.M. Hodgetts (2004), *Entrepreneurship: Theory, Process, Practice*, 6th edn, Stamford, CT: Thomson South-Western.

Kyrö, P. (2001), 'To grow or not to grow? Entrepreneurship and sustainable development', *International Journal of Sustainable Development and World Ecology*, **8** (1), 15–28.

Larson, A.L. (2000), 'Sustainable innovation through an entrepreneurship lens', *Business Strategy and the Environment*, **9** (5), 304–17.

Latour, B. (1987), *Science in Action*, Cambridge, MA: Harvard University Press.

Latour, B. (1996), *Aramis, or the Love of Technology*, Cambridge, MA: Harvard University Press.

Latour, B. (2005), *Reassembling the Social: An Introduction to Actor-Network Theory*, Oxford: Oxford University Press.

Latour, B. and S. Wolgar (1979), *Laboratory Life: The Social Construction of Scientific Facts*, Beverley Hills, CA: Sage.

Laville, J.-L. and M. Nyssens (2001), 'The social enterprise: towards a theoretical socio-economic approach', in C. Borzaga and J. Defourney (eds), *The Emergence of Social Enterprise*, Abingdon and New York: Routledge.

Lawson, C. (1999), 'Towards a competence theory of the region', *Cambridge Journal of Economics*, **23**, 151–66.

Leadbeater, C. (1997), *The Rise of the Social Entrepreneur*, London: Demos.

Leadbeater, C. (1999), *Living in Thin Air: The New Economy*, London: Viking Books.

Leana, C.R. and H.J. Van Buren (1999), 'Organizational social capital and employment Practices', *Academy of Management Review*, **24**, 538–54.

Lechner, C. and M. Dowling (2003), 'Firm networks: external relationships as sources for the growth and competitiveness of entrepreneurial firms', *Entrepreneurship and Regional Development*, **15** (1), 1–26.

Lefebvre, H. (1991), *The Production of Space*, translated by Norman Kemp Smith, New York: St Martin's Press.

Leitner, H. (1990), 'Cities in pursuit of economic growth: the local state as entrepreneur', *Public Geography Quarterly*, **9**, 146–70.

Leitner, H. and E. Sheppard (1998), 'Economic uncertainty, inter-urban competition and the efficacy of entrepreneurialism', in T. Hall and P. Hubbard (eds), *The Entrepreneurial City*, Chichester: John Wiley & Sons Ltd.

Li, J. (2008), 'Small firm networking: contents and nature of knowledge sharing and Learning', *International Journal of Knowledge Management Studies*, **2** (3), 272–84.

Liedman, S.-E. (2002), *Ett oändligt äventyr* [*An Eternal Adventure*], Stockholm: Albert Bonniers Förlag.

Lindgren, M. (2009), '*Gränsöverskridande entreprenörskapsforskning: entreprenörskap som process, projekt och emanicipering*' [*Entrepreneurial Research Crossing Borders: Entrepreneurship as Process, Project and Emancipation*], in C. Holmquist (ed.), *Entreprenörskap på riktigt. Teoretiska och praktiska perspektiv* [*Entrepreneurship for Real. Theoretical and Practical Perspectives*], Lund, Sweden: Studentlitteratur.

Lindgren, M. and J. Packendorff (2007), *Konstruktion av entreprenör-skap* [*Constructing Entrepreneurship*], Örebro Sweden: Forum för småföretagsforskning.

Linnanen, L. (2002). 'An insider's experience with environmental entrepreneurship', *Greener Management International*, **38** (Summer), 71–80.

Ljungbo, K. (2010), *Language as a Leading Light to Business Cultural Insight*, doctoral thesis, Stockholm University School of Business.

Luhmann, N. (1979), *Trust and Power*, Chichester: John Wiley & Sons.

Lukermann, F. (1964), 'Geography as a formal intellectual discipline and the way in which it contributes to human knowledge', *Canadian Geographer*, **8** (4), 167–72.

Lundvall, B.-Å. (ed.) (1992), *National Systems of Innovation: Towards a Theory of Innovation and Interactive Learning*, London: Pinter.

Macey, S.L. (1994), *Encyclopedia of Time*, New York: Garland Publishing.

MacKinnon, D., A. Cumbers and K. Chapman (2002), 'Learning, innovation and regional development: a critical appraisal of recent debates', *Progress in Human Geography*, **26** (3), 293–311.

MacLeod, G. (1998), 'In what sense a region? Place hybridity, symbolic shape, and institutional formation in (post-)modern Scotland', *Political Geography*, **17**, 833–63.

Madsen, H., H. Neergaard and J.P. Ulhøi (2008), 'Factors influencing the establishment of knowledge-intensive ventures', *International Journal of Entrepreneurial Behavior & Research*, **14** (2), 70–84.

Maillat, D. (1998), 'From the industrial districts to the innovative milieu: Contribution to an analysis of territorialised productive organisations', *Recherches Economiques de Lovain*, **64**, 111–29.

Mair, J. and E. Noboa (2006), 'Social entrepreneurship: how intentions to create a social venture are formed', in J. Mair, J. Robinson and K. Hockerts (eds), *Social Entrepreneurship*, Basingstoke and New York: Palgrave Macmillan.

Mair, J., J. Robinson and K. Hockerts (eds) (2006), *Social Entrepreneurship*, Basingstoke, UK and New York: Palgrave Macmillan.

Malmberg, A. and P. Maskell (1997), 'Toward an explanation of regional specialization and industry agglomeration', *European Planning Studies*, **5**, 25–41.

Malpas, J.E. (1999), *Place and Experience: A Philosophical Topography*, Cambridge: Cambridge University Press.

Mariavelias, C. (2009), 'Freedom, opportunism and entrepreneurialism in post-bureaucratic organizations', in D. Hjorth and C. Steyaert (eds), *The Politics and Aesthetics of Entrepreneurship*, Cheltenham, UK and Northampton, MA, USA: Edward Elgar.

Mariotti, S. and C. Glackin (2010), *Entrepreneurship*, 2nd edn, Upper Saddle River, NJ: Prentice Hall.

Markusen, A. (2008), 'Sticky places in slippery space: a typology of industrial districts', in R. Martin (ed.), *Economy: Critical Essays in Human Geography*, Aldershot and Burlington, VT: Ashgate, reprinted in *Economic Geography*, 1996, **72**, 293–313.

Marshall, A. (1898), *Principles of Economics*, London: Macmillan.

Martin, F. and M. Thompson (2010), *Social Enterprise: Developing Sustainable Businesses*, Basingstoke: Palgrave Macmillan.

Martin, R. (1994), 'Economic theory and human geography', in D. Gregory, R. Martin and G. Smith (eds), *Human Geography. Society, Space and Social Science*, Basingstoke: Macmillan.

Martin, R. (1999a), 'The new "geographical turn" in economics: some critical reflections', *Cambridge Journal of Economics*, **23**, 65–91.

Martin, R. (1999b), 'The "new economic geography": challenge or irrelevance?', *Transactions of the Institute of British Geographers*, **24**, 387–91.

Martin, R. (2008), 'Introduction', in R. Martin (ed.), *Economy: Critical Essays in Human Geography*, Aldershot and Burlington, VT: Ashgate, reprinted in *Economic Geography*, 1996, **72**, 293–313.

Martin, R. and P. Sunley (2008), 'Paul Krugman's geographical economics and its implications for regional development theory: a critical assessment', in R. Martin (ed.), *Economy. Critical Essays in Human Geography*, Aldershot and Burlington, VT: Ashgate, reprinted in *Economic Geography*, 1996, **3**, 259–92.

Mascanzoni, D. and M. Nonotny (2000), *Lokomotivföretagen i Italien* [*The Locomotive Companies in Italy*], Rådet för arbetslivsforskning, report no. 12.

Maskell, P. and A. Malmberg (1999a), 'Localised learning and industrial competitiveness', *Cambridge Journal of Economics*, **23**, 167–85.

Maskell, P. and A. Malmberg (1999b), 'The competitiveness of firms and regions. "Ubiquitification" and the importance of localized learning', *European Urban and Regional Studies*, **6**, 9–25.

Massey, D. (1995a), *Spatial Divisions of Labour: Social Structures and the Geography of Production*, London: Macmillan.

Massey, D. (1995b), 'The conceptualization of place', in D. Massey and P. Jess (eds), *A Place in the World*, Oxford: Oxford University Press.

Massumi, B. (1992), *A User's Guide to Capitalism and Schizophrenia. Deviations from Deleuze and Guattari*, Cambridge, MA: The MIT Press.

Matten, D. and J. Moon (2008), '"Implicit" and "explicit" CSR: a conceptual framework for a comparative understanding of corporate social responsibility', *Academy of Management Review*, **33** (2), 404–24.

Mawson, A. (2008), *The Social Entrepreneur: Making Communities Work*, London: Atlantic Books.

May, J. and N. Thrift (eds) (2001), *Timespace: Geographies of Temporality*, New York: Routledge.

Mayer, M. (1995), 'Urban governance in the post-Fordist city', in P. Healey et al. (eds), *Managing Cities: The New Urban Context*, Chichester: John Wiley & Sons.

McClelland, D. (1961), *The Achieving Society*, Princeton, NJ: D. van Nostrand.

McDonald, C. and G. Marston (2001), 'Fixing the niche? Rhetorics of the community sector in the neo-liberal welfare regime', paper presented at workshop 'Social entrepreneurship: whose responsibility is it anyway?', Centre of Full Employment and Equity (CofFEE) and the Department of Social Work.

McKnight, D.H., L.L. Cummings and N.L. Chervany (1998), 'Initial trust formation in new organizational relationships', *Academy of Management Review*, **3**, 473–90.

McLeod, H. (1997), 'Cross-over: the social entrepreneur', *Inc. Special Issue: State of Small*, **19** (7), 100–104.

McWilliams A., and D. Siegel (2001), 'Corporate social responsibility: a theory of the firm perspective', *Academy of Management Review*, **26** (1), 117–27.

Mehra, M. and A.-M. Jørgensen (eds) (1997), *Towards Sustainable Development for Local Authorities: Approaches, Experiences and Sources*, Copenhagen: European Environment Agency.

Merleau-Ponty, M. (1962), *Phenomenology of Perception*, London: Routledge.

Merrifield, A. (2000), 'Henri Lefebvre: a socialist in space', in M. Crang and N. Thrift (eds), *Thinking Space*, London and New York: Routledge.

Metro (2001), 'Trängsel ger framgång' [*Crowdedness Brings Success*], 29 May, 14.

Meyerson, D., K.E. Weick and R.M. Kramer (1996), 'Swift trust and temporary groups', in R.M. Kramer and T.R. Tyler (eds), *Trust in Organizations: Frontiers of Theory and Research*, Thousand Oaks, CA: Sage.

Miles, M. (1997), *Art, Space and the City*, London: Routledge.

Mirowski, P. (1989), *More Heat than Light: Economics as Social Physics, Physics as Nature's Economics*, Cambridge: Cambridge University Press.

Mollenkopf, J.H. (1983), *The Contested City*, Princeton, NJ: Princeton University Press.

Monge, P.R. and N.S. Contractor (2001), 'Emergence of communication networks', in F.M. Jablin and L.L. Putnam (eds), *The New Handbook of Organizational Communication*, Thousand Oaks, CA: Sage.

Moore, H. (2002), 'Building the social economy', accessed 22 November 2010 at www.fathom.com/feature/35515/.

Morgan, K. (1997), 'The learning region: institutions, innovation and regional renewal', *Regional Studies*, **31**, 491–503.

Mort, G., J. Weerawardena and K. Carnegie (2003), 'Social entrepreneurship: towards conceptualization', *Nonprofit and Voluntary Sector Marketing*, **8** (1), 76–88.

Mosey, S. and M. Wright (2007), 'From human capital to social capital: a longitudinal study of technology-based academic entrepreneurs', *Entrepreneurship: Theory and Practice*, **31** (6), 909–35.

Motte, A. and F. Cajori (1934), *Sir Isaac Newton's Mathematical Principles of Natural Philosophy and his System of the World*, Berkeley, CA: University of California Press.

Mulgan, G. (2006), 'Cultivating the other invisible hand of social entrepreneurship: comparative advantage, public policy, and future research priorities', in A. Nicholls (ed.), *Social Entrepreneurship: New Models of Sustainable Social Change*, Oxford: Oxford University Press.

Murdoch, J. (2008), 'Inhuman/nonhuman/human: actor-network theory and the prospects for the nondualistic and symmetrical perspective on nature and society', in C. Philo (ed.), *Theory and Methods. Contemporary Foundations of Space and Place*, Aldershot and Burlington, VT: Ashgate, reprinted in J. Murdoch (1997), *Environment and Planning D: Society and Space*, **15**, 731–56.

Murtha, T.P., S.A. Lenway and J.A. Hart (2001), *Managing New Industry Formation: Global Knowledge Formation and Entrepreneurship in High Technology*, Stanford, CA: Stanford University Press.

Nahapiet, J. and S. Ghoshal (1998), 'Social capital, intellectual capital and the organizational advantage', *Academy of Management Review*, **23**, 242–67.

Naisbitt, J., N. Naisbitt and D. Philips (2001), *High Tech High Touch: Our Accelerating Search for Meaning*, London: Nicholas Brealey Publishing.

Nancy, J.-L. (1991), *The Inoperative Community*, Minneapolis, MN: University of Minnesota Press.

Newman, J. (2001), *Modernising Governance: New Labour, Policy and Society*, London: Sage.

Nicholls, A. (2006), 'Social entrepreneurship', in S. Carter and D. Jones-Evans (eds), *Enterprise and Small Business. Principles, Practice and Policy*, 2nd edn, Harlow: Pearson Education.

Nicolini, D., S. Gherardi and D. Yanow (eds) (2003), *Knowing in Organizations: A Practice-Based Approach*, Armonk, NY: M.E. Sharpe.

Nijkamp, P. (2003), 'Entrepreneurship in a modern network economy', *Regional Studies*, **37** (4), 395–405.

Nilsson, J.-E. (2002), 'Entreprenörskapets dynamik och regionala förankring – generella drag' ['The dynamics and regional connection of entrepreneurship – general characteristics'], in P. Aronsson and B. Johannisson (eds), *Entreprenörskapets dynamik och regionala förankring* [*The Dynamics and Regional Connection of Entrepreneurship*], Växjö, Sweden: Växjö University Press.

Noë, A. (2004), *Action in Perception*, Cambridge, MA: The MIT Press.

Normann, R. (2001), *Reframing Business. When the Map Changes the Landscape*, Chichester: John Wiley & Sons.

NUTEK (2001), *Regionala vinnar Kluster* [Regional Winning Clusters]

Nyström, L. (2002), 'Det tredje Sverige' [The third Sweden], in P. Aronsson and B. Johannisson (eds.), *Entreprenörskapets dynamik och regionala förankring* [The dynamics and regional connection of entrepreneurship], Växjö, Sweden: Växjö University Press.

O'Gorman, C. (2006), 'Strategy and the small business', in S. Carter and D. Jones-Evans (eds), *Enterprise and Small Business. Principles, Practice and Policy*, 2nd edn, Harlow: Pearson Education.

Ohmae, K. (1993), 'The rise of the region state', *Foreign Affairs*, **72**, 78–87.

Öhrström, B. (2005), 'Urban och ekonomisk utveckling. Platsbaserade strategier i den postindustriella staden' ['Urban and economic development. Place-based strategies in the postindustrial city'], in O. Sernhede and T. Johansson (eds), *Storstadens omvandlingar. Postindustrialism, globalisering och migration. Göteborg och Malmö* [*Transformations of Big Cities. Postindustrialization, Globalization and Migration. Gothenburg and Malmoe*], Göteborg, Sweden: Daidalos.

Oinas, P. (1999), 'Voices and silences: the problem of access to embeddedness', *Geoforum*, **30**, 351–61.

Orlikowski, W.J. (2000), 'Using technology and constituting structures: a practice lens for studying technology in organizations', *Organization Science*, **13** (3), 249–73.

Orlikowski, W.J. (2002), 'Knowing in practice: enacting a collective ability in distributed organizing', *Organization Science*, **13**, 249–73.

Osborne, D. and T. Gaebler (1992), *Reinventing Government: How the Entrepreneurial Spirit is Transforming the Public Sector*, Reading, MA: Addison-Wesley.

Osborne, D. and P. Plastrik (1997), *Banishing Bureaucracy: The Five Strategies for Reinventing Government*, Reading, MA: Addison-Wesley.

Ostgaard, T.A. and S. Birley (1994), 'Personal networks and firm competitive strategy – a strategic or coincidental match?', *Journal of Business Venturing*, **9**, 281–305.

O'Toole, J. and W. Bennis (1992), 'Our federalist future', *California Management Review*, **70** (6), 59–72.

Otto, M.A.C. (1992), *Der Ort: Phänomenologische Variationen*, Freiburg, Germany: Alber.

Paasi, A. (2008), 'Bounded spaces in the mobile world: deconstructing "Regional Identity"', in J.N. Entrikin (ed.), *Regions: Critical Essays in Human Geography*, Aldershot and Burlington, VA: Ashgate, reprinted in *Tijdschrift voor Economische en Sociale Geografie*, 2002, **93**, 137–48.

Painter, J. (1998), 'Entrepreneurs are made, not born: learning and urban regimes in the production of entrepreneurial cities', in T. Hall and P. Hubbard (eds), *The Entrepreneurial City*, Chichester: John Wiley & Sons.

Paquet, G. (1994), 'Reinventing governance', *Opinion Canada*, **2** (2), 1–5.

Paredo, A.M. and J.J. Chrisman (2006), 'Toward a theory of community-based enterprise', *Academy of Management Review*, **31** (2), 309–28.

Pastakia, A. (2002), 'Assessing ecopreneurship in the context of a developing country: the case of India', *Greener Management International*, **38** (Summer), 93–108.

Peck, J. (1991), 'Labour and agglomeration: vertical disintegration, skill formation and flexibility in local labour markets', mimeo, School of Geography, University of Manchester.

Peck, J. (1995), 'Moving and shaking: business elites, state localism and urban privatism', *Progress in Human Geography*, **19**, 16–46.

Pereira, A.A. (2004), 'State entrepreneurship and regional development. Singapore's industrial parks in Batam and Suzhou', *Entrepreneurship and Regional Development*, **16**, March, 129–44.

Perrini, F. and C. Vurro (2006), 'Social entrepreneurship: innovation and social change across theory and practice', in J. Mair, J. Robinson and K. Hockerts (eds), *Social Entrepreneurship*, Basingstoke and New York: Palgrave Macmillan.

Petersen, A., I. Barns, J. Dudley and P. Harris (1999), *Poststructuralism, Citizenship and Social Policy*, London: Routledge.

Petranker, J. (2007), 'The presence of others: network experience as an antidote to the subjectivity of time', in R. Hassan and R.E. Purser (eds), *24/7: Time and Temporality in the Network Society*, Stanford, CA: Stanford University Press.

Pfeffer, J. (1981), 'Management as symbolic action: the creation and maintenance of organizational paradigms, in L.L. Cummings and B.M. Shaw (eds), *Research in Organizational Behaviour*, vol. 3, 117–135.

Philo, C. (1989), 'Contextuality', in A. Bullock, O. Stallybrass and S. Trombly (eds), *The Fontana Dictionary of Modern Thought*, London: Fontana Press.

Philo, C. (2000), 'Foucault's geography', in M. Crang and N. Thrift (eds), *Thinking Space*, London and New York: Routledge.

Piore, M.J. and C.F. Sabel (1984), *The Second Industrial Divide: Possibilities for Prosperity*, New York: Basic Books.

Plato (2008), *Timaios*, translated by Robin Waterfield, Oxford: Oxford University Press.

Polanyi, M. (1966), *The Tacit Dimension*, London: Routledge & Kegan Paul.

Porter, M.E. (1990), *The Competitive Advantage of Nations*, Basingstoke: Macmillan.

Porter, M. (1998a), 'The Adam Smith address: location, clusters, and the "new" microeconomics of competition', *Business Economics*, January, 7–13.

Porter, M.E. (1998b), 'Clusters and the new economics of competition', *Harvard Business Review*, **76**, Nov/Dec, 77–90.

Portes, A. and J. Sensenbrenner (1993), 'Embeddedness and immigration: notes on the social determinants', *American Journal of Sociology,* **98**, 1320–50.

Pouder, R. and C. St. John (1996), 'Hot spots and blind spots: geographical clusters of firms and innovation', *Academy of Management Review*, **21**, 1192–225.

Powell, W.W. and L. Smith-Doerr (1994), 'Networks and economic life', in N. Smelser and R. Swedberg (eds), *Handbook of Economic Sociology*, Princeton, NJ: Princeton University Press.

Power, D. and S.J. Scott (2004) (eds), *Cultural Industries and the Production of Culture*, London: Routledge.

Putnam, R.D., R. Leonardi and R.Y. Nanetti (1993), *Making Democracry Work: Civic Traditions in Modern Italy*, Princeton, NJ: Princeton University Press.

Quinn, J. (1997), 'Personal ethics and business ethics: the ethical attitude of owner/managers of small business', *Journal of Business Ethics*, **16** (2), 119–27.

Ramírez, J.L. (1995), *Skapande mening – en begreppsgenealogisk undersökning av rationalitet, vetenskap och planering* [*Creative Meaning – A Contribution to a Human-Scientific Theory of Action*], Stockholm: Nordplan.

Rämö, H. (1999), 'An Aristotelian human time-space manifold: from chronochora to kairotopos', *Time and Society*, **8**, 309–28.

Rämö, H. (2002), 'Doing things right and doing the right things: time and timing in project', *International Journal of Project Management*, **20**, 569–74.

Rämö, H. (2004a), 'Moments of trust: temporal and spatial factors of trust in organizations', *Journal of Managerial Psychology*, **19** (8), 760–75.

Rämö, H. (2004b), 'Spatio-temporal notions and organized environmental issues – an axiology of action', *Organization*, **11** (6), 849–72.

Rämö, H. (2007), 'Finding time and place for trust in ICT network organizations', in R. Hassan and R.E. Purser (eds), *24/7: Time and Temporality in the Network Society*, Stanford, CA: Stanford Business Books.

Rämö, H. (2010), 'Three facets of management research: theoretical sophistication, explaining practice and reflective understanding', *International Journal of Management Concepts and Philosophy*, **4** (1), 60–70.

Redding, S.G. (1993), *The Spirit of Chinese Capitalism*, Berlin: Walter de Gruyter.

Rehn, A. and S. Taalas (2004), 'Acquaintances and connections – *Blat*, the Soviet Union and mundane entrepreneurship', *Entrepreneurship and Regional Development*, **16**, May, 235–50.

Reich, R.B. (2001), *The Future of Success: Work and Life in the New Economy*, London: Heinemann.

Relph, E. (1976), *Place and Placelessness*, London: Pion.

Renzulli, L.A., H. Aldrich, and J. Moody (2000), 'Family matters: gender, networks, and entrepreneurial outcomes', *Social Forces*, **79** (2), 523–46.

Ricardo, D. (1817), *On the Principles of Political Economy*, London: John Murray.

Rindova, V., D. Barry and D.J. Ketchen (2009), 'Entrepreneurship as emancipation. Introduction to special topic forum', *Academy of Management Perspectives*, **34** (3), 477–91.

Rivlin, A. M. (1992), *Reviving the American Dream: The Economy, the States and the Federal Government*, Washington, DC: Brookings Institution.

Rogers, E. and D. Kincaid (1981), *Communication Networks*, New York: Free Press.

Romer, P. (1986), 'Increasing returns and long-run growth', *Journal of Political Economy*, **94**, 23–33.

Rooks, G., A. Szirmai and A. Sserwanga (2009), 'The interplay of human and social capital in entrepreneurship in developing countries. The case of Uganda', United Nations University Research Paper no. 2009/09.

Rorty, R. (1981), *Philosophy and the Mirror of Nature*, Princeton, NJ: Princeton University Press.

Rose, C. (1980), 'Human interpretation as text interpretation', in A. Buttimer and D. Seamon (eds), *The Human Experience of Space and Place*, London: Croom Helm.

Rosenberg, N., R. Landau and D. Mowery (1992), *Technology and the Wealth of Nations*, Palo Alto, CA: Stanford University Press.

Rothwell, R. (1991), 'External networking and innovation in small and medium-sized manufacturing firms in Europe', *Technovation*, **11** (2), 93–111.

Rowan, D. (1997), 'Lastword: glossary for the 90s', *Guardian*, Guardian Weekend, 15 February, T67.

Ruef, M. (2010), 'Entrepreneurial groups', in H. Landström and F. Lohrke (eds), *Historical Foundations of Entrepreneurship Research*, Cheltenham, UK and Northampton, MA, USA: Edward Elgar.

Sack, R. (1997), *Homo Geographicus*, Baltimore, MD: Johns Hopkins University Press.

Salomon, L.M. and H.K. Anheier (1994), *The Emerging Sector Revisited: An Overview*, Baltimore, MD: John Hopkins Institute for Policy Studies.

Salomon, L.M. and H.K. Anheier (1997), 'The civil society sector', *Society*, **34** (2), 60–65.

Sanner, L. (1997), 'Trust between entrepreneurs and external actors: sensemaking in organizing new business ventures', doctoral thesis, Göteborgs universitet Department of Business Administration.

Savage, M. and A. Warde (1993), *Urban Sociology, Capitalism and Modernity*, Basingstoke: Macmillan.

Savitch, H.V. and P. Kantor (1995), 'City business: an international perspective on marketplace politics', *International Journal of Urban and Regional Studies*, **19**, 495–512.

Saxenian, A. (1994), *Regional Advantage. Culture and Competition in Silicon Valley and Route 128*, Cambridge, MA and London: Harvard University Press.

Say, J.B. (1855), *A Treatise on Political Economy*, 4th edn, Philadelphia, PA: Lippincott, Grambo & Co.

Sayer, A. (1989), 'Post-Fordism in question', *International Journal of Urban and Regional Research*, **13** (4), 666–95.

Sayer, A. (1992), *Method in Social Science*, London: Routledge.

Schaltegger, S. (2002), 'A framework for ecopreneurship: leading bioneers and environmental managers to ecopreneurship', *Greener Management International*, **38** (Summer), 45–58.

Schaper, M. (2002), 'The essence of ecopreneurship', *Greener Management International*, **8** (Summer), 26–30.

Schaper, M. (2010), 'Understanding the green entrepreneur', in M. Schaper (ed.), *Making Ecopreneurs: Developing Sustainable Entrepreneurship*, Aldershot: Ashgate Gower.

Schatzki, T.R. (1997), 'Practices and actions: a Wittgensteinian critique of Bourdieu and Giddens', *Philosophy of the Social Sciences*, **27** (3): 283–308.

Schatzki, T.R. (2003), 'A new societist social ontology', *Philosophy of the Social Sciences*, 2003, **33**, 174–202.

Schatzki, T.R. (2005), 'The sites of organizations', *Organization Studies*, **26** (3), 465–84.

Schatzki, T.R. (2006), 'The time of activity', *Continental Philosophy Review*, **39**, 155–82.

Schatzki, T.R., K. Knorr Cetina and E. von Savigney (eds) (2001), *The Practice Turn in Contemporary Theory*, London: Routledge.

Schon, D. (1983), *The Reflective Practitioner: How Professionals Think in Action*, New York: Basic Books.

Schumpeter, J. (1934), *The Theory of Economic Development*, Cambridge, MA: Harvard University Press.

Schutz, A. (1962), *Collected Papers*, vol I, M. Natanson (ed.), The Hague: Martinus Nijhoff.

Schuyler, G. (1998a), 'Social entrepreneurship: profit as a means, not an end', accessed February 2009 at www.celcee.edu/products/digest/Dig98-7.html.

Schuyler, G. (1998b), 'Merging economic and environmental concerns through entrepreneurship', *Digest* of the Ewing Marion Kauffman Foundation, Center for Entrepreneurial Leadership, **98** (8), 3–4.

Scott, A.J. (2000), 'Economic geography: the great half-century', in G.L. Clark, M. Feldman and M. Gertler (eds), *Oxford Handbook of Economic Geography*, Oxford: Oxford University Press, reprinted in *Cambridge Journal of Economics*, 1999, **24**, 483–504.

Scott, A.J (2006), *Geography and Economics*, Oxford: Oxford University Press.

Seelos, C. and J. Mair (2005), 'Social entrepreneurship – the contribution of individual intrapreneurs to sustainable development', IESE Business School working paper no. 553.

Shamir, B. and Y. Lapidot (2003), 'Trust in organizational superiors: systemic and collective considerations', *Organization Studies*, **3**, 463–91.

Shapero, A. and L. Sokol (1982), 'The social dimension of entrepreneurship', in C.A. Kent, D.L. Sexton and K.H. Vesper (eds), *Encyclopedia of Entrepreneurship*, Englewood Cliffs, NJ: Prentice Hall.

Shapin, S. (1995), 'Here and everywhere: sociology of scientific knowledge', *Annual Review of Sociology*, **21**, 289–321.

Sharpe, L.J. (1976), 'The role and functions of local government in modern Britain', in Layfield Report, *The Relationship Between General and Local Government*, London: HMSO, 203–20.

Shaw, E. (1997), 'The real networks of small firms', in D. Deakins, P. Jennings and C. Mason (eds), *Small Firms: Entrepreneurship in the 1990s*, London: Paul Chapman Publishing.

Shaw, E. (1998), 'Social networks: their impact on the innovative behaviour of small service firms', *International Journal of Innovation Management*, **2** (2), 201–22.

Simon, H.A. (1991), 'Bounded rationality and organizational learning', *Organization Science*, **2** (1), 125–34.

Skloot, E. (1995), *The Nonprofit Entrepreneur*, New York: Foundation Center.

Smircich, L. and C. Stubbart (1985), 'Strategic management in an enacted world', *Academy of Management Review*, **10** (4), 724–36.

Smith, J.E. (1969), 'Time, times, and the "right time", *Chronos* and *Kairos*', *The Monist*, **53**, 1–13.

Smith, J.E. (1986), 'Time and qualitative time', *Review of Metaphysics*, **40**, 3–16.

Snow, C.P. (1959), *The Two Cultures*, Cambridge: Cambridge University Press.

Snyder, G. (1968), *The Back Country*, New York: New Directions Press.

Snyder, M. and N. Cantor (1998), 'Understanding personality and social behaviour: a functionalist strategy', in D.T. Gilbert, S.T. Fiske and G. Lindsey (eds), *The Handbook of Social Psychology*, 4th edn, Boston, MA: McGraw-Hill.

Soja, E.W. (1989), *Postmodern Geographies: The Reassertion of Space in Critical Social Theory*, London: Verso.

Soja, E.W. (1996), *Thirdspace. Journeys to Los Angeles and Other Real-and-Imagined Places*, Oxford: Blackwell.

Soja, E.W. (2008), 'Writing the city spatially', in C. Lévy (ed.), *The City: Critical Essays in Human Geography*, Aldershot and Burlington, VT: Ashgate, reprinted in *City*, 2003, **7**, 269–80.

Spence, L. (1999), 'Does size matter? The state of the art in small business ethics', *Business Ethics: A European Review*, **8** (3), 163–74.

Spence, L. and R. Rutherford (2003), 'Small business and empirical perspectives in business ethics: editorial', *Journal of Business Ethics*, **47** (1), 1–5.

Spinosa, C., F. Flores and H. Dreyfus (1997), *Disclosing New Worlds*, Cambridge, MA: The MIT Press.

Stark, D. (2000), 'For a sociology of worth', paper presented at the Conference on Economic Sociology at the Edge of the Third Millennium, Moscow.

Stevenson, H.H. and J.C. Jarillo (1990), 'A paradigm of entrepreneurship: entrepreneurial management', *Strategic Management Journal*, **11**, 17–27.

Steyaert, C. (1997), 'A qualitative methodology for process studies of entrepreneurship: creating local knowledge through stories', *International Studies of Management and Organization*, **27** (3), 13–33.

Steyaert, C. (2000), 'Entre-concepts: conceiving entrepreneurship', paper presented at the RENT-conference XIV, Prague.

Steyaert, C. (2004), 'The prosaic of entrepreneurship', in D. Hjorth and C. Steyaert (eds), *Narrative and Discursive Approaches to Entrepreneurship*, Cheltenham, UK and Northampton, MA, USA: Edward Elgar.

Steyaert, C. (2007), '"Entrepreneuring" as a conceptual attractor? A review of process theories in 20 years of entrepreneurship studies', *Entrepreneurship and Regional Development*, **19** (6), 453–77.

Steyaert, C. and J. Katz (2004), 'Reclaiming the space for entrepreneurship in society: geographical, discursive and social dimensions', *Entrepreneurship and Regional Development*, **16**, May, 179–96.

Stoffaes, C. (1987), *Fins de mondes*, Paris: Editions Odile Jacob.

Storey, D. (1980), *Job Creation and Small Firms Policy in Britain*, London: Centre for Environmental Studies.

Storey, D. (1994), *Understanding the Small Business Sector*, London: Routledge.

Storper, M. (1992), 'The limits to globalization: technology districts and international trade', *Economic Geography*, **28**, 60–93.

Storper, M. (1993), 'Regional worlds of production: learning and innovation in the technology districts of France, Italy and the USA', *Regional Studies*, **27** (5), 433–55.

Storper, M. (1997), *The Regional World: Territorial Development in a Global Economy*, New York: Guilford Press.

Storper, M. and R. Walker (1989), *The Capitalist Imperative. Territory, Technology, and Institutional Growth*, New York and: Oxford: Basil Blackwell.

Storper, M. and B. Harrison (1991), 'Flexibility, hierarchy and regional development: the changing structure of industrial production systems and their forms of governance in the 1990s', *Regional Policy*, **20**, 407–22.

Sundin, E. (2009), 'Det dolda samhällsentreprenörskapet – omsorgsmotiv i småföretag' ['Hidden social entrepreneurship – caring motives among small firms'], in M. Gawell, B. Johannisson and M. Lundqvist (eds), *Samhällets entreprenörer* [*Society's Entrepreneurs*], Stockholm: KK-stiftelsen.

Sunley, P. (1996), 'Context in economic geography: the relevance of pragmatism', *Progress in Human Geography*, **20**, 338–55.

Swedberg, R. (2006), 'Social entrepreneurship: the view of the young Schumpeter', in C. Steyaert and D. Hjorth (eds), *Entrepreneurship as Social Change*, Cheltenham, UK and Northampton, MA, USA: Edward Elgar.

Taylor, M. (2003), *Public Policy in the Community*, Basingstoke and New York: Palgrave Macmillan.

Thake, S. and S. Zadek (1997), *Practical People, Noble Causes: How to Support Community-based Social Entrepreneurs*, London: New Economics Foundation.

Thalbuder, J. (1998), 'How nonprofit and for-profit differ', accessed February 2008 at www.socialentrepreneurs.org/entredef.html.

Thompson, J. (2002), 'The world of the social entrepreneur', *The International Journal of Public Sector Management*, **15** (5), 412–31.

Thompson, J., G. Alvy and A. Lees (2000), 'Social entrepreneurship – a new look at the people and potential', *Management Decision*, **38** (5), 338–48.

Thompson, K. and H. Smith (1991), 'Social responsibility and small business: suggestions for research', *Journal of Small Business Management*, **29** (1), 30–44.

Thornton, P.H. (1999), 'The sociology of entrepreneurship', *Annual Review of Sociology*, **25**, 19–46.

Thrift, N.J. (1989), 'The perils of transition models', *Environment and Planning D: Society and Space*, **13** (4), 127–9.

Thrift, N. (2005), *Knowing Capitalism*, London: Sage.

Tichy, N.M., N.L. Tushman and C. Forbrun (1979), 'Social network analysis for organisations', *Academy of Management Review*, **4** (4), 507–19.

Till, K. (1993), 'Neotraditional towns and urban villages: the cultural production of a geography of "Otherness"', *Environment and Planning D: Society and Space*, **11** (6), 709–32.

NUTEK (2003), 'Tillväxt i småföretag' [Growth among small firms], Swedish Agency for Economic and Regional Growth.

Timmons, J. (1999), *New Venture Creation: Entrepreneurship for the 21st Century*, 5th edn, New York: Irwin/McGraw-Hill.

Todling, F. (1991), 'The geography of innovation: transformation from Fordism towards post-Fordism?', mimeo, Institute of Urban and Regional Studies, University of Economics and Business Administration, Vienna.

Tomkins, C. (2001), 'Interdependencies, trust and information in relationships, alliances and networks, *Accounting, Organizations and Society*, **26**, 161–91.

Törnqvist, G. (1991), 'Swedish contact routes in the European urban landscape', mimeo, Department of Social and Economic Geography, University of Lund, Sweden.

Trädgårdh, L. (2000), 'Utopin om den sociala ekonomin' ['The social economy as Utopia'], in F. Wijkström and T. Johnstad (eds), *Om kooperation & social ekonomi. Röster i ett nordiskt samtal* [*About cooperation and social economy. Voices in a Nordic conversation*], Stockholm: Föreningen kooperativa studier.

Tschumi, B. (1994), *Event-Cities*, Cambridge, MA: The MIT Press.

Tuan, Y.-F. (1974a), *Topophilia: A Study of Environmental Perception, Attitudes, and Values*, Englewood Cliffs, NJ: Prentice Hall.

Tuan, Y.-F. (1974b), 'Space and place: humanistic perspective', *Progress in Human Geography*, **6**, 211–52.

Tuan, Y.-F. (1977), *Space and Place. The Perspective of Experience*, Minneapolis, MN and London: The University of Minnesota Press.

Tuan, Y.-F. (1979), 'Space and place: humanistic perspectives', in S. Gale and G. Olsson (eds), *Philosophy and Geography*, Dordrecht, The Netherlands: D. Reidel.

Uzzi, B. (1996), 'The sources and consequences of embeddedness for the economic performance or organizations: the network effect', *American Sociological Review*, **61**, 674–98.

Uzzi, B. (1997), 'Social structure and competition in interfirm networks: the paradox of embeddedness', *Administrative Science Quarterly*, **42**, 35–67.

Vasi, I.B. (2009), 'New heroes, old theories? Toward a sociological perspective on social Entrepreneurship', in R. Ziegler (ed.), *An Introduction to Social Entrepreneurship*, Cheltenham, UK and Northampton, MA, USA: Edward Elgar.

Venkataraman, S. (1997), 'The distinctive domain of entrepreneurship research', in J.A. Katz (ed.), *Advances in Entrepreneurship, Firm Emergence and Growth*, vol. 3, Greenwich, CT: JAI Press.

Vestrum, I.K. and O.J. Borch (2006), 'Dynamics of entrepreneurship culture', paper presented at ESU2006 Conference at the University of Tampere in Hämeenlinna, Finland.

von Wright, G.H. (1971), *Explanation and Understanding*, London: Routledge & Kegan Paul.

Vyakarnam, S., A. Bailey, A. Myers and D. Burnett (1997), 'Towards an understanding of ethical behaviour in small firms', *Journal of Business Ethics*, **16** (15), 1628–36.

Walley, E.E. and D. Taylor (2002), 'Opportunists, champions, mavericks . . .? A typology of green entrepreneurs', *Greener Management International*, **38** (Summer), 31–43.

Watson, J.B. (1970), *Behaviourism*, New York: Norton.

Watson, S. (1991), 'Gilding the smokestacks: the new symbolic representations of deindustrialised regions', *Environment and Planning D: Society and Space*, **9**, 59–70.

WCED (World Commission on Environment and Development) (1987), 'Our common future, "The Brundtland Report"', Oxford: Oxford University Press.

Weber, M. (1975), *Makt og byråkrati* [Power and bureaucracy], 2nd edn, Oslo: Gyldendal Norsk Forlag.

Weick, K.E. (1979), 'Cognitive processes in organizations', *Research in Organizational Behaviour*, vol. 1, 41–74.

Weick, K.E. (1995), *Sensemaking in Organizations*, Thousand Oaks, CA: Sage.

Weiskopf, R. and C. Steyaert (2009), 'Metamorphoses in entrepreneurship studies: towards an affirmative politics of entrepreneuring', in D. Hjorth and C. Steyaert (eds), *The Politics and Aesthetics of Entrepreneurship*, Cheltenham, UK and Northampton, MA, USA: Edward Elgar.

Wenger, E. (1998), *Communities of Practice. Learning, Meaning and Identity*, Cambridge: Cambridge University Press.

Werlen, B. (2008), 'Space and causality, or whatever happened to the subject?', in C. Philo (ed.), *Theory and Methods: Critical Essays in Human Geography*, Aldershot, and Burlington, VT: Ashgate, reprinted in Werlen, B. (1993), *Society, Action and Space: An Alternative Human Geography*, London: Routledge, pp. 1–20, 209-10, 210a, 210b.

Westerdahl, H. (2001), *Business and Community*, Göteborg, Sweden: Bokförlaget BAS.

Westlund, H. (2001), 'Social economy and employment. The case of Sweden', paper presented at Uddevalla Symposium 2001: Regional Economies in Transition, Vänersborg, Sweden.

Westlund, H. and S. Westerdahl (1997), *Contribution of the Social Economy to Local Employment*, Östersund/Stockholm: Institutet för social ekonomi/Koopi.

Westlund, H. and R. Bolton (2003), 'Local social capital and entrepreneurship', *Small Business Economics*, **21**, 77–113.

White, E.C. (1987), *Kaironomia: On the Will-To-Invent*, Ithaca, NY: Cornell University Press.

Wickham, P.A. (2006), *Strategic Entrepreneurship*, 4th edn, Harlow: Pearson Education.

Wigren, C. and L. Melin (2009), 'Fostering a regional innovation system – looking into the power of policy-making', in D. Hjorth and C. Steyaert (eds), *The Politics and Aesthetics of Entrepreneurship*, Cheltenham, UK and Northampton, MA, USA: Edward Elgar.

Wikipedia (2007), 'CSR', accessed 29 May at http://en.wikipedia.org/wiki/Corporate_social_responsibility.

Williams, R. (1965), *The Long Revolution*, London: Penguin.

Winch, P. (1958), *The Idea of a Social Science and its Relation to Philosophy*, London: Routledge & Kegan Paul.

Worthington, I. and C. Britton (2009), *The Business Environment*, 6th edn, Harlow: Prentice Hall.

Wriston, W.B. (1992), *The Twilight of Sovereignty*, New York: Scribner's.

Zerbinati, S. and V. Souitaris (2005), 'Entrepreneurship in the public sector: a framework of analysis in European local governments', *Entrepreneurship and Regional Development*, **1**, 3–19.

Zimmerer, T.W. and N.M. Scarborough (2002), *Essentials of Entrepreneurship and Small Business Management*, 3rd edn, Upper Saddle River, NJ: Prentice Hall.

Index